AF478623

ANTONIO MANUEL
I WANT TO ACT, NOT REPRESENT!

This publication is produced in conjunction with the exhibition *Antonio Manuel: I Want to Act, Not Represent!*, co-curated by Claudia Calirman and Gabriela Rangel, on view at the Americas Society Art Gallery from September 15 to December 10, 2011.

The publication is produced by Americas Society in conjunction with Associação para o Patronato Contemporâneo (APC).

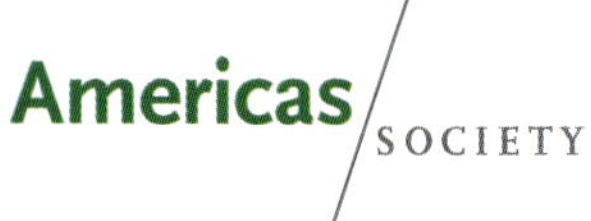
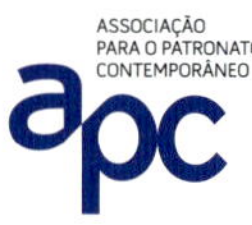

Americas Society gratefully acknowledges the following donors for their generous support of the exhibition *Antonio Manuel: I Want to Act, Not Represent!* as well as its catalogue:

Full Comex Trading, Petrobas, the Ministry of Foreign Affairs, Brazil and the Consulate General of Brazil in New York, Credit Suisse, Itaú BBA, the Tinker Foundation, Andrea and José Olympio Pereira and in part by an award from the National Endowment for the Arts.

In-kind support is provided by Galeria Nara Roesler, Associação para o Patronato Contemporâneo (APC) and Arte al Día.

Americas Society's Visual Arts Program is also supported by Sharon Schultz Simpson and in part by public funds from the New York City Department of Cultural Affairs, in partnership with the City Council.

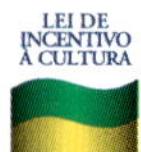
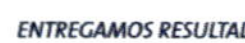
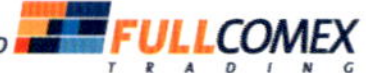
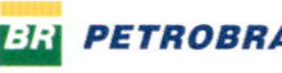
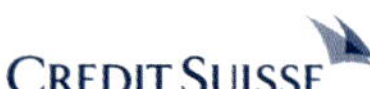
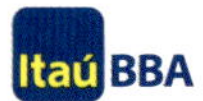
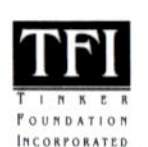
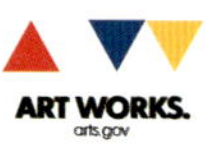
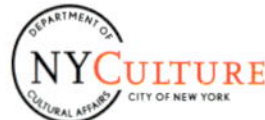
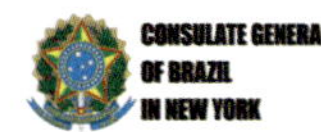
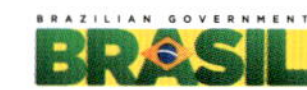
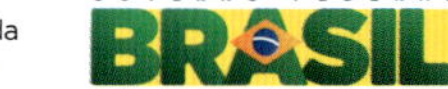

EDITORS
Claudia Calirman, Alexandra García and Gabriela Rangel

ASSISTANT EDITOR
Christina De León

RESEARCH and PUBLICATION COORDINATOR
Natalie Bunnell

EXHIBITION PROJECT COORDINATORS, GALERIA NARA ROESLER, SÃO PAULO
Marli Matsumoto
Rafaela Ferreira

GRAPHIC DESIGNER
Kate Johnson

COPYEDITORS
Michele Faguet
Leticia Lima

TRANSLATORS
Valeria Souza Cruz
Mari Hayman
John Laudenberger
Michele Markowitz
Monica Vieira

CHIEF EXHIBITION PREPARATOR
Arturo Sánchez

PRE-PRESS
GHP

PRINTING
Midas Printing

ISBN: 1-879128-40-3
ISBN 13: 978-1-879128-40-8

PUBLISHED BY:
Americas Society
680 Park Avenue
New York, NY 10065

New York / São Paulo

AND
Associação para o Patronato Contemporâneo (APC)
Rua Doutor Oliveira Pinto, 145
Jardim Paulistano
São Paulo, SP 01444-010

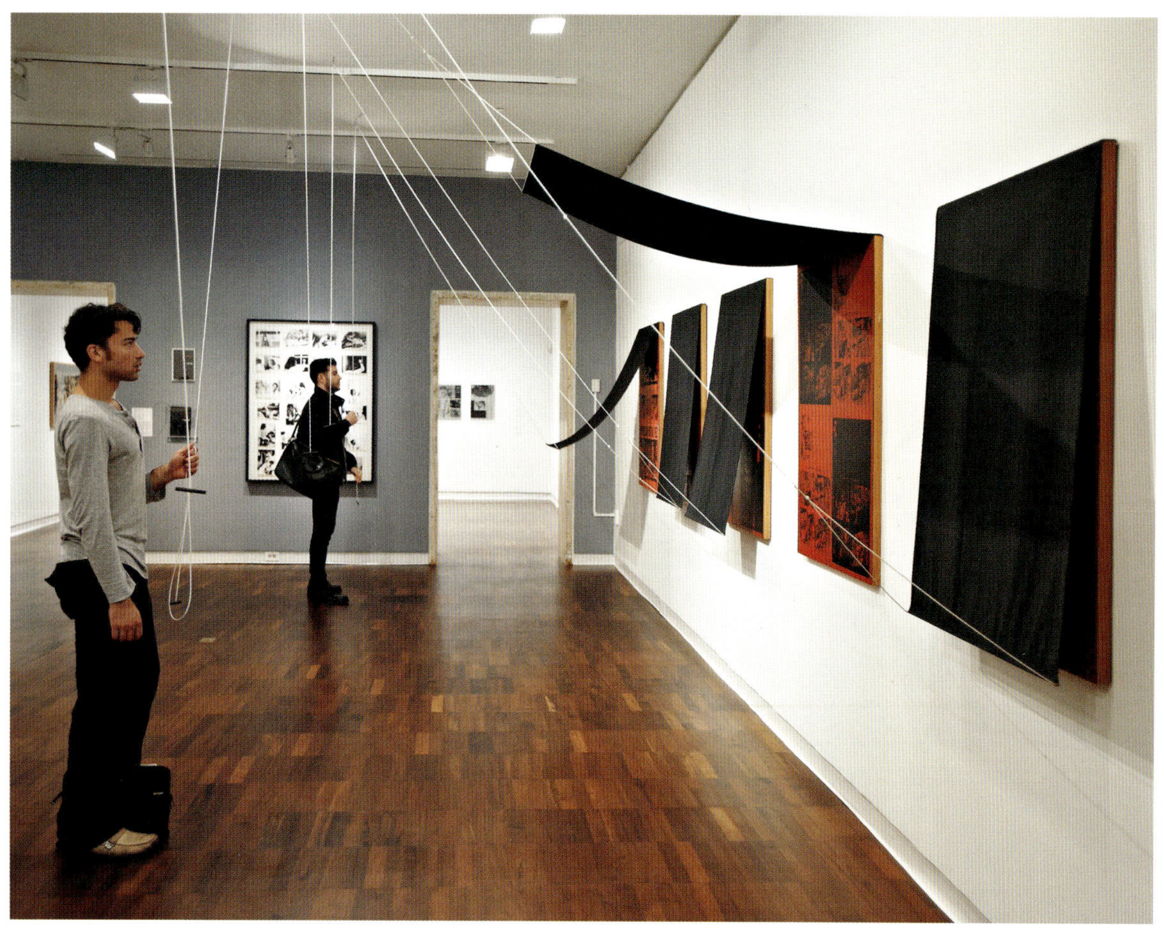

Installation view of *Antonio Manuel: I Want to Act, Not Represent!*

Americas Society's Visual Arts program has held a longstanding commitment to present exhibitions, which focus on artists who deserve greater attention in the United States. For more than forty years the organization's mission has been to foster a deeper understanding of the significant cultural production occurring throughout the Western hemisphere. *Antonio Manuel: I Want to Act, Not Represent!,* curated by Claudia Calirman and Gabriela Rangel is an important addition to this groundbreaking legacy.

Antonio Manuel began his career in the late 1960s in the midst of the Brazilian military dictatorship. The title of the exhibition and catalogue is a reference to his first solo show in Rio de Janeiro in 1967, when the Brazilian critic Ronaldo Brito wrote: "More than an artistic debut, it was a statement of intentions: 'I don't want to represent, I want to Act.'" Within this historical context Antonio Manuel privileged his artistic freedom of expression over the systematic fear that was enforced upon him. Since the end of the military regime in 1985, Brazil has undergone significant growth, emerging as an influential force in the international political and cultural scene.

Americas Society is proud to present Antonio Manuel's first solo exhibition in the United States. Well known in Europe and throughout Latin America, *Antonio Manuel: I Want to Act, Not Represent!* is a long overdue tribute to the artist's pioneering efforts in the visual arts. This book published jointly with Associação para o Patronato Contemporâneo (APC) includes materials documenting the artist's performances, as well as the artistic collaborative spirit which flourished in Brazil during the 1970s. I would like to thank Beverly Adams, Michael Asbury and Judith Rodenbeck for their tremendous contributions, which will provide new scholarship to North American audiences.

I thank our generous donors Full Comex Trading, Petrobras, the Ministry of Foreign Affairs, Brazil and the Consulate General of Brazil in New York, Credit Suisse, Itaú BBA, the Tinker Foundation, Andrea and José Olympio Pereira and the National Endowment for the Arts. In-kind support was also provided by Galeria Nara Roesler, Associação para o Patronato Contemporâneo (APC) and Arte al Día.

I wish to extend my deepest gratitude to Antonio Manuel, Claudia Calirman, and Gabriela Rangel. This exhibition would not have been possible without the support of Nara Roesler, Daniel Roesler, Marli Matsumoto, Alexandra Garcia, and Rafaela Ferreira of Galeria Nara Roesler, who together produced this successful and exciting project with the Americas Society staff: Christina De León, Theodora Doulamis, Andrea Sanseverino Galan, Ragnhild Melzi, Arturo Sánchez and Monica Vieira, along with our dedicated interns Seth Becker and Natalie Bunnell.

Susan L. Segal
President and CEO, Americas Society

ANTONIO MANUEL: THE POLITICS OF IRREVERENCE

CLAUDIA CALIRMAN

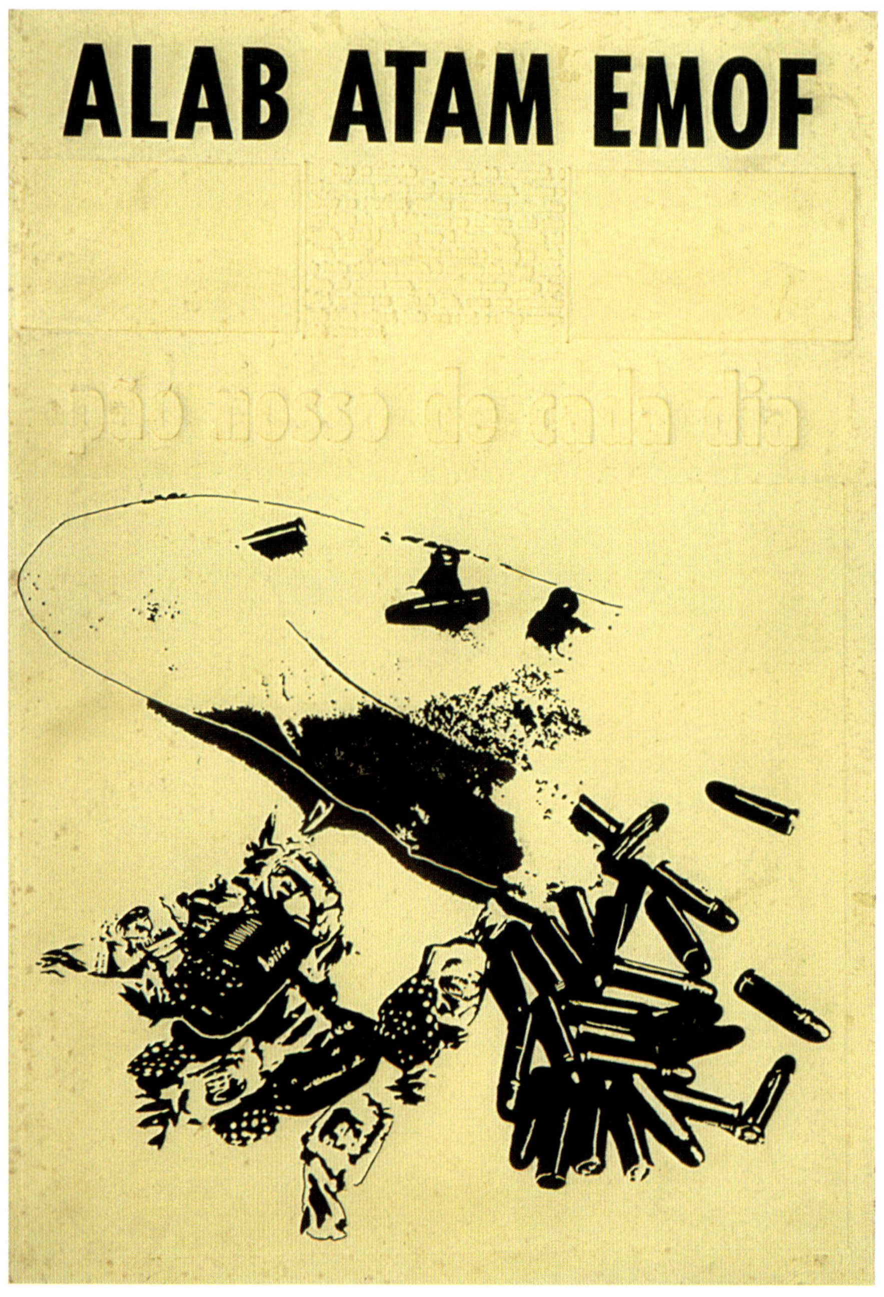

Bala mata fome (Bullet Kills Hunger), 1975. From the *Flan* series, ink on papier-mâché stereotype mold, 22 x 15 in. Courtesy the artist

The late 1960s and early '70s, the most repressive period of the military dictatorship that ruled Brazil for two decades, coincided with rapid and dramatic changes to the country's art scene. Visual artists, under pressure from both the authoritarian regime and fearful art institutions, struggled to avoid being paralyzed by a state of self-imposed censorship. They rallied against conformity in their work and pushed artistic boundaries as they incorporated nontraditional mediums and flaunted the rules imposed by art institutions.

Born in Portugal in 1947, Brazilian artist Antonio Manuel is one of the artists who best combined innovative and provocative artistic forms with a political undercurrent, embodying the desire to reconcile new artistic practices with a concern for local politics. Faced with the dilemma of how to exercise freedom of expression in a country where civil liberties were endangered, Antonio Manuel's appropriations of the media and his interventions using his own body aimed to subvert and critique the forces of repression as well as to question institutional policy.

In 1973, at the height of the dictatorship's most violent period,[1] Antonio Manuel shot *Loucura & Cultura* (Madness & Culture), a ten-minute, 35mm black-and-white short film that touched on some of the most pressing issues of the era: madness, violence, repression and self-expression. Based on a debate titled "Amostragem da Cultura Loucura-Brasileira" (Sampling of Brazilian Culture-Madness), which took place at the Museum of Modern Art of Rio de Janeiro (MAM RJ) on June 10, 1968,[2] the film features Rogério Duarte, Lygia Pape, Caetano Veloso, Luiz Carlos Saldanha and Hélio Oiticica—all central figures in the Brazilian cultural landscape at that time. Duarte, Pape and Veloso, who participated in the debate at MAM, are captured individually in front, profile and back views, mimicking the composition of police mug shots. Filmmaker Saldanha, who was jailed in Rome when the work was filmed,[3] is represented by a blank shot, while Oiticica, living abroad in New York at the time, is pictured as a still photograph, in profile.[4] The participants' images do not necessarily match their own voices: when Pape appears, sometimes it is Duarte who speaks; when Veloso appears, at times it is Duarte's voice we hear.

The film opens with a still image of Duarte, a graphic designer and one of the gurus of the Tropicália movement,[5] accompanied by a voiceover: "Attention! I need to speak. Attention! Attention! I want to speak." The film also contains excerpts from the actual debate at MAM, followed by a recording of "La Marseillaise," sung in operatic mode. Once

1   The country was experiencing the so-called *anos de chumbo* (leaden years) under General Emílio Garrastazú Médici, who ruled from 1969 to 1974.
2   The debate was organized by Frederico Morais, Rogério Duarte and Hélio Oiticica.
3   Luiz Carlos Saldanha's imprisonment was not related to political issues.
4   *Loucura & Cultura* was awarded "Best Film" at the second Jornal do Brasil/INC Short Film Festival.
5   Rogério Duarte, who came from the state of Bahia, was at the center of the Tropicália movement in the late 1960s and '70s. A multimedia musician, composer, filmmaker and poet, he is best known for his graphic designs for the covers of Tropicália's records and for posters advertising Cinema Novo films, including Glauber Rocha's *Deus e o Diabo na Terra do Sol* (Black God, White Devil), 1964. The Tropicália movement employed an interdisciplinary approach to the arts, branching out into music, the visual arts, theater, literature and cinema. It attempted to merge the modern and the archaic, national elements and international trends, grassroots and vanguard art.

the rallying call of the French Revolution, "La Marseillaise" is today the official national anthem of France; in Antonio Manuel's film it stands in for the Brazilian anthem, as it was strictly forbidden to use the national hymn for anything other than patriotic purposes.

Loucura & Cultura is a portrait of a generation attempting to define itself—artistically, politically, intellectually—amid the atmosphere of fear created by the military dictatorship. On December 13, 1968, the Ato Institucional No. 5 (Institutional Act No. 5) was established by the military government. The AI-5, as it became known, was undoubtedly the most severe in a succession of increasingly repressive measures issued by the military regime. The dictate was intended to be in effect for one year, but, in fact, it would come to define the relationship between Brazilian civilians and their government for a decade. Suspending political and civil rights and sanctioning torture as a means of intimidating political opponents,[6] the AI-5 marked a drastic change in the country's political and cultural atmosphere. Immediate results were the widespread arrest of students, intellectuals, politicians, artists and journalists and the censorship of the media and the arts. Brazil after the AI-5 was a changed nation, marked by disillusionment with traditional politics and rejection of the military regime and its authoritarianism.[7]

In *Loucura & Cultura,* Antonio Manuel interweaves disparate elements to depict the afflictions of the time: fear of persecution, a state of self-imposed censorship and madness. To this end, he utilizes sound bites from the debate that pointed to the dilemma of self-expression under the dictatorship: "Maybe my function is to play the role of a clown in this big farce that is Brazilian culture;" "Every creative process is an act of madness;" "Violence is implied in all acts of creation." We hear that a woman in the audience accused the artists of practicing "intellectual masturbation." The artist is presented as a marginal figure: a clown or jester of society. Madness is discussed as a necessary step in the process of

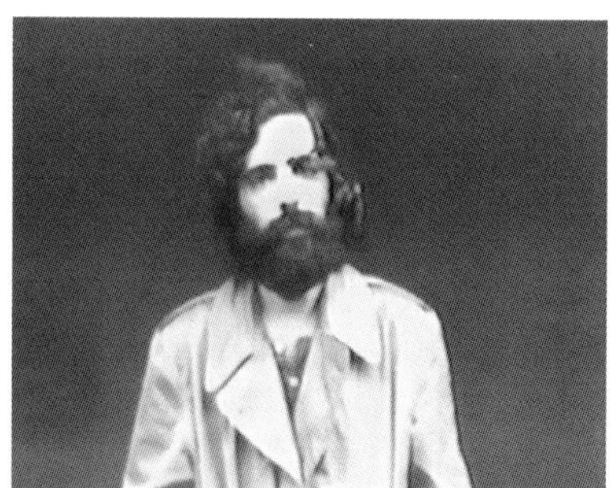 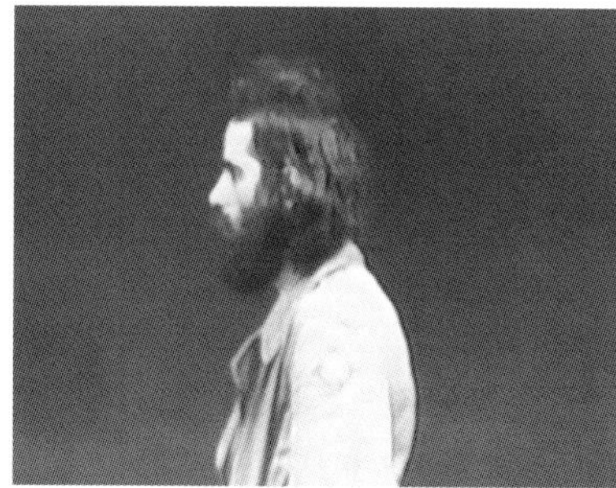 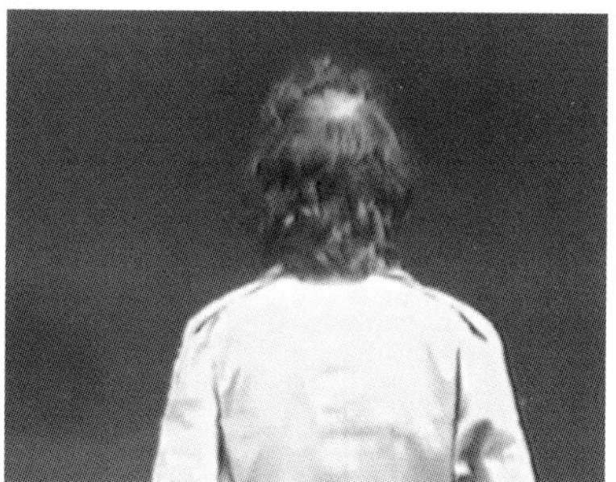

Stills from *Loucura & Cultura* (Madness & Culture), 1973. B&W with sound, 10 minutes, 35mm. Courtesy the artist

6   Elio Gaspari, interviewed by the author, July 30, 2003, São Paulo. A comprehensive account of the political events in Brazil under the military dictatorship can be found in journalist Elio Gaspari's four-part series about the period, *A Ditadura Escancarada* (São Paulo: Companhia das Letras, 2002); *A Ditadura Envergonhada* (São Paulo: Companhia das Letras, 2002); *A Ditadura Derrotada* (São Paulo: Companhia das Letras, 2003); and *A Ditadura Encurralada* (São Paulo: Companhia das Letras, 2004).

7   A study on the visual arts during the *anos de chumbo* is forthcoming in Claudia Calirman's book, *Brazilian Art under Dictatorship: Antonio Manuel, Artur Barrio, and Cildo Meireles* (Duke University Press, 2012).

creation; its marginal connotations, its alienation and lack of reason—all yield creative power. The daily violence under military rule—street demonstrations between the police and the students, censorship, arbitrariness and authoritarianism—is suggested in the film by the mug shots of artists.

In fact, there was a direct and literal connection between the violence imposed by the dictatorship and madness: in many cases, incarceration and torture resulted in mental illness. Perhaps the most notorious case was the 1968 imprisonment of Rogério Duarte following his arrest (along with his brother Ronaldo) at a street demonstration in Rio de Janeiro. The brothers were taken into custody by military officials and tortured; over the next three years, Rogério would be interned in three psychiatric hospitals as a result.[8] The artistic community was also shaken in 1972 when Torquato Neto, a poet, journalist and one of the key lyricists of the Tropicália movement, committed suicide, at age twenty-eight, following a stay in a mental hospital.[9]

In his essay "A antropologia de nós mesmos" (The Anthropology of Ourselves), film critic Jean-Claude Bernadet points out that the artists in *Loucura* & *Cultura* are mute and petrified. He then asks, "Are they mute because they are not allowed to speak, or because they have nothing—except for the confusing call to freedom, as abstract as it is fossilized— left to say?"[10] Indeed much of Antonio Manuel's work is underscored by a feeling of angst rooted in the need to articulate what cannot be said—the call to communicate what is being censored, suppressed, or effaced. It is not by coincidence that his most compelling works consist of interventions in, or disruptions of, the tools of mass media; it is in the cracks and fissures of the media that Antonio Manuel's work finds its most compelling platform.

BREAKING THE NEWS

Antonio Manuel's first interventions in the media, in 1966, comprised silhouettes drawn with black ink and crayon over printed pages of newspapers. In some of these untitled drawings, he depicts doll-like figures that resemble automatons, some gesticulating or appearing perplexed, others with mouths agape, trying to give voice to what is being censored. Appropriating mass media venues to modify, highlight and unveil or infiltrate his own messages was a strategy Antonio Manuel would explore in many different forms during this repressive period.

After drawing directly on the printed pages of newspapers, Antonio Manuel became interested in the actual mechanisms of production and publication. In this series titled *Flans,* 1968, he maintains the same layout and size of a newspaper page while emphasizing the brutality of the forces of repression. In later *Flans* from the mid-1970s, Antonio Manuel recreates the layout of the newspaper in a freer mode and plays with words as visual

8   Rogério Duarte discloses his imprisonment and torture by the military regime, and his three internments in psychiatric hospitals that followed, in his book *Tropicaos* (Rio de Janeiro: Azougue Editorial, 2003), 23–48.

9   Torquato Neto died by gas asphyxiation in his apartment in Rio de Janeiro on November 10, 1972. He had come from a period of internment in the psychiatric hospital Pedro II in Rio de Janeiro. In 1973, the poet Waly Salomão joined with Torquato Neto's widow, Ana Maria Duarte, to organize his poetry, lyrics and articles from his column "Geléia Geral" (General Jam) in the newspaper *Última Hora* (Rio de Janeiro), and excerpts from his diary while he was interned at the psychiatric hospital in the posthumous book *Os Últimos Dias de Paupéria*—a play on *The Last Days of Pompeii.* In 1982, Salomão and Duarte reissued a second, revised and enlarged edition of the book (Rio de Janeiro: Max Limonad, 1982).

10   Jean-Claude Bernardet, "A Antropologia de nós mesmos," in *Anos 70-Cinema,* no. 4, (Editora Europa, 1979–80), *The Social Documentary in Latin America,* ed. Julianne Burton, (Pittsburgh: University of Pittsburgh Press, 1990), 95.

poems—eliminating text, using letters both upside down and backwards—while emphasizing the white spaces of the page, sometimes even infusing them with color. In *Bala Mata Fome* (Bullet Kills Hunger), 1975, he writes the words in reverse (Alab Atam Emof) as if to enigmatically distill the violence and aggression recorded in the newspapers.

Images of the violent clashes between police and students (drawn from the front pages of the São Paulo newspaper *Última Hora*) assume a monumental scale in Antonio Manuel's *Repressão outra vez – Eis o saldo* (Repression Once Again – Here is the Outcome), 1968, an installation comprising five panels featuring graphic images and headlines from the daily news media. Each silkscreened panel, printed in black ink on a red background, is covered with black cloth attached to a rope mechanism that the viewer engages to reveal the lurid images underneath. The installation was to be exhibited in May 1969 at MAM for the Pre-Paris Biennial, an exhibition intended as a preview of the works chosen to represent Brazil at the *VI Biennale de Paris* later that year.[11] However, Brazilian audiences would not see Antonio Manuel's work—or any of the other submissions—as the works were deemed subversive by the military regime and the show was shut down by the police before it opened to the public. Beyond its immediate impact—at the time it was by far the most blatant example yet of the regime's policy of censorship regarding the arts—the banning of the Pre-Paris Biennial set events in motion that led to the major international boycott against the *X Bienal de São Paulo* in 1969.[12] This was not an isolated instance in which Antonio Manuel's work was censored, though it was probably the one that provoked the most lasting consequences.

TRANSGRESSIVE ACTIONS

Although ubiquitous, censorship of the arts and the media during the military regime lacked clear criteria. It could be imposed on something obvious and banal, like an image of Che Guevara, or could be more subjective—for instance, in some cases the color red was considered to have communist connotations and black to be an allusion to anarchism. Censorship was not only imposed on works of art considered to be politically subversive but also on artworks that did not conform to the norms. That lack of definition generated a constant sense of fear, leading to self-imposed censorship among artists. The arbitrary nature of the regime was itself a form of insanity. It did not provide a clear definition for what was considered subversive, and thus could react to the author of a supposedly provocative work of art with either a mild reprimand or a burst of rage.

At the opening night of the *XIX Salão Nacional de Arte Moderna* at MAM in April 1970, Antonio Manuel performed an impromptu act that would become memorable as a symbol of artistic resistance, an act of transgression and a political act of irreverence.

11   The *VI Biennale de Paris* took place at the Musée d'Art Moderne de la Ville de Paris, October–November 1969. During the Biennial, the space dedicated to Brazil was left empty to show that the country's representation had been censored. The only category with participation was Architecture and Urbanism, represented by a delegation from the state of Paraná. See Frederico Morais, *Cronologia das Artes Plásticas no Rio de Janeiro, 1816–1994* (Rio de Janeiro: Top Books, 1995), 307–08.

12   A detailed account of the national and international boycott of the *X Bienal de São Paulo* (1969) is forthcoming in the author's *Brazilian Art under Dictatorship: Antonio Manuel, Artur Barrio, and Cildo Meireles* (Duke University Press, 2012).

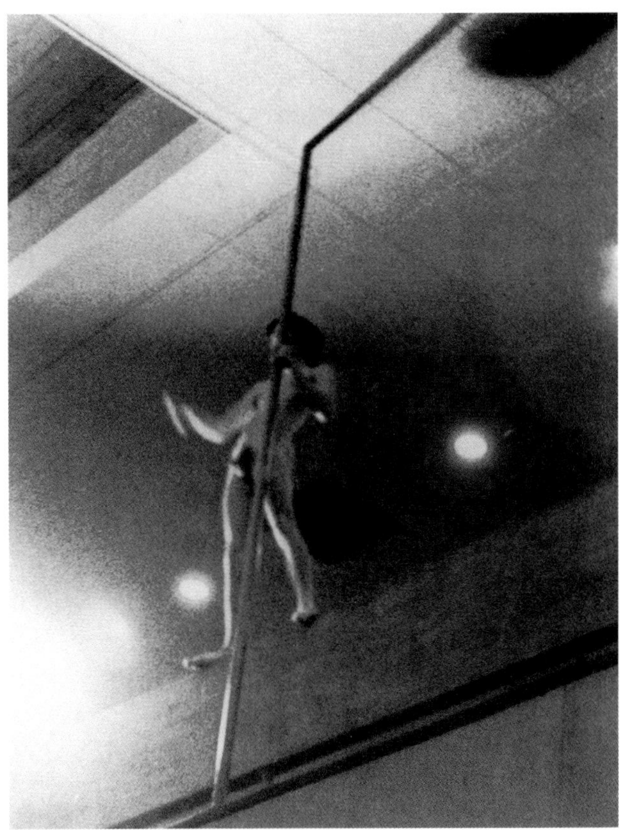

O corpo é a obra (The Body Is the Work), 1970. C-Print, 12.6 x 10 in.
Courtesy the artist

Weeks earlier Antonio Manuel had submitted his own body as a work of art to the Salon,
titling it *O corpo é a obra* (The Body Is the Work) and listing the official measurements as
his own height and weight. It was unanimously rejected by the Salon's jury.[13] At the Salon's
opening, which he attended solely as a guest, Antonio Manuel removed his clothing and
climbed the staircase of the museum. After being forced to flee the museum, he sought
shelter with the renowned art critic Mário Pedrosa, who supported and praised him, coining
the expression "Experimental Exercise of Freedom" in reference to Antonio Manuel's
unexpected and irreverent action.[14] According to Pedrosa in a recorded interview, "[Antonio
Manuel's] attitude presented the work of art itself—the act—as irresistible and at the same
time irrepressible. Nobody can impose exclusion. There are no rules that can forbid the
work of art to be made, the act to exist."[15]

13   The jury of the Salão Nacional de Arte Moderna was composed of Frederico Morais, Edila Mangabeira and Loio Pérsio. The Salão
Nacional, organized by the Ministry of Culture and Education, was an annual event with official sponsorship by the state. Its major prize was
a two-year international traveling grant.

14   Pedrosa's conversation that evening was taped by a cassette recorder brought by photographer Hugo Denizart, who was among the group
of artists who left the museum with Antonio Manuel. See *Antonio Manuel, Entrevista a Lúcia Carneiro e Ileana Pradilla, Série Palavra do
Artista* (Rio de Janeiro: Lacerda Ed., 1999). A translation of the interview can be found in *Antonio Manuel*, ed. Michael Asbury and Garo
Keheyan (Cyprus: Pharos Centre for Contemporary Art), 112–13.

15   *Antonio Manuel* (Rio de Janeiro: Funarte / Instituto Nacional de Artes Plásticas, 1984), 16, author's translation. Following Pedrosa's
account, art critic Ronaldo Brito wrote that at Antonio Manuel's first solo exhibition at Galerie Goeldi in Rio de Janeiro, in 1967, the artist had
already expressed in his work a statement of intentions: "I don't want to represent, I want to act." Ronaldo Brito, "Fluido Labirinto," in
Antonio Manuel, trans. Paulo Henriques Britto (Rio de Janeiro: Centro Cultural Hélio Oiticica, 1997), 13. This same phrase, which in many
ways exemplifies Antonio Manuel's overarching artistic practice, also inspired the title of this exhibition at the Americas Society: *Antonio
Manuel: I Want to Act, Not Represent!*

The only surviving documentation of Antonio Manuel's action at the XIX Salão Nacional de Arte Moderna at MAM is a series of photographs taken by the press. However, two months after his body was rejected as a work of art by the Salon Antonio Manuel transformed his ephemeral performance into a permanent object of art with the installation *Corpobra* (Bodywork), 1970. He built a life-size rectangular wooden box with straw at the bottom and Plexiglas on top. Inside he placed a black-and-white photograph of his naked body on the staircase of the museum. Covering his genitals, a piece of black cardboard (like those used to censor nude photographs) bears the inscription "Corpobra." Behind the box is a rope mechanism that, when pulled, reveals another photograph of Antonio Manuel's fully naked body.

Antonio Manuel kept exercising his right to act, whether solicited or not, and remained committed to communicating a reality that was forcibly being suppressed in the media. His next step was to interfere directly in the creation and dissemination of the news. He created, printed and circulated his own news after gaining access to the printing room of *O DIA* (the most sensationalist and popular newspaper in Rio de Janeiro). This time he would include his own headlines such as "Confusão no MAM: Pintor Mostra Pós-Arte" (Confusion at MAM: Painter Shows Post-Art).[16] These modified pages of newspapers, titled *Clandestinas* (Clandestines), 1973, constituted Antonio Manuel's most audacious intervention in the media. He was careful to maintain the design, layout and official logo of *O DIA,* keeping the remaining print pages—with their equally sensationalist headlines—intact.[17] He wanted his modified pages to look exactly like the original ones, despite the additions of his own disturbing elements. He produced a series of ten modified pages with a circulation of two to three hundred copies each. He then distributed a few copies of each issue to newsstands in Rio de Janeiro's main neighborhoods. Antonio Manuel pretended that he was officially delivering authentic copies of *O DIA,* and people bought the papers unaware of their origin. Through this irreverent act of rebellion, he exposed flaws inherent to the media under censorship—not only its gaps and omissions, its daily inventions and suppressions of reality, but also its vulnerability to being infiltrated using its own system of distribution and circulation.[18]

In 1973 Antonio Manuel appropriated the media again following the cancellation of his exhibition at MAM, which was most likely a consequence of the staff's fear of reprisal from the military regime. (By that time, it had become common to assess exhibitions in advance to avoid any conceivable firestorms.) All but one of the works submitted by Antonio Manuel for this exhibition had been censored by the institution. Surprisingly, the only one approved by MAM for the planned show was *O bode* (The Goat), 1973, in which a live black goat

16　Through his personal connection and friendship with the newspaper owner's younger son, the journalist Ivan Chagas Freitas, Antonio Manuel was granted permission to use the newspaper as a public art project of sorts. When Ivan's father, Antônio de Pádua Chagas Freitas, discovered Antonio Manuel's activities in *O DIA,* he immediately expelled him from the newspaper's printing room. As told by Antonio Manuel to the author, August 22, 2002, Rio de Janeiro.

17　Some of the headlines of the *Clandestinas* included "Homem Apresenta-se Nu no Museu Como Obra de Arte" (Man Presents himself Naked in Museum—As Work of Art), accompanied by the photograph of the artist naked holding a pole at the Museum; "Amarrou um Bode na Dança do Mal" (Tied a Goat in the Dance of Evil), next to a photograph of a goat; and "Pintor Mostra Pós-Arte" (Painter Shows Post-Art), showing Antonio Manuel naked in the museum.

18　In conjunction with the exhibition *Antonio Manuel: I Want to Act, Not Represent!,* Americas Society and Columbia University organized a joint symposium titled "The Politics of Camouflage in Artistic Practices from the 1970s," October 2011. The symposium addressed ways in which artists around the world infiltrated and disguised politically engaged art in the context of repression.

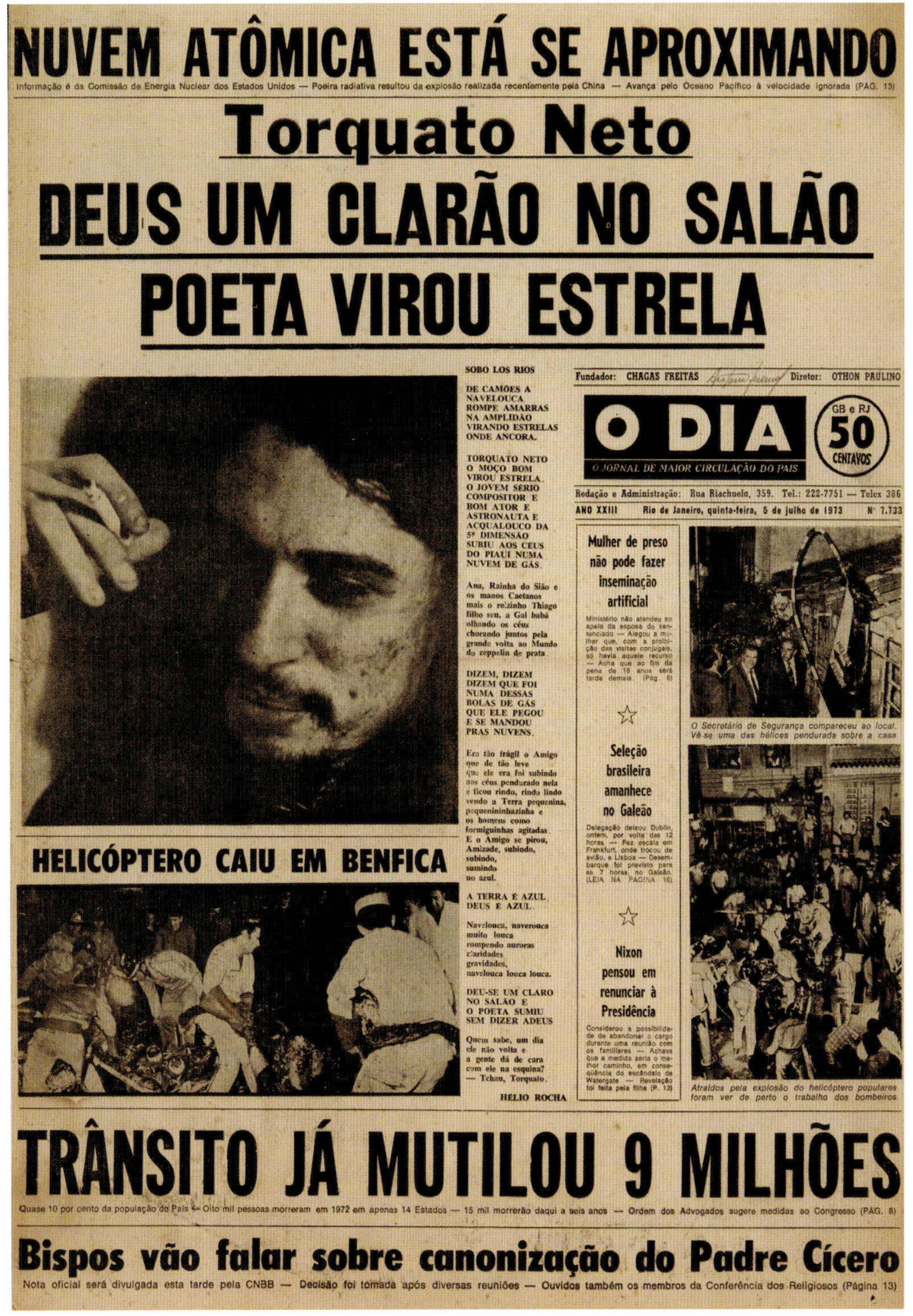

Deus um clarão no salão poeta virou estrela (A Flash in the Salon, Poet Became a Star), 1973. From the *Clandestina* series, newspaper, 22 x 15 in. Courtesy the artist was to sit in the center of a red enclosure. The goat created an opportunity for a double entendre in the work's title, as the Portuguese *bode* can signify both "goat" and "bad vibes." It was also a reference to performance and body art because *bode* sounds similar to the word "body" in English.

The goat is one of the animals sacrificed in certain rituals of Umbanda and Quimbanda, syncretic Afro-Brazilian religions. In these traditions, sacrificial animals are offered as sacred food to the various *orixás* (deities) during public ceremonies. Antonio Manuel offered the black goat as a metaphor for both the bad spirits and the heavy tension of a repressive era, and for its ludic connotations and carefree nature.[19] During the dictatorship it was not uncommon for artists to use animals (sometimes even sacrificing them) as a symbol for the torture carried out by the regime. In the historical exhibition *Do Corpo à Terra* (From the Body to the Earth), 1970, curated by Frederico Morais at the Municipal Park of Belo Horizonte, in the state of Minas Gerais, Artur Barrio disposed his *trouxas ensanguentadas* (bloody bundles), made out of cows' meat and bones and wrapped with blood-stained rope. At the same event, Cildo Meireles burned live chickens as a metaphor for the torture and killing of political prisoners, which provoked strong reactions from politicians.

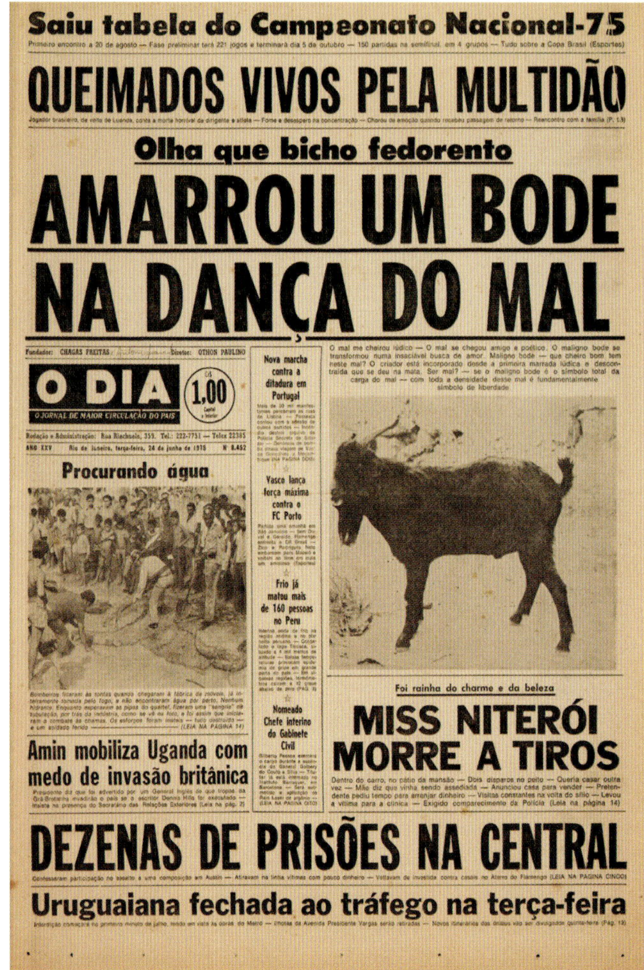

Amarrou um bode na dança do mal (Tied up a Goat to Do the Dance of Evil), 1975.
From the *Clandestina* series, newspaper, 22 x 15 in. Courtesy the artist

    19 *Antonio Manuel,* 46.

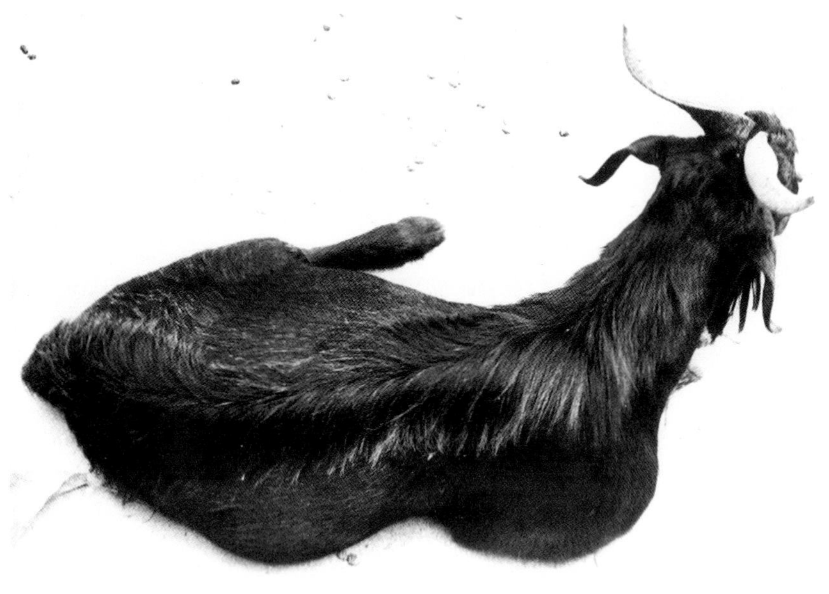

O bode (The Goat), 1973. Gelatin silver print, 7.2 x 9.5 in. Courtesy the artist

Eventually *O bode* was censored as well, leading to the cancellation of the entire exhibition at MAM. The museum's somewhat bizarre justification for banning *O bode* was that it was not typical of Antonio Manuel's work. As when his own body had been rejected as a work of art, Antonio Manuel refused to passively accept being stifled. In a bold challenge to this decision, he used the media to publish his censored exhibition. At Antonio Manuel's request Washington Novaes, the editor of the Rio de Janeiro newspaper *O Jornal,* published images of the censored works, devoting the paper's entire six-page Sunday Arts & Leisure supplement to the artist on July 15, 1973. The Sunday edition, which had a national circulation of sixty thousand, titled the supplement *Exposição de Antonio Manuel — De 0 à 24 horas* (Exhibition of Antonio Manuel — From 0 to 24 Hours). It was an ephemeral exhibition, "on view" for twenty-four hours, the same duration as a daily newspaper. Again, Antonio Manuel used the immediacy of the medium, its broad distribution and its power of communication to convey his ideas in an immediate and intuitive manner.

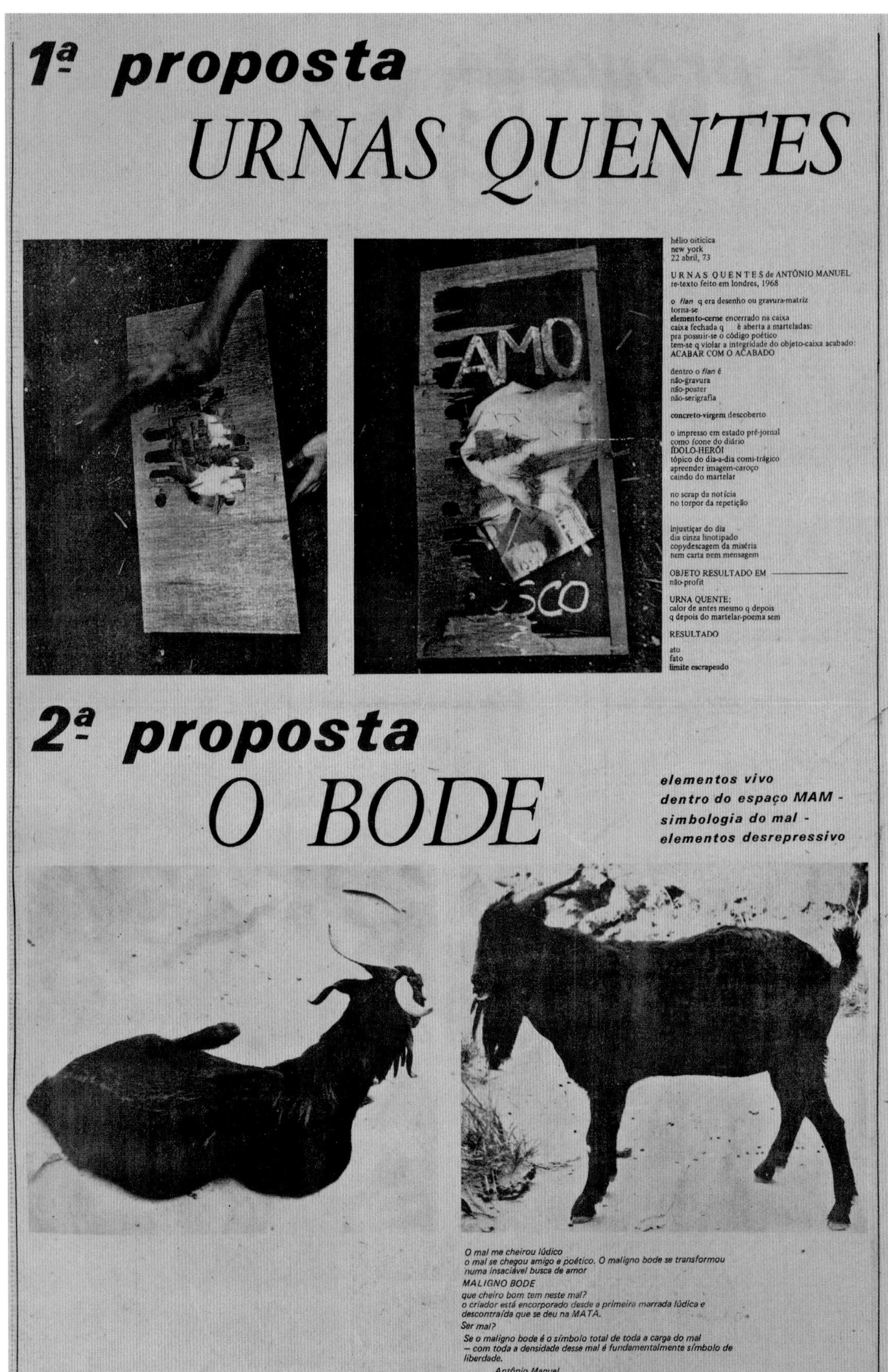

Exposição Antonio Manuel – De 0 a 24 horas (Exhibition of Antonio Manuel – From 0 to 24 Hours), 1973. Newspaper, 22 x 15 in. Courtesy the artist

4ª proposta

CLANDESTINAS

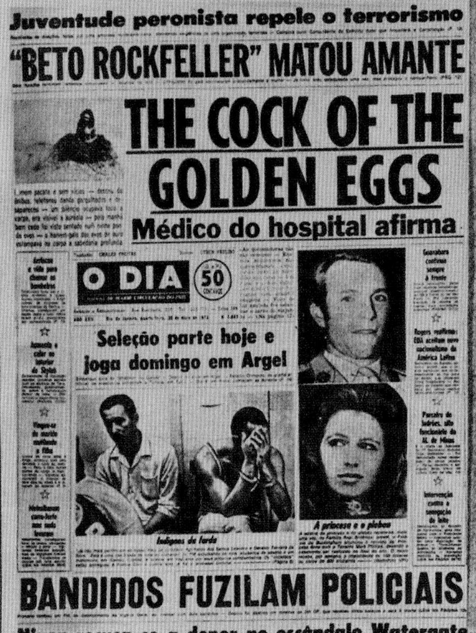

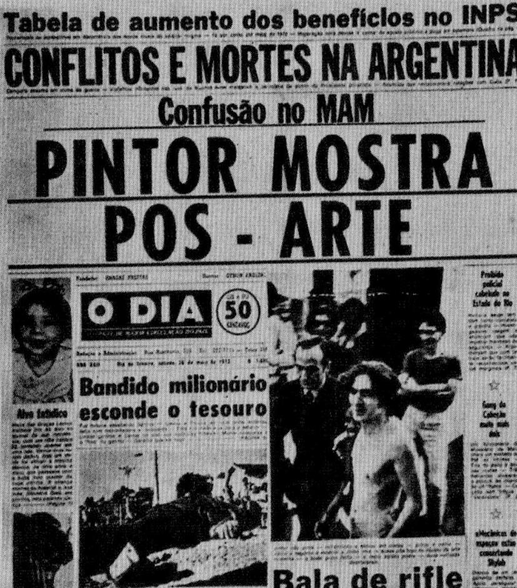

antônio manuel se projeta novo antônio manuel. pode ser múltiplos, mas preferé ser único, ou, pelo menos, único bem poucos.

depois da notícia, news, para os outros, público e audiência, milhões, uns poucos resolvem transformar-se em notícia para uns poucos: anti-notícia de um anti-comportamento para um anti-público — os três, notícia, comportamento e público, quase clandestinos e altamente sofisticados.

o sistema usando o artista pode ser trágico; o contrário, pelo menos, engraçado. o sistema se supõe normalmente racional; o artista-evento, normalmente irracional, um ruído, em todo caso, o primeiro detém o dinheiro junto com uma fajuta tábua de valores; o segundo recusa-se a ganhá-lo, se não engulirem, ou fingirem engulir, a sua anti-tábua.

os atos quotidianos são como as vielas de veneza: suportáveis porque conduzem à apoteose de uma praça são marcos. o artista os suporta, rotina marginal, até o glorioso tempo lugar de representar o ato para si mesmo — e para uma coisa-medium e/ou testemunho que o registre.

ao projetar-se ato, o artista já se projeta signo — uma compulsão: ele é um sign-addict. virado linguagem, pode manipular simulacros, modelos, de integração social e se insere manchete de jornal, em tiragem limitada ou separata, junto a outras gentes-signos de sua eleição, os chamados marginais de um público maior.

aqui, a suburra transa com os salões e museus e bancos e marchands. o modelo criado pelos românticos, vie de bohème, revolução industrial, — a volta à natureza, ontem; a ecologia, hoje — mantém-se, sincrônico.

a leucemia da linguagem não deixa vaza para o que se chama vida e homem. o andróide é o homem-signo projetado pela aspiração ou compulsão de progresso do homem.

talvez que a noção corrente de reificação deva ser revista. se o homem era o homem do antropóide, o andróide é o homem do homem. um novo humanismo implica o fim do progresso linear. o homem tem que estruturar-se, projetar-se sincrônico para superar o projeto de progressão androidante.

o biológico ainda é um evento surpreendente. o ato sexual é a sua piazza san marco. ou matar. ou morrer. tem o mesmo grau de surpresa — e de liberdade de uma pantera num zoológico.

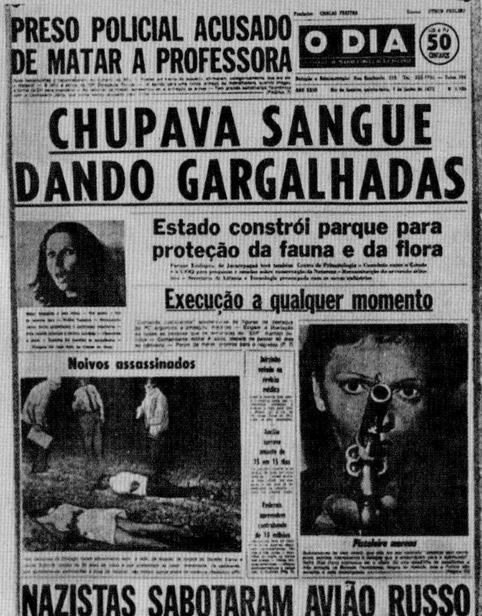

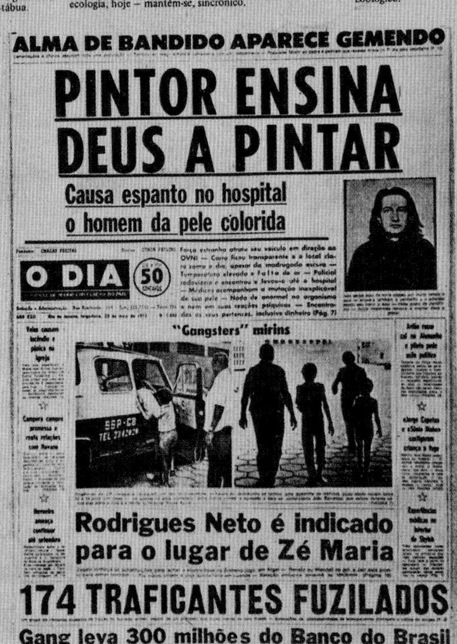

AFFIRMING THE CULTURE OF MARGINALITY

The appropriation of the media in a variety of innovative forms led Antonio Manuel to experiment with the format of the *fotonovela,* resulting in an artist's book titled *A arma fálica* (A Phallic Weapon).[20] *Fotonovelas*—illustrated novels with sensationalist stories—were very popular at the time. Hélio Oiticica, who had briefly returned to Brazil from London, starred as Guru, the main character in *A arma fálica.* Guru had spent many years in London, but his wife Neném had stayed behind in Rio de Janeiro. Upon his return, he catches her having an affair with Paulomarginal, an outcast from Mangueira Hill, one of the oldest shantytowns of Rio de Janeiro. A crime is then committed: Guru kills Paulomarginal with a phallic weapon.

A arma fálica's sensationalistic plot has many similarities to the story lines from Brazilian Cinema Marginal, also known as Udigrudi (taken from the English word "underground"). Challenging the tenets of Cinema Novo filmmakers, such as Glauber Rocha and his neorealist "aesthetics of hunger," Cinema Marginal filmmakers aimed to create their own aesthetic based on the underpinnings of debauchery and violence. According to Ivana Bentes, "What is at stake in Cinema Marginal is a new relationship with the emerging urban imaginary, which refuses or is suspicious of high culture … it seeks to submerge itself in mass culture, popular culture, the circus, *chanchada,* variety shows, television, erotic films … in comic books, radio soap opera, the tabloid press, carnival music, sentimental ballads, kitsch, and the Jovem Guarda."[21] Adopting strategies similar to those of his filmmaking peers, Antonio Manuel borrowed a medium from mass culture, incorporating parody, pastiche and dark humor in his *fotonovela* to explore violence and life on the margins of society.

The notion of marginality (the artist as an outcast) was central to the collective consciousness of the time, with Oiticica's banner "seja marginal, seja herói" (be an outcast, be a hero) acting as an unsung mantra of the age. Criminals, artists, homosexuals, transvestites and political prisoners all belonged to a different sector of society that was targeted by the military regime and marginalized by much of the country's conservative population.

Antonio Manuel also paid homage to figures on the margins of society in such works as *Caixa poema* (Poem Box), 1973, a sculptural installation in which two rotating boxes display photographs of two transvestites caught by the police.[22] The images are juxtaposed with the poem "o rei mandou dizer que ninguém toque nas frutas do seu pomar" (the king demanded that nobody touch the fruits of his orchard), seemingly a reference to the transvestites as forbidden fruit. Another, more recent and poetic work, *Pêndulo* (Pendulum), 1995/2010, consists of a small tin can attached to the wall with a piece of black charcoal hanging from it by a thread. *Pêndulo* is a condensed record of Antonio Manuel's earlier

---

20   Antonio Manuel, *A arma fálica,* graphic project by Luciano Figueiredo (Rio de Janeiro: Rio Arte, 1995). The text of *A arma falica* was written by Antonio Manuel with some dialogues supplied by Lygia Pape along with photographs by Lygia Clark's nephew, Marcos Lins Andrade (known as Kiko). Antonio Manuel only had twenty-four shots to complete the *fotonovela.* It was supposed to be published in an independent newspaper (*O Pasquim*) at the time, but was not published until some twenty-five years after it was created. *A arma fálica* was set at Oiticica's home in the neighborhood of Jardim Botânico in Rio de Janeiro and at the docks of Praça Mauá, where, a year earlier, Antonio Manuel had bid Oiticica farewell when he first departed on a ship for London.

21   Ivana Bentes, "Multitropicalism, Cinematic-Sensation, and Theoretical Devices," in *Tropicália: A Revolution in Brazilian Culture,* ed. Carlos Basualdo (São Paulo: Cosac Naify, 2005), 122.

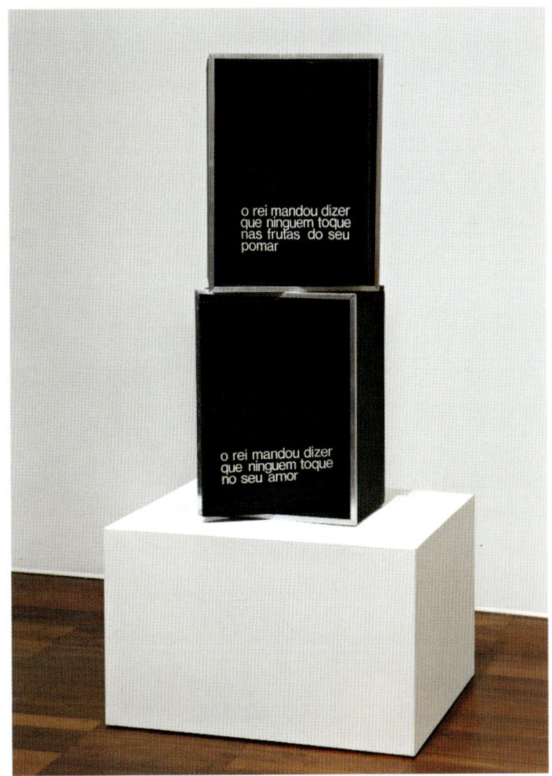

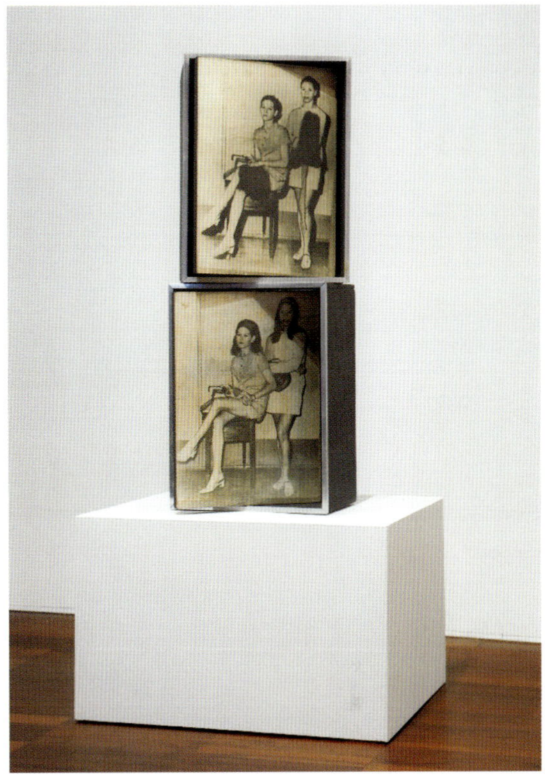

Caixa poema (Poem Box), 1973. Wood and gelatin silver print, 17 x 13 x 7.5 in. Courtesy the artist

installation *Fantasma* (Ghost), 1994, in which pieces of charcoal hang from the ceiling while flashlights illuminate a photograph of a witness of the massacre of the Vigário Geral favela in Rio de Janeiro (1993) with a photograph of his head covered with a white sheet during a press conference, so that his lost identity resembles a ghost, a non-person, an effaced figure.

Of his moving image works, a potent visual sociological portrait of the culture of marginality, with its exacerbated urban violence, can be found in *Semi Ótica* (Semi Otics / Optics), 1975, a seven-minute, 35mm, black-and-white short film. It opens with a shot of Antonio Manuel's photographic installation *The Cock,* 1972, which depicts the artist, half-naked, on top of a large nest made of straw and placed upon a dune of seashells. Despite its vitality and upright posture, the "cock" is in a permanent state of impotence[23] because it is unable to lay eggs; thus it is much like the silenced and marginalized artist. The camera segues through a precarious-looking house at the top of Morro do Borel (Borel Hill), a favela of Rio de Janeiro. A Brazilian national flag is painted across the facade of the house. When the window opens, the painted flag breaks apart and becomes a dark hole. The camera focuses on the space of the black hole to reveal a series of newspaper photographs

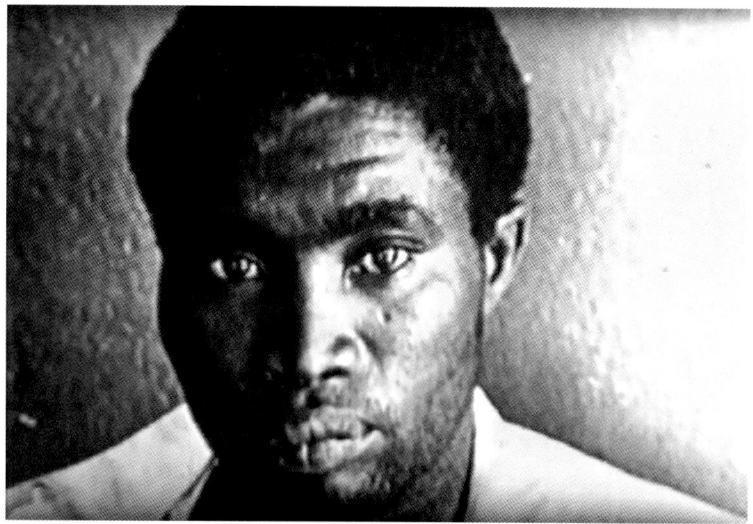

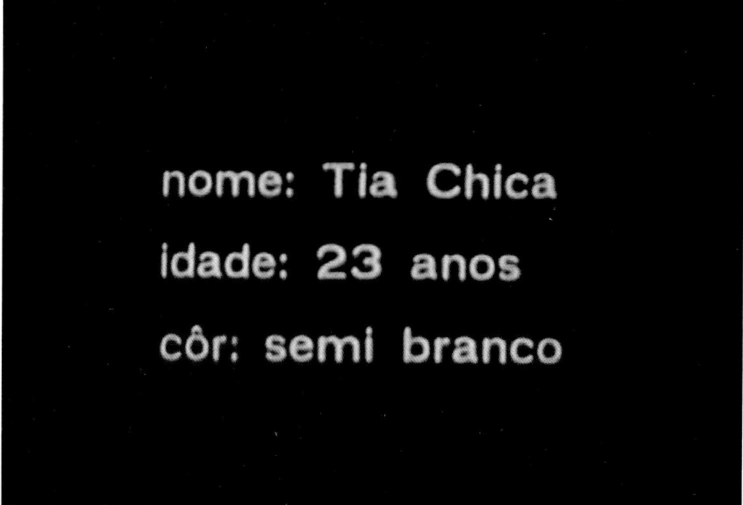

Stills from *Semi Ótica* (Semi Otic/Optic), 1975. B&W, with sound, 35 mm, 7 minutes.
Courtesy the artist

of victims of the death squads, made up of policemen "unofficially" sanctioned to kill criminals.[24] Superimposed onto each photograph is a short inscription indicating the person's fictional name or nickname, age and a "semi-color" associated with them, taken from the colors of the Brazilian flag (green, yellow, blue and white) along with black. These semi-colors (semi-green, semi-yellow, semi-blue, semi-white and semi-black) are ambiguous in their intention: they depict colors from the Brazilian flag, and at the same time they also address issues of race and class. The images reveal "quasi-peoples," pariahs from society, individuals who lack civil rights and are considered to be only partial citizens. Made during the most repressive time of the dictatorship, the film poignantly captures the many contradictions of the period—for example, that the dictatorship counted on and was supported

23 *Antonio Manuel*, 47.
24 *Semi Ótica* was awarded "Best Social-Anthropological Film" at the fifth Short Film Festival of Bahia. The images were found in the archives of the newspaper *O DIA*.

by many segments of the population, including the lower classes, who benefitted from an economic boom and the growth of domestic consumer goods. Moreover, Brazil's 1970 World Cup victory temporarily lifted public moral, encouraging such expressions of nationalism as the display of the flag on a shoddy house in an impoverished neighborhood. Behind the scenes, the death squads were targeting not only marginalized sectors of the population but also political opponents of the regime. In this short film, as in his media-based series like *Flans* and *Clandestinas* (Clandestines), Antonio Manuel vividly presents the current state of violence through the cuts, cracks and fissures, communicating what has been censored or effaced.

Antonio Manuel's work is characterized by a tension between seemingly divergent forces—political content versus formal composition, ephemeral performance versus material art object, order versus disorder—and among the most iconic examples of this dynamic is *Urnas quentes* (Hot Ballot Boxes), 1968–2004. First exhibited in 1968, the series included twenty sealed wooden boxes, meant to be broken open by viewers in a cathartic, physical manifestation of the public's anger and rage. Inside the boxes were images and texts taken from contemporary newspapers and photographic archives, as well as poems. Each box required a rather brutal act—the public had to crack them open with a hammer—in order to view the contents. Because of the violence inherent in these pieces, they functioned as a metaphor for the harsh, hostile actions of the regime. The title of the work "hot" ballot boxes also served as an ironic reminder of the suppression of elections in Brazil during the dictatorship.[25]

Antonio Manuel's irreverent actions invariably include an impeccable formal presentation even as they confront violent realities. He intervenes in the pages of newspaper to modify their messages and content, while allowing their layout and form to remain intact (*Clandestinas*). He takes off his clothes in a museum, but then transforms his unexpected action into a formal sculpture (*Corpobra*). He reproduces graphic images of police violence in bold red-and-black screen prints, then conceals them under minimalist panels and places the power of unveiling into the viewer's hands (*Repressão outra vez – Eis o saldo*). He collects clippings of current events in a tidy wooden box and then invites the public to engage in an act of violence to reveal them (*Urnas quentes*). His art moves between the rational (the geometric grid of the *Flans* and newspapers, the packaging of crates, the geometric structure of boxes and cans) and the rebellious and irreverent (questioning the truth of newspapers, taking off his clothes, publishing his censored exhibition). Visually it has all the formal qualities of a man dressed in a tuxedo; in its intent, however, it is closer to the man who unexpectedly takes off his clothes in public. It is here, in the space between order and disorder, that Antonio Manuel's work asserts its ultimate power.

---

25   In 1975, Antonio Manuel remade and sealed one of his *Urnas quentes*. He planned to break it after thirty years, but in 2005, when the time arrived, he decided to leave it untouched. In 2004 he remade another *Urna quente*, which is the one exhibited at his solo exhibition at Americas Society.

URNA QUENTE

ANTONIO MANUEL

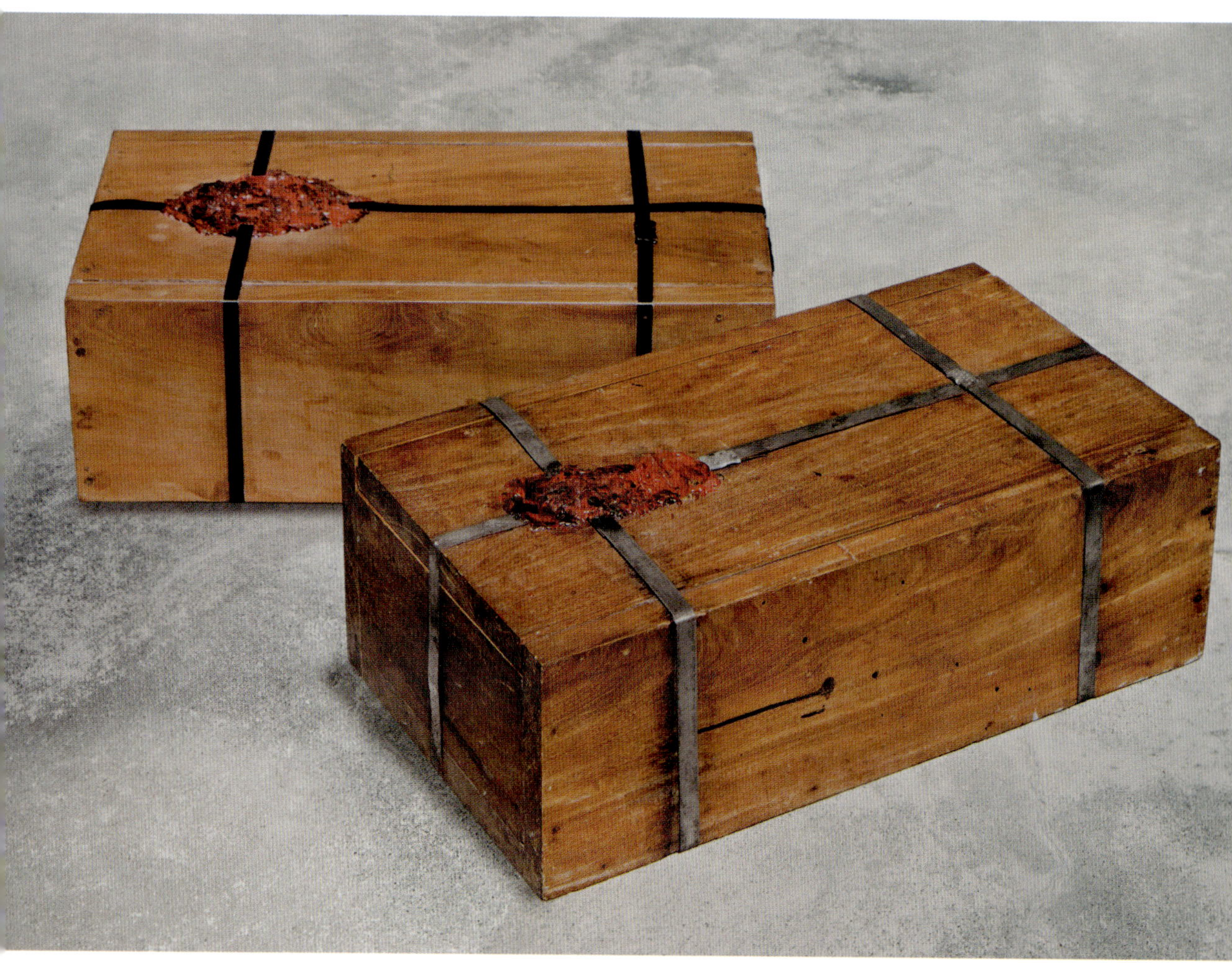

Urnas quentes (Hot Ballot Boxes), 1975 (right) and 2004 (left). Wood, sealing wax and tape, both 24 x 13 x 8 in. Courtesy the artist

At times I felt compelled to create variations of pieces, so that the works could be seen and reach the public. In 1968, I created the first *Urnas quentes* (Hot Ballot Box), presented at Aterro do Flamengo in the event, *Apocalipopótese* (Apocalypopothesis). The boxes were broken by people with curiosity and a desire to discover what was inside of them.

In 1975, I produced a new *Urna quente* out of hardwood, sturdy and one-hundred times thicker than the first *Urnas,* hermetically shut with tape and seal. On the seal, while hot, I stamped my name. I wanted this *Urna* to stay shut for many years, I thought about thirty years. I went to the notary and produced a document called *Urna quente–1975,* not to be violated with thrashings, but to remain permanently shut.

In 2004, I was invited by curator Lynn Zelevansky to participate in the exhibition *Beyond Geometry.* The work chosen was *Urna quente–1975.* Lynn came to Brazil, we met at my studio, and she formally invited the *Urn*a to participate in the travelling exhibition throughout the United Sates. However, this occurred during the George W. Bush administration, shortly after September 11. The paranoia created by the administration, along with a question of homeland security, generated a great concern on my part about the possibility of the *Urna* being officially opened by the United States government. In Brazil, I consulted a lawyer who confirmed that the Department of Homeland Security could open the *Urna* and reveal its secret, thus destroying the work.

The possibility of the *Urna* being opened by the United States government was real, and in order to not take such a risk, I decided to create a new *Urna,* similar on the outside to the *Urna* of 1975, but different on the inside. This second *Urna* was sent to the exhibition *Beyond Geometry,* in secret, as if it were the one from 1975.

I thought about writing something about the creation of this *Urna.* I never did, so I am now. However, long ago, I met with art critic Ronaldo Brito and told him about this *Urna.* When Michael Asbury, another art critic, was in Brazil, I shared the same story. So, three people knew the work existed: Ronaldo, Michael, and I. Motivated by the exhibition at the Americas Society and the fact that the *Urna* will be exhibited again in the United States, I called Lynn and told her the whole story.

The *Urna quente,* 2004 comes out of hiding to gain a life of its own, as language, and as a means of communication and experience.

Rio de Janeiro, 2011

URNA QUENTE - 75

hermeticamente fechada. não mais para
ser violentada a porretadas.

a ideia da URNA QUENTE - 75 é de   en
cerrar por muito tempo coisas.
lacrada encerra o que não pode ser re
velado.

antonio manuel   25/2/1975

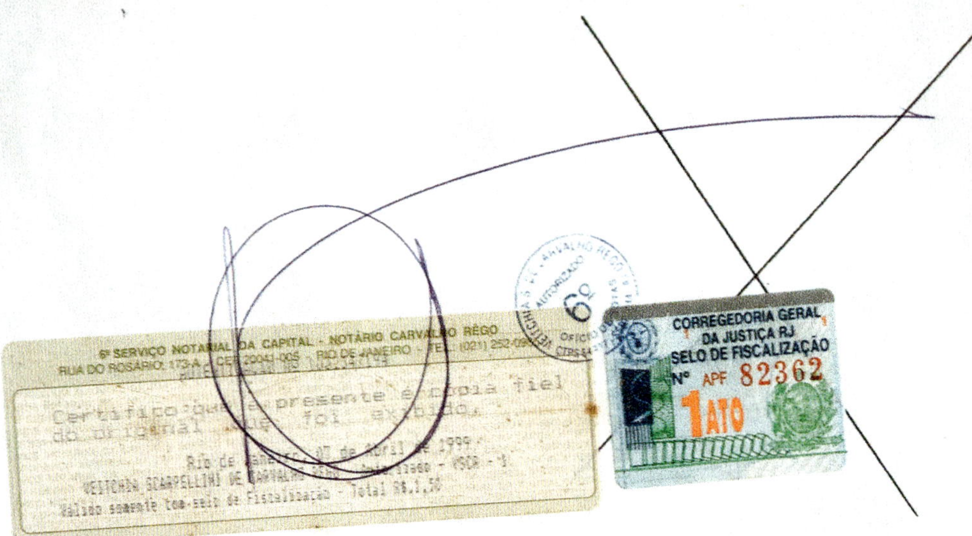

Notarized document for *Urna quente – 1975* (Hot Ballot Box – 1975). Courtesy the artist

Page 25:

1–3: Images of *Urna quente* (Hot Ballot Box), 1975. C-Print. Courtesy the artist

4–5: Stills from *Urna quente* (Hot Ballot Box), 1968. Short film directed by Raimundo Amado: 16 mm, B&W. Courtesy the artist

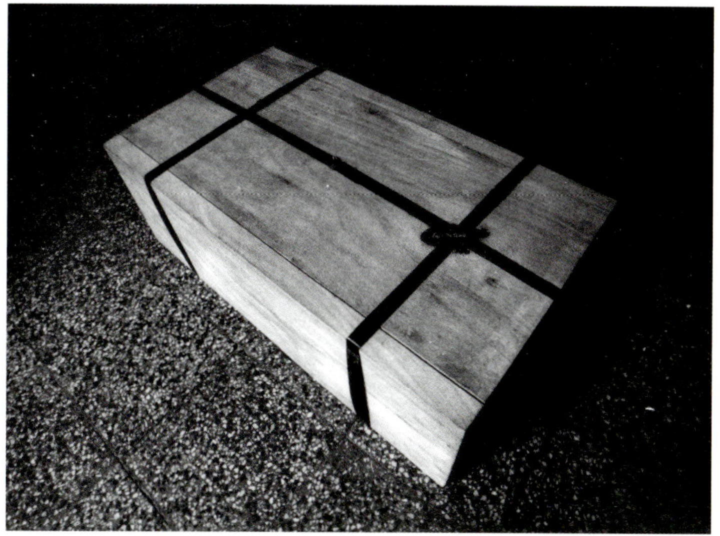

1

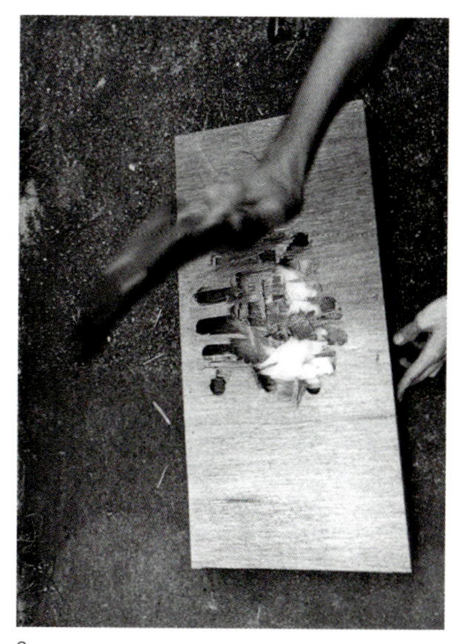

2

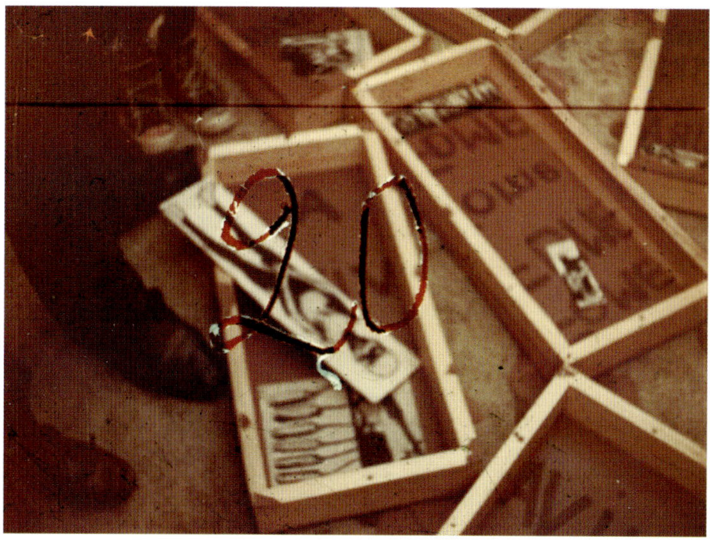

3

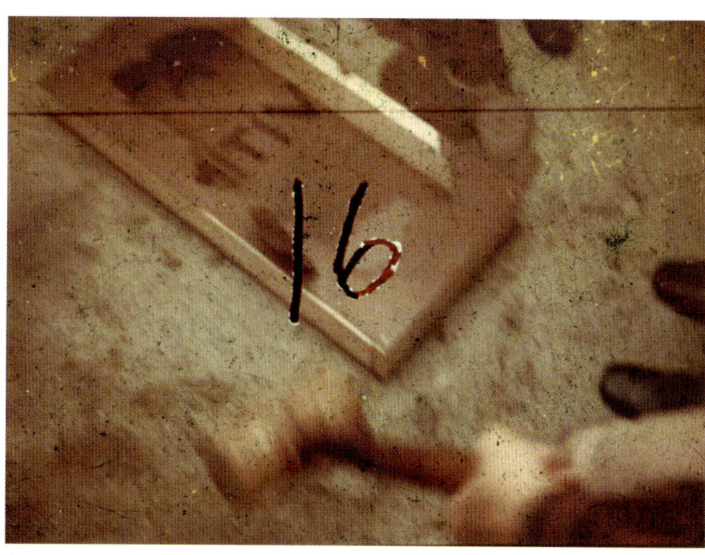

4

5

FLANS, URNAS QUENTES AND THE RADICALISM OF A CORDIAL MAN

MICHAEL ASBURY

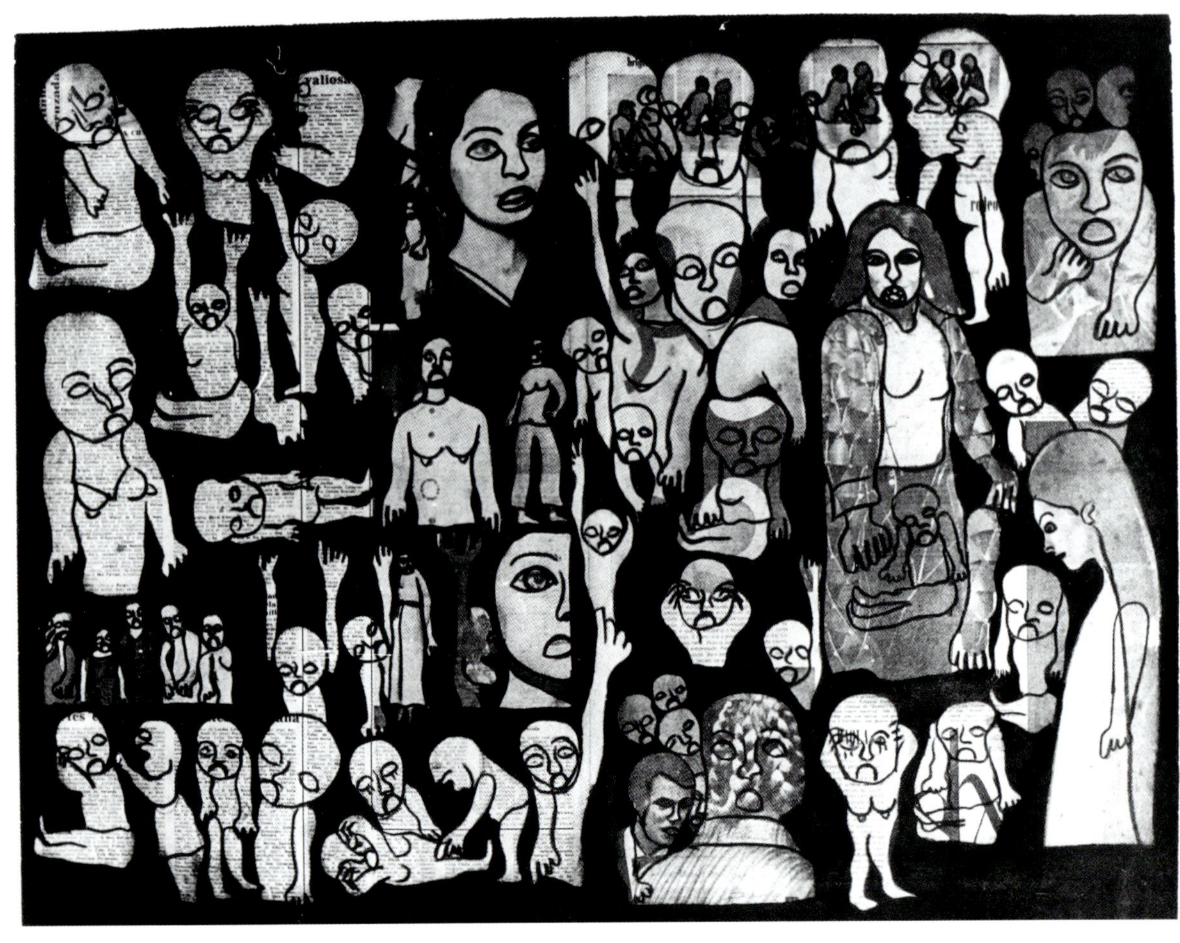

Untitled, 1966. Crayon on newsprint paper, 22 x 31 in. Courtesy the artist

Among the artists of his generation in Brazil, Antonio Manuel is arguably the one most closely associated with the drive to express (and therefore denounce) the violence perpetrated by the military dictatorship that took power in the 1964 coup. This overt political dimension of his early work often labels him, particularly when considered from outside Brazil, as the anti-institutional rebellious artist par excellence.

With the widening of geographical boundaries of the art historical canons, 1960s and '70s experimental and conceptual practices in Brazil—and more broadly in Latin America— are often considered as intrinsically political in nature, distinguishing them from conceptual art produced in the Northern-Western hemisphere.[1] Within this dichotomy, conceptualism in the North has been perceived as more autonomous in its concerns, while the affinities that radical practices from Latin America had with international events—such as the struggles for independence throughout the colonized world, the civil rights movement, the war in Vietnam and the events of May '68 in Paris—are perhaps unintentionally overshadowed. It is true to say that the art produced in Brazil at that moment was limited by a cultural milieu still in the process of consolidating its institutions, which were afflicted by state and even self-censorship. Experimentally inclined artists were therefore forced to find alternative means of dissemination, which in turn informed their innovative approaches toward artistic media bringing their practice closer to the "praxis of everyday life"—a concept articulated by Peter Bürger in his discussion of the European avant-garde.[2] This local specificity within a global moment of political radicalism is further enhanced in Antonio Manuel's case by his friendship and collaboration with artists such as Hélio Oiticica and Lygia Pape, and critics such as Mário Pedrosa, emphasizing his connection to the current understanding of Brazilian art within the recently expanded art historical canon.

Without glossing over its local specificity, which is indeed helpful in dislodging old assumptions of creative derivation, there are nevertheless certain problems that emerge from such an approach. First, it may undermine the critical ambivalence held by such artists in relation to those emerging institutions. Furthermore, the piecemeal process of inclusion that has characterized the expansion of the art historical canon tends to isolate individual contributions at the expense of the collective dynamic to which their work belonged. Finally (and perhaps most significantly in the case of Antonio Manuel), the association between artistic practice and the radicalism of the 1960s and '70s tends to fix the artist's overall practice in time, framing all subsequent work within the specificity of one historical moment.

1   For an overview of recent publications on this subject see Robin Adèle Greeley, "Art and Politics in Contemporary Latin America," *Oxford Art Journal* 32, no. 1 (2009).

2   Peter Bürger, *Theory of the Avant-Garde*, trans. M. Shaw (Minneapolis: University of Minnesota, 1984). It is worth mentioning Bürger here in relation to Hal Foster's critique in *Return of the Real* (MIT 1996), which brilliantly argues that the historic avant-gardes held a relation of deferred action upon the neo-avant-gardes. As I have argued before, Foster's argument nevertheless affirms the very teleology it sets out dismantle once examples from the southern hemispheres are considered. See M. Asbury, "Neoconcretism and Minimalism: On Ferreira Gullar's Theory of the Non-Object," in Kobena Mercer, *Cosmopolitan Modernisms* (London, UK and Cambridge, MA: InIVA and MIT), 2005.

This essay will explore these three issues primarily, but not exclusively, in relation to two series of works by Antonio Manuel, *Flans* and *Urnas quentes* (Hot Ballot Boxes), examining how these correspond to a fluid creative praxis that was the product of successive political events and art historically placed at the crossroads of what conventionally could be categorized as Neoconstructivism, Pop art, and Conceptualism.

With its cheap material, graphic quality, and the possibility of relating to events in "real life," the newspaper has a crucial place in Antonio Manuel's career as an artist. His early drawings of human forms arranged in a seemingly random manner across the newspaper page displayed, at first, little relation to the background other than emphasizing his disregard for perspective through the flatness imposed by the printed matter. However, the somewhat *art brut* quality of those early experiments soon gave way to a more direct engagement with the actual content of the page.

Like many other artists of his generation, Antonio Manuel would frequent the Museu de Arte Moderna in Rio de Janeiro (MAM RJ), which although still under construction throughout the 1960s, had become a crucial meeting place for artists and intellectuals. One day, while walking toward the museum, a sensationalist headline at a newspaper stand caught his attention. It read: "Matou o cachorro e bebeu o sange. Mulher vampira age em Impanema" ("Killed the dog and drank its blood. Vampire lady on the loose in Impanema"). The front page included images of two women: one was associated with the headline while the other was a bikini-clad beauty pageant contestant. Sitting at the museum's canteen, he began drawing over the newspaper page, emphasizing the ambiguity that he saw between the images and the headline and obscuring irrelevant information by interfering with the text and photographs—a process that would inform the first *Flans* series. Hélio Oiticica happened to pass by at that moment and was very much taken by this work; he invited Antonio Manuel to show his drawings on newspaper in conjunction with the installation *Tropicália* that he was working on for a forthcoming exhibition at MAM in 1967 entitled *Nova Objetividade Brasileira* (New Brazilian Objectivity).

This was the third in a series of groundbreaking annual exhibitions held at MAM, following *Opinião 65* and *Opinião 66.* These exhibitions signaled a new approach in art production that significantly distinguished itself from the previous Constructivist-oriented groups. *Opinião 65,* 1965, associated the Brazilian new figuration group and former Constructivist artists with international tendencies such as Pop art and to a certain extent Nouveau Réalisme through an emphasis on painting and its capacity for sociopolitical commentary. The bringing together of the Constructivist legacy and the growing interest in popular culture was further developed in *Opinião 66* and would culminate in *Nova Objetividade Brasileira* the following year. As articulated in Oiticica's catalogue essay, the exhibition articulated a national response to the international advent of Pop and Op art by contextualizing the imagery of mass media within the national crisis, the reality of underdevelopment, and the conditions of life under a military regime on the eve of its repressive climax.[3]

---

3   Hélio Oiticica, "Esquema Geral da Nova Objetividade," in *Nova Objetividade Brasileira* (Rio de Janeiro: Museu de Arte Moderna, 1967), reprinted and translated in: *Hélio Oiticica* (Rotterdam: Witte De With, 1992).

Antonio Manuel's own relation to the newspaper, and by extension to mass media, undertook a profound transformation during 1967. Although he admired its intrinsic qualities, he had become frustrated with the fragility and limitations of the newspaper page. This led him to request that the *Jornal do Brasil* press reprint selected newspaper pages on more robust paper. This direct intervention with the press earned him greater familiarity with printing processes, leading to his "discovery" of the flan.[4] In fact, it was only possible to reprint an already published newspaper page because the *Jornal do Brasil* archived its used flans for a period of time.[5] According to Antonio Manuel, the flans were enveloped in an aluminum foil container that kept them moist until they were used. Once they had captured the text and images from the linotype, they were burned; the clay and plaster composition would then harden enough to make an imprint on the soft plumb rotary mold. Flans were then usually discarded.[6]

Antonio Manuel found this discarded material interesting as an object: a monochrome surface containing hidden information that would be made temporarily visible by applying talc over it. The first *Flans* series were made between 1967 and 1968: Antonio Manuel made late-night or early-morning visits to newspaper presses in Rio, where he would recover and select the discarded items and later make interventions on them in his studio. In the wake of May 1968, the first *Flans* series relates primarily to newspaper pages that documented the discontent with the military regime manifested through riots between workers, students and the police. The artist's intervention consisted in applying ink over the flan, emphasizing the relation between image and text and selecting what should remain visible and what should not: a form of reversal of the act of censuring that could be considered as a premonitory characteristic of the work's own historical trajectory.

The variety of newspapers combined with the type of access that reprinting "copies" required suggests that by 1967 the artist had established, even if on an informal level, a trusting relationship with employees of newspaper presses around Rio de Janeiro. In addition to *Jornal do Brasil,* these included the *Correio da Manhã, O DIA* and *O Pais.*[7] Each newspaper used different brands of flans as well as presenting their own distinct graphic, photographic and journalistic signatures; these distinct qualities appealed to Antonio Manuel as much as the political content itself.[8] This is evident in the headlines "As armas do diálogo" (The Weapons of Dialogue) from *Correio da Manhã,* June 2, 1968, as well as in the cropped photograph on a page from *Jornal do Brasil* that same year that partially captures a political slogan on a wall, transforming the graffiti "Ditadura Assassina" (Assassin Dictatorship) into "Dura assassina" (Hard Assassin). It is clear by this printed material that

---

4   Lower case will be used to distinguish flans used in the newspaper press from Antonio Manuel's series of *Flans.*

5   The flan was developed in the nineteenth century (between 1822 and 1829) to solve the problem of producing curved molds. It is located within the printing process as the stage between the flat linotype and the curved plumb mold whose rotation imprints the newspaper sheets that are fed into it. The graphic information on the flan is therefore positive, as in the actual final newspaper print, as opposed to the inverted image on the plumb mold. Now made obsolete by the introduction of computer technology, it consisted of an initially flexible surface formed by "layers of paper with a composition of clay and plaster in between." James Moran, *Printing Presses: History and Development from the Fifteenth Century to Modern Times* (Berkeley: University of California Press, 1973), 181.

6   The artist in conversation with the author, Rio de Janeiro, April 18, 2011.

7   To collect the discarded flans required Antonio Manuel to "knock on the door and ask." Ibid.

8   *Jornal do Brasil*'s graphic design had been completely reconfigured over the course of the 1950s by Amilcar de Castro under the editorship of Reynaldo Jardim. Both became members of the Neoconcrete group in 1959. Antonio Manuel would have been aware of this indirect relation his work had with Neoconcretism. A selection of "facsimile" pages from the Neoconcrete period has been translated into English and is available for download at: https://docs.google.com/fileview?id=0B-5FWqyX6FKWNjBlZWQ3ZGYtODVhYy00ZTIzLWI1OgtZGQxZjlkY mJhYzlk&hl=en, (accessed August 1, 2011).

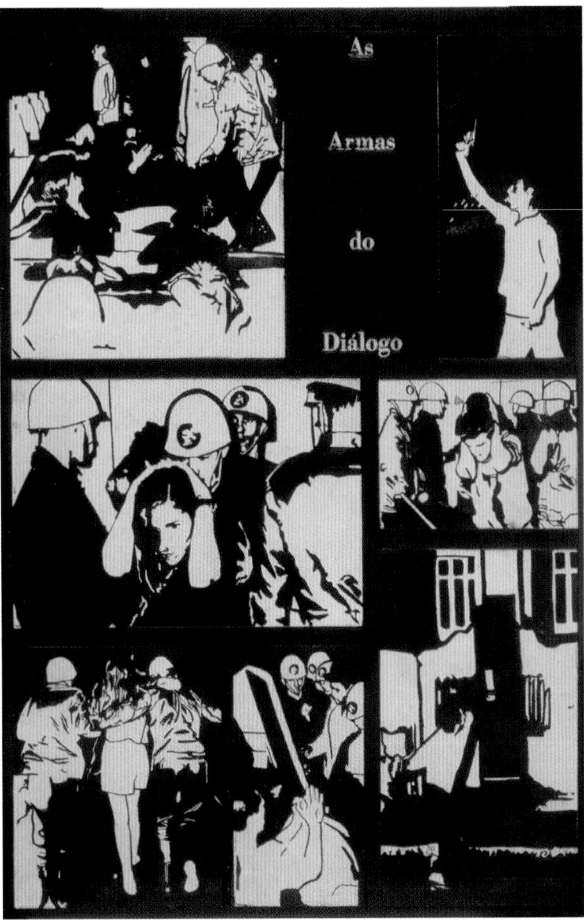

As armas do diálogo (The Weapons of Dialogue), 1968. From the
Flan series, ink on papier-mâché stereotype mold, 22 x 15 in.
Courtesy the artist

at the time of production the so-called political content of the work did not go beyond
that which was already within the public domain. Equally, it would be misleading to assume
that Oiticica's invitation to Antonio Manuel to participate in the *Tropicália* environment was
merely the act of an older artist discovering and promoting the work of a younger one.

From the very beginning Antonio Manuel was officially recognized for his work. He first
sold a drawing at the 1965 *Salão dos Adolescentes* to one of the officials from *O Globo*
newspaper, the event's sponsor. The following year he won a prize for a wax crayon drawing
on newspaper at the *XXIII Salão Paranaense de Belas Artes*. In 1967, the year *Nova
Objetividade Brasileira* took place, Antonio Manuel had his first solo exhibition at the Goeldi
Gallery in Rio and participated in the *IX Bienal de São Paulo* and was awarded the acquisition prize for a drawing in Indian ink on newspaper. In this way it would be simplistic to
associate the content of his imagery with a general rebellious and anti-institutional attitude,
at least not up to this point. Instead, it would be more precise to consider the case of an
officially recognized young artist becoming caught within a situation of hardening political
repression and responding to this through both his work and his character. His subsequent

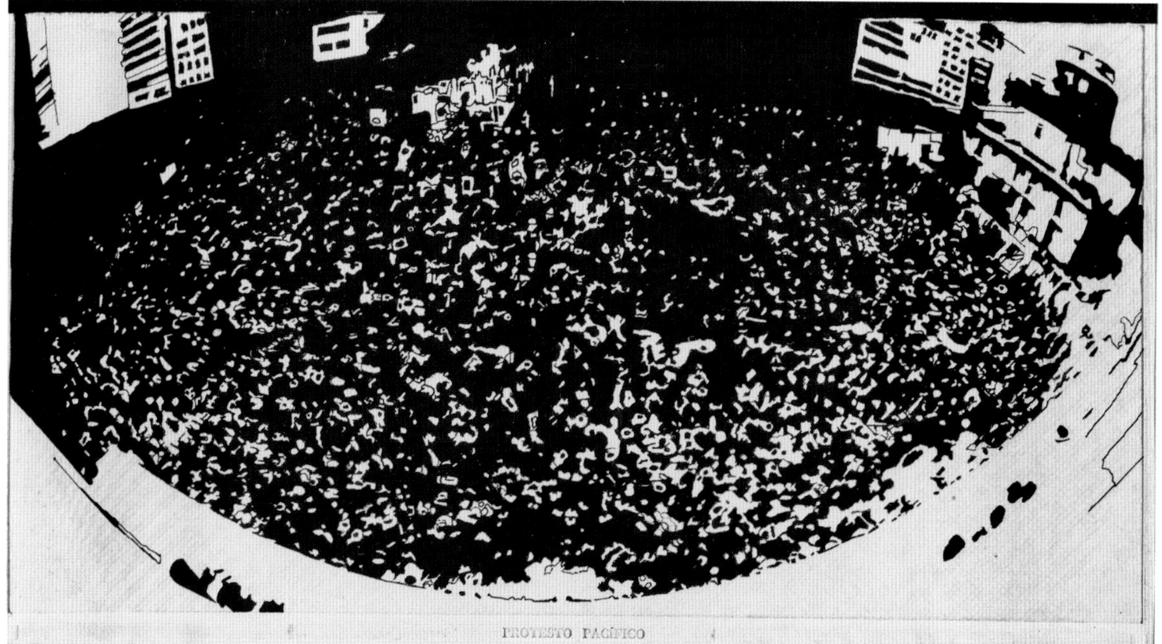

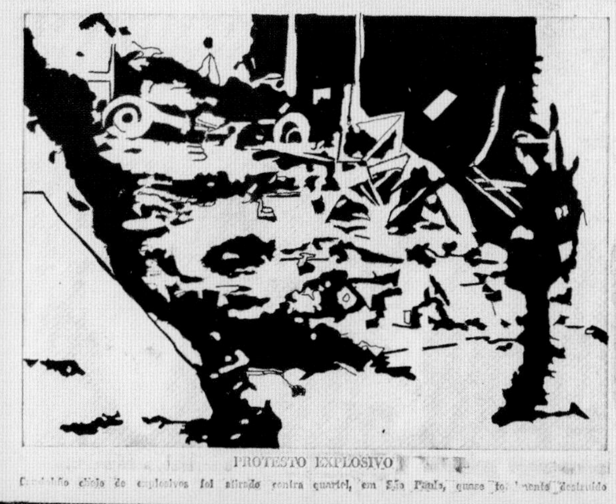

Por seis horas, mais de 100 mil cariocas protestaram contra o Govêrno, apoiando o movimento dos estudantes que, conforme o previsto, foi sem incidentes, com dezenas de discursos de universitários, operários, professôres e padres, que definiram "o compromisso histórico da Igreja com o povo".

Com perfeito dispositivo de segurança, os estudantes garantiram a realização da passeata, sem depredações, chegando a prender e soltar um policial que incitava a que fôsse apedrejado o prédio do Conselho de Segurança Nacional. A concentração começou às 10 horas, com os primeiros grupos de padres e estudantes, sem qualquer policiamento ostensivo.

Entre os primeiros oradores estava o representante da Igreja, ressaltando que "calar os moços é violentar nossas consciências". Presentes cêrca de 150 padres, inclusive o bispo-auxiliar do Rio de Janeiro, Dom Castro Pinto, que acompanhou a passeata, durante os 32 minutos de travessia da Av. Rio Branco. Na Candelária, falou Wladimir Palmeira, lembrando o assassinato do secundarista Édson Luís, "que um dia será vingado".

A manifestação seguiu para o Palácio Tiradentes, onde houve novos discursos, inclusive de um representante dos favelados, o mais aplaudido, ao afirmar que agora êles também "estavam na luta". No local foi queimada uma bandeira dos Estados Unidos, um policial tentou prender Wladimir Palmeira, mas não ocorreram incidentes. Ficou decidido dar o prazo de uma semana ao Govêrno, para atender às reivindicações, entre elas a da liberdade para todos os presos políticos. Marcaram também, para hoje, encontro de tôda a liderança estudantil, com o objetivo de analisar os resultados.

Informou a Secretaria de Segurança que ninguém foi detido, mas o DOPS prendeu cinco estudantes que distribuíam panfletos. A Polícia Federal pediu ao CONTEL que proibisse a exibição de filmes e transmissão de reportagens em rádio e televisão que "mostrem tumultos em que se envolveram os estudantes", e o governador Negrão de Lima, cêrcado por 100 soldados da PM, acompanhou, através de informações, todo o movimento, declarando-se satisfeito com os rumos da manifestação.

Em Belo Horizonte, a polícia atacou e foi repelida por estudantes que saíram às ruas, em duas passeatas, enquanto que, em frente à Universidade Federal do Ceará, os agentes também reprimiram, com violência, protesto dos universitários. No Rio Grande do Sul estudantes programam para hoje passeatas, em solidariedade aos cariocas.

Última página

GOVERNADORES PELO DIALOGO

Dez governadores da ARENA fizeram, ontem à noite, um apêlo ao presidente Costa e Silva, em Brasília, em reunião que durou 2 horas, no sentido de que o Govêrno mude o tratamento em relação aos estudantes e adote medidas que representem na prática "a recuperação do prestígio popular do Govêrno federal, som o retôrno ao convencionalismo político de antes da revolução". O marechal Costa e Silva respondeu ser esta precisamente a preocupação do Govêrno, e exemplificou com o trabalho realizado nas áreas da Reforma Universitária e Administrativa do Ministério da Educação. Antes dêsse encontro, alguns governadores e convencionais arenistas decepcionaram-se com a omissão do presidente da República, em analisar a crise que abala o País, nos dois discursos que fêz, na Convenção, o escrito o o improvisado, passando a criticar a indefinição do Govêrno. No improviso, o marechal anunciou a formulação de uma nova política de Segurança Nacional, contida em um documento "em grande parte de natureza ultra-secreta". E, entre os "Objetivos Permanentes", incluiu a prática da Justiça Social. Essa referência e uma breve alusão ao "aprimoramento nas relações com o Legislativo" foram as únicas concessões do presidente em comentar as crises política e social.

Páginas 3, 5, 7, 10, 11, 12, 14, 15, última e editorial

1, 2, 3, 4 e última do segundo Caderno

Marcha reúne cem mil (March Brings Together One Hundred Thousand), 1968. From the *Flan* series, ink on papier-mâché stereotype mold, 21 x 15 in. Courtesy the artist participation in official exhibitions was symptomatic of this shift. An early *Flan* entitled *Guevara* was "lost" after being exhibited at the *IV Salão Nacional de Arte Moderna* in Brasilia[9] in 1967 and in December 1968 a large silkscreen depicting clashes between police and students was seized and, according to Pierre Restany, subsequently burned following the police closure of the *II Bienal da Bahia* the day after its inauguration.[10] Antonio Manuel's account provides a vivid depiction of the general atmosphere of fear that emerged:

> I had made several silkscreen prints of *Guevara* a little while before, in order to help political activists who needed money. That was when I saw a headline in the *Jornal da Bahia* newspaper, which read: "Weapons Arsenal Found in a Political Hideout," and next to that headline there was a picture of the silkscreen print. Serious incidents involving the censors started to occur and I was continuously leaving myself exposed, by publicly debating the issue of the closing of the show, and so on. I soon felt as if I was being tailed, to such a degree that I was advised to return to Rio immediately. [The painter] Vanda Pimentel took me to the bus station. I caught a coach and returned under a cloud of fear. I put a piece of paper into a matchbox; on it I had written my name, telephone number, address, and a brief summary of the situation I was in. I stayed awake the entire journey, holding the matchbox in my hand. If something happened to me, I planned to let it fall surreptitiously to the ground, in the hope that someone would find it. That box was like an *Urna quente* in my hand.[11]

Following the coup in 1964, political activists and union and student leaders had been persecuted while the art circuit, with its perceived detachment, modest size and association with "elite" sectors of society had been left relatively unaffected. However, with the growing interventions by the regime, the cultural sector's dissatisfaction had been strongly expressed in a mass demonstration in Rio known as the "Marcha dos cem mil" (March of the One Hundred Thousand) in June of 1968. After the decree of Institutional Act No. 5 or "AI-5" six months later, the military decisively turned against the intelligentsia. A preview exhibition had been organized by MAM, Rio de Janeiro, in May 1969 to showcase the forthcoming Brazilian representation at the *IV Biennale de Paris* due to take place later that year. As one of the selected artists, Antonio Manuel produced a series of works using silkscreened

---

9   Although I was unable to determine which month the Salon took place, a review discussing the deliberations of the jury by Mário Pedrosa (*Correio da Manhã*, December 17, 1967) suggests that the exhibition took place following the death of Che Guevara on October 9, 1967. This indicates that Antonio Manuel's lost flan of Guevara followed in the tradition of Oiticica's *Bólide caixa "Homenagem a Cara de Cavalo"* (Box Bólide "Homage to Cara de Cavalo") produced the previous year using newsprint images of his outlaw friend murdered by police squads. In 1968 (in the context of the *Domingo de bandeiras* (Flag Sunday) event discussed in this essay) Claudio Tozzi would produce a flag entitled Guevara Dead or Alive while Oiticica appropriated a newspaper image of another executed "criminal," famously declaring "Seja marginal, seja herói."

10   Antonio Manuel, *Entrevista a Lúcia Carneiro e Ileana Pradilla*, Série Palavra do Artista (Rio de Janeiro: Lacerda Editores, 1999). For an English translation of the interview, see *Antonio Manuel*, ed. Michael Asbury and Garo Keheyan (Nicosia, Cyprus: Pharos Publishers, 2006). No references could be found as to the precise day the Bienal da Bahia opened so one can only assume that its closure followed the AI-5 decree on December 13, 1968. The Bienal da Bahia was reopened from January 17 to February 15, 1969.

11   Ibid.

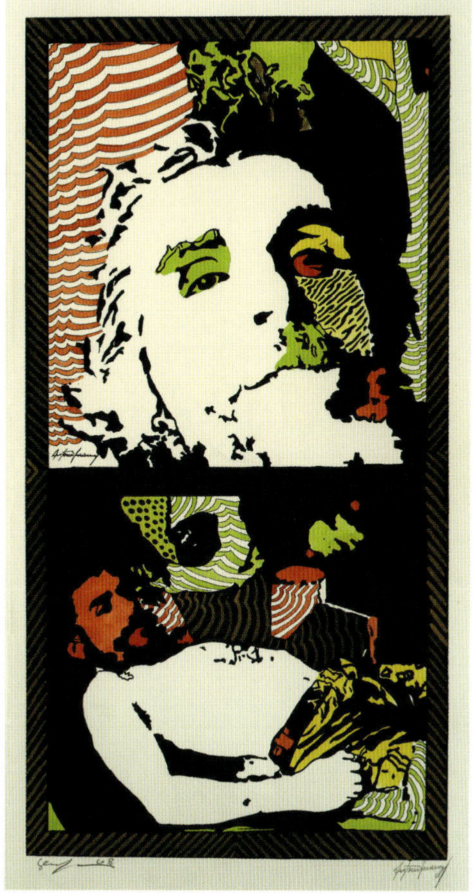

Antonio Manuel and Ivan Serpa, *Guevara,* 1968. Mixed media. Courtesy the artist and Luiz Chrysostomo collection

newspaper imagery entitled *Repressão outra vez – Eis o saldo* (Repression Once Again – Here is the Outcome). Before the exhibition could even open, armed army officers had closed the museum:

> Days later, Niomar Muniz Sodré, who I didn't know personally, telephoned and asked me to meet her. She told me that having heard of the closing of the exhibition, she had asked the staff at MAM to hide as many works as possible. I was sitting on her sofa when she said, "Look, your paintings are behind you." It was a work for which there was a search warrant out to seize it, and she had hidden it in her office. This episode became a significant moment in my life. Through it, I came to know Niomar, founder of MAM and owner of the *Correio da Manhã* newspaper, a great lady of Brazilian culture, who became my friend.[12]

12   Ibid.
Correio da Manhã, given its association with rebel federal deputies, along with its general critical stand toward the regime, was arguably the newspaper most affected by the repression that followed the AI-5. In fact, it never quite recovered from the assaults, eventually closing in 1974.   **33**

Given these circumstances, the Associação Brasileira de Críticos de Arte (Association of Brazilian Art Critics) wrote a letter to its members advising them to avoid future participation as salon and exhibition jury members. This would lead the association's president, Mário Pedrosa, to organize the international mobilization for the boycott of the *Bienal de São Paulo* later that year. A respected art critic since the 1930s and political militant since the 1920s, Pedrosa's role was fundamental in the worldwide condemnation of the repression and torture perpetrated by the regime. Oiticica, who had left Brazil in December 1968 to work on the production of his exhibition at the Whitechapel Gallery in London the following year, mobilized European artists through an open letter that addressed the ethical problem of participating at that year's *Bienal de São Paulo.*[13] With many artists, musicians, and intellectuals either in prison or in exile, the spirit of solidarity within the cultural sphere spread in this way beyond the national borders, and by 1969 the international boycott severely disrupted the staging of the *Bienal de São Paulo.* The French critic Pierre Restany visited Brazil during the 1960s and '70s and would later write critical accounts of the situation in Brazil and the plight of its artists.[14] Hans Haacke wrote a letter to György Kepes—who was responsible for the selection of artists from the U.S.—stating his adherence to the boycott, in keeping with his refusal to represent a nation perpetrating an immoral war in Vietnam and that supported fascist regimes in Latin America.

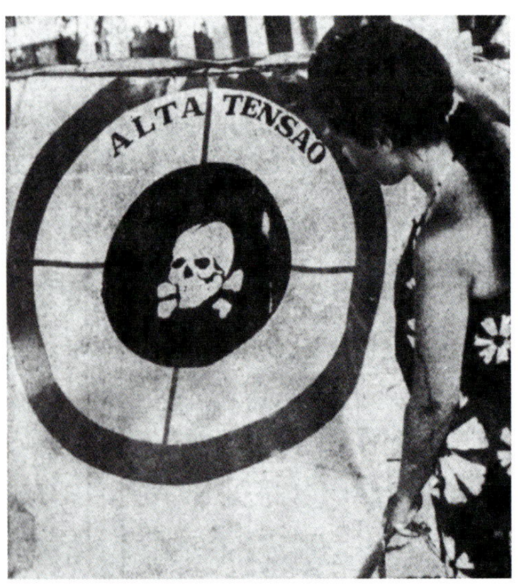

Anna Maria Maiolino's *Alta tensão* (High Tension), 1967. Published in *Jornal do Brasil*. Courtesy Anna Maria Maiolino

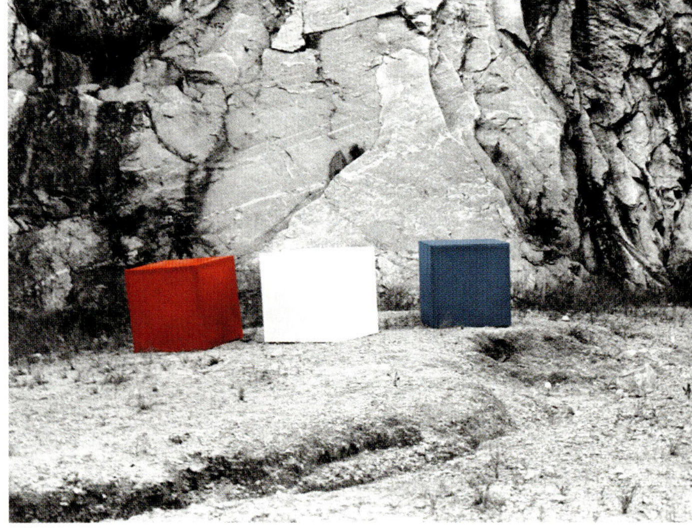

Lygia Pape's performance *Trio do embalo maluco* (Crazy Rocking Trio), 1968. Courtesy Projeto Lygia Pape

13   Oiticica, "Lettre ouverte aux sélectionnés," June 16, 1969, Guy Brett archive. Pedrosa himself attended Oiticica's opening in London. See Asbury, "This Other Eden," in *Oiticica in London,* ed. Guy Brett and Luciano Figueiredo (London: Tate Publishers, 2007).
14   Pierre Restany, "L'art bresilien dans les sables mouvants," in *Domus,* no. 544 (March 1975): 17–25.

This sense of solidarity went beyond the issue of political action and is reflected in Oiticica's letter from London to Lygia Clark, stating that he wasn't interested in disseminating his work abroad unless it was associated with other artists, writers, and musicians, such as Rubens Gerchman, Lygia Pape, Raimundo Amado, Antonio Manuel, Roberto Amaro Lanari, Caetano Veloso and Gilberto Gil.[15] These ties of friendship are evident in his other correspondence, in which he routinely inquired about the problems and controversies that mired Brazilian cultural and political life while also offering practical help and guidance—as in the case of Antonio Manuel, following his censured participation at the 1969 *Biennale de Paris.*[16]

If in the political sphere one can identify the *Marcha dos cem mil* as a point of convergence of diverse social and cultural sectors against the regime, in hindsight, *Nova Objetividade Brasileira* in 1967 could be understood as fulfilling a similar role within the specific field of art. Many artists from São Paulo and Rio, who had been so hostile a decade earlier particularly within the Concrete and Neoconcrete groups, became reconciled under what Oiticica had outlined as the general scheme of the Brazilian avant-garde in the exhibition catalogue.[17]

That same year, artists Nelson Leirner and Flávio Motta proposed an urban intervention in São Paulo entitled *Domingo das Bandeiras* (Flag Sunday) in which artists would produce flags to be sold in the streets to passersby for a low, fixed price. The São Paulo municipality prohibited the event, arguing that it constituted an unpatriotic provocation. The event was thus transferred to Rio and took place in February the following year at the General Osório Square in Ipanema.[18] It received an enthusiastic response from local artists, among them Oiticica who displayed his flag "Seja marginal, seja herói" (Be an Outcast, Be a Hero)[19] and Anna Maria Maiolino with her flag proclaiming "Alta Tensão" (High Tension). In July 1968 Frederico Morais, an art critic at the *Diário das Noticias,* organized a month-long program of public art sponsored by the newspaper and held at the Aterro do Flamengo, near MAM. Oiticica coordinated an event that Rogério Duarte named *Apocalipopótese* (Apocalypopothesis), a neologism suggesting the hypothesis of apocalypse. The event gathered a diverse group of artists: Pape with her *Trio do embalo maluco* (Crazy Rocking Trio), white box-like recipients out of which people would burst; Duarte with a demonstration of trained dogs; Jackson Ribeiro with his large scrap metal sculptures; Oiticica with dancers from the Mangueira samba school wearing *Parangolés;* and Antonio Manuel with the *Urnas quentes.* Other artists included Sami Mattar, Roberto Lanari, the Poema-Processo group and Torquato Neto.[20]

15   Oiticica, Letter to Lygia Clark, London, April 18, 1969, reprinted in *Lygia Clark – Hélio Oiticica: Cartas,* 1964–1974, ed. Luciano Figueiredo (Rio de Janeiro: Editora UFRJ, 1996), 94.

16   See Asbury, "This Other Eden." For a translated segment of Oiticica's letter to Antonio Manuel, see Asbury, "Antonio Manuel: Occupations/Discoveries," in *Antonio Manuel,* ed. Michael Asbury and Garo Keheyan (Cyprus: Pharos Publishers, 2006), 37–38.

17   Oiticica, "Esquema Geral da Nova Objetividade."

18   Paulo Roberto de Oliveira Reis, "Exposições de Arte – Vanguarda e Política entre os anos 1965 e 1970" (PhD diss., Federal University of Paraná, Curitiba, Brazil, 2005), 172.

19   Editors' Note: The word "marginal" in "Seja marginal, seja herói" may be translated as "outcast" or "outlaw."

20   John Cage was later recognized (through photographs) as having attended the event, a fact that reportedly Cage himself confirmed. Antonio Manuel in conversation with the author, Rio de Janeiro, April 19, 2011.

Prior to the event organizational meetings were held at Oiticica's house where Antonio Manuel and Duarte discussed a possible collaboration. They planned a structure entitled *Cabine do amor* (Love Shack), which the viewer could enter and then peer through gaps in the wood panels to see images of bodies projected within another compartment. A fascination with the relation between inside and outside and an engagement with the "spectator" as active participant became key issues for many artists including Antonio Manuel. According to the artist, the actual structure had already been constructed by Oiticica but Duarte's other commitments disrupted the project.[21] Antonio Manuel developed an alternative project that he entitled *Urnas quentes,* consisting of several wooden boxes of simple construction containing images, newspaper cutouts, poems and slogans.[22] As the boxes were sealed, their content could only be revealed through a destructive act. However, Antonio Manuel later admitted being surprised by the public's violent enthusiasm for destruction.[23]

Urnas quentes translates literally into English as "Hot Ballot Boxes" but as Guy Brett has argued, the translation does little justice to the term: "In English the word 'urn' no longer has any connection with ballot-boxes. The association with ashes, with death and the coldness of cemeteries, is still there and therefore the title *Hot Urns* has a contradictory impact."[24] Brett goes on to quote Cynthia Canejo in arguing that the etymological disconnection between "ballot-box" and "urn" means that the English translation misses the "'suggestion that the information inside was 'current and needed to be opened while hot.'"[25] Moreover,

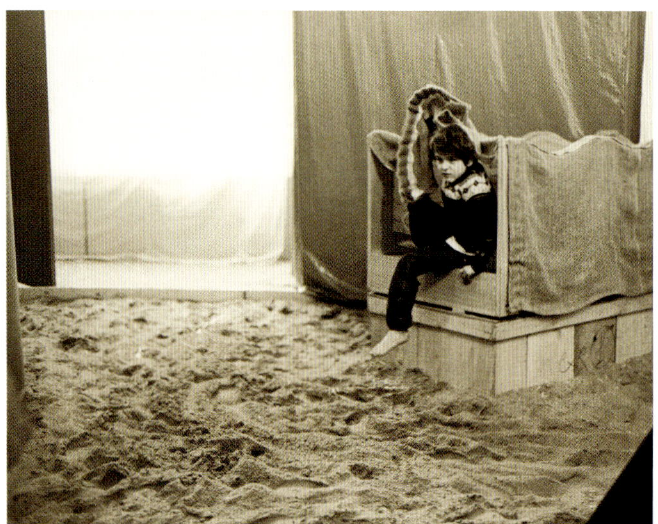

Hélio Oiticica, *Bólide cama 1 – Suprasensorial* (Bed Bólide 1
– Supersensorial), 1968. Courtesy Projeto Hélio Oiticica

21   The artist in conversation with the author, Rio de Janeiro, August 14, 2005.
22   Antonio Manuel recalls constructing twenty or twenty-five of these boxes at Jackson Ribeiro's studio in the Lapa neighbourhood of Rio. Ibid. Ribeiro was the person responsible for introducing Oiticica to the Mangueira favela during a project to construct carnival floats. It was from the experience at Mangueira that works such as the *Parangolé* would emerge.
23   Antonio Manuel, *Entrevista a Lúcia Carneiro e Ileana Pradilla.*
24   Brett, "I don't want to represent, I want to Act," in *Antonio Manuel* (Porto: Fundação de Serralves, 2000), 24.
25   Ibid in Cynthia Canejo, "Antonio Manuel: A Dialectical Response to Brazilian Developments in Modern Art," (MA Diss., University of California at Santa Barbara, 1998).

being "hot" also suggests that they contained illicit or prohibited material: a common sentiment for those experiencing the paranoia that the regime installed, whereby at any moment one could be stopped and searched for subversive or illegal material.

With the *Urnas quentes* a number of new elements were introduced within Antonio Manuel's practice. The issue of violence shifted from being a representation of reality mediated by the newspaper to the concealment of information whose unveiling then becomes a participatory element in the work.[26] As Brett argues, there is an affinity that connects Antonio Manuel to the experience of other artists who developed in their practice a dialectic of revealing and concealing such as Oiticica, Clark, Piero Manzoni, as well as Ferreira Gullar with his Neoconcrete poems.[27] Antonio Manuel recollects, for instance, how he enjoyed entering Oiticica's *Bólide cama 1 – Suprasensorial* (Bed Bólide 1 – Supersensorial)[28] where one became aware of everything that happened around while remaining concealed from those outside.[29] The mutual appreciation of each other's work is perhaps best exemplified by the collaborative piece *Parangolé P22, Cape 18, Nirvana,* 1968, which incorporated imagery contained within an *Urna quente* destroyed during *Apocalipopótese.* The image was that of a young famine victim from Biafra. The example is pertinent since like the *Urna quente* itself, the *Parangolé*'s malleable structure enabled the wearer to both conceal and reveal the image.

The vast web of friendships and relationships that were established during those difficult years between Antonio Manuel—who was from a modest Portuguese immigrant family—and people from diverse levels of society, invites speculation about the artist's character. A clue can perhaps be found in a much later work. For an artist so closely associated with appropriation and found imagery, it might seem strange that he would exhibit the installation *Fantasma* (Ghost) at the *XXIV Bienal de São Paulo* in 1998, curated by Paulo Herkenhoff around the theme of anthropophagy.[30] The sheer scale of the installation overwhelmed the single photographic print placed at the end of the room. Audience members, curious to enter the installation in order to view the small image, did so at their own peril, as their clothes risked being stained by the numerous pieces of charcoal suspended from the ceiling. The image depicted a witness to an indiscriminate massacre perpetrated by members of the police force in one of Rio's favelas; fearful of revealing his identity, the witness covered

26   Camillo Osório argues that Antonio Manuel's *Urnas Quentes* could be considered as a precedent to the violation of the walls in Oc. Their content being revealed through the act of violence is equated with the experience of breaching the walls through the passage opened by the artist. The curator also raises the connection that *Ocupações-Descobrimentos* (Occupations-Discoveries) has with Oiticica's *Penetrables.* Luiz Camillo Osorio in *Antonio Manuel: Ocupações/Descobrimentos* (Niteroi: Museu de Arte Contemporânea, 2002), 6.

27   The latter was a critic and poet who until 1961 was the main spokesman for the Neoconcrete movement.

28   *Bólide cama 1: Suprasensorial,* 1968.

29   The artist in conversation with the writer, Rio de Janeiro, August 13, 2005. See Asbury, "Antonio Manuel: Occupations/Discoveries."

30   In 1928 the poet Oswald de Andrade published his "Manifesto Antropofágico," which equated the Brazilian propensity toward appropriating European culture with the cannibalistic rituals of the original Brazilian Tupi natives. Devouring [the culture of] the other thus became understood not as a sign of dependency but as an intrinsic national characteristic.

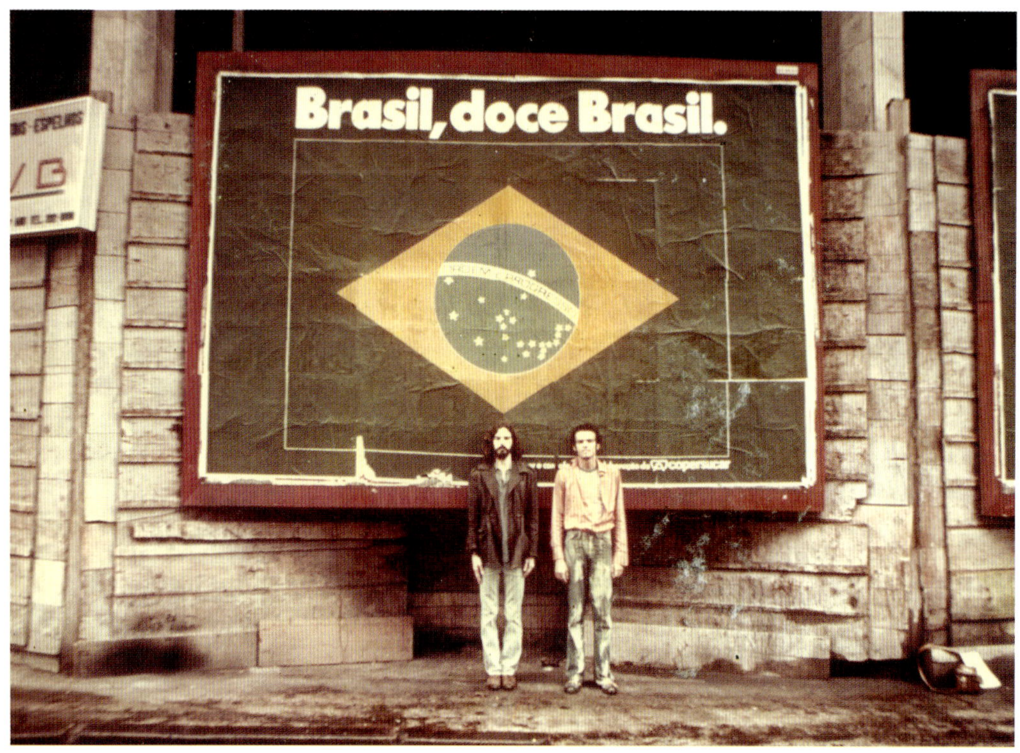

Antonio Manuel and Raymundo Colares, used in *Sabor doce para bocas amargas* (Sweet Taste for Bitter Mouths), c. 1975. Courtesy the artist

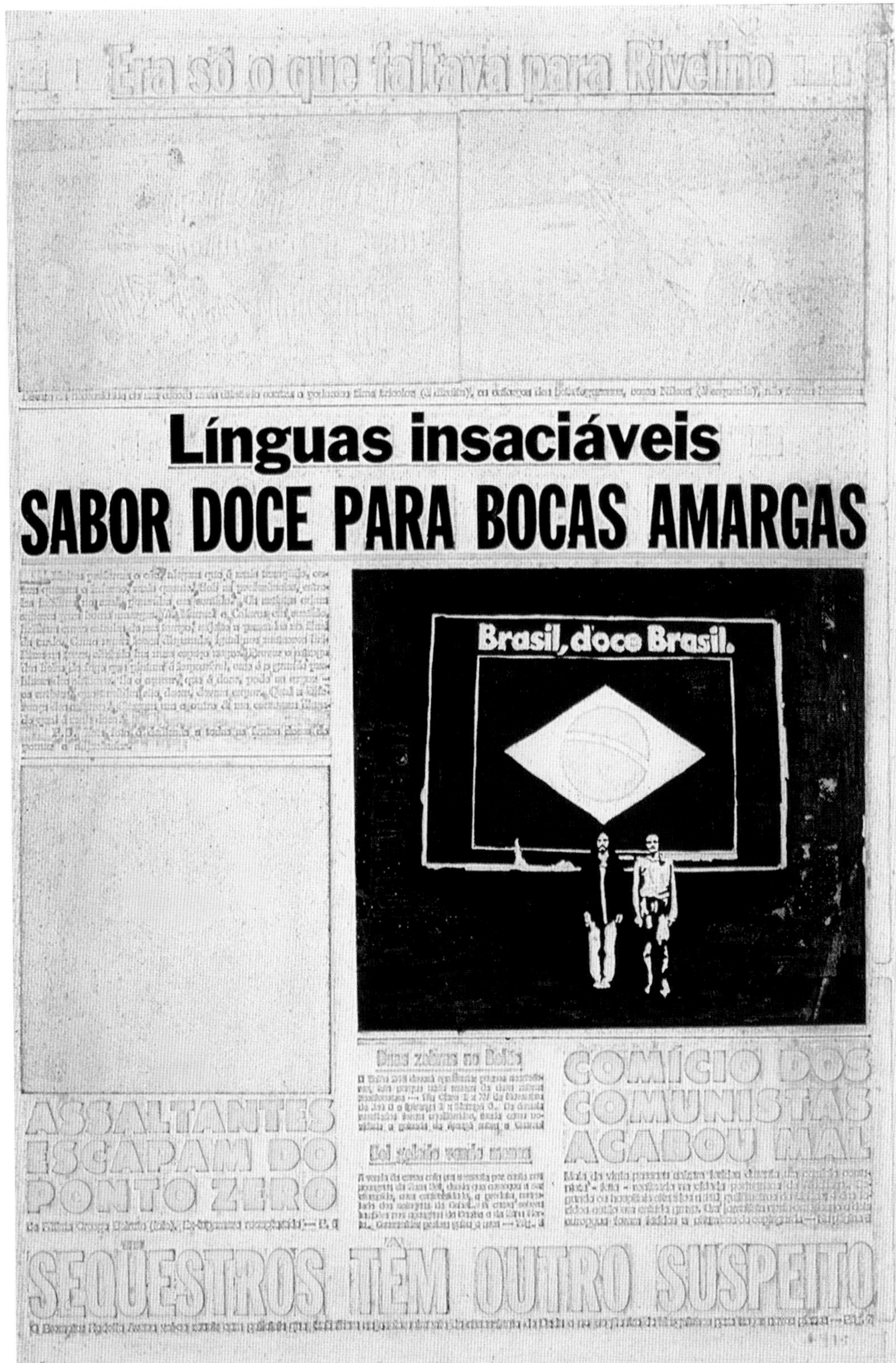

Sabor doce para bocas amargas (Sweet Taste for Bitter Mouths), 1975. From the *Flan* series, ink on papier-mâché stereotype mold, 22 x 15 in. Courtesy the artist

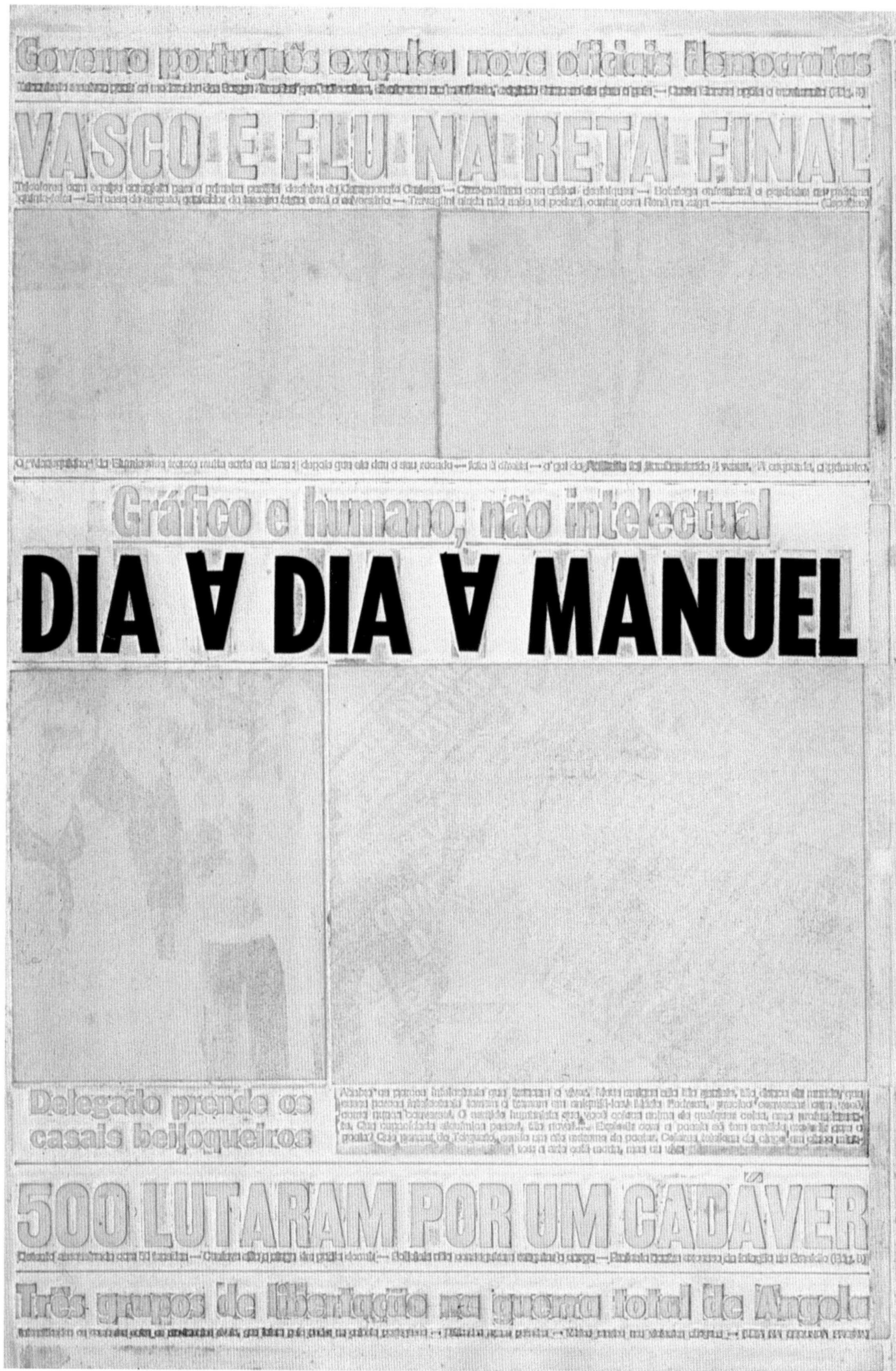

Dia a dia Manuel (Day by Day Manuel), 1975. From the *Flan* series, ink on papier-mâché stereotype mold, 21 x 14.5 in. Courtesy the artist himself with a white sheet during an interview with the media. Antonio Manuel's description of how that image disturbed him brings to mind Sérgio Buarque de Holanda's categorization of the Brazilian man [sic] as intrinsically cordial.[31] Cordiality here should not be considered as equivalent to politeness. On the contrary, while polite formalities tend to safeguard the individual from the wider social sphere, cordiality denotes the individual's will to become absorbed by the social. According to Buarque de Holanda, Brazilians tend to favor a greater intimacy that privileges first names over surnames and allows a particular form of sociability whereby the individual craves familiarity, whether amicable or otherwise. Antonio Manuel (or should I say Mr. de Oliveira?) demonstrated an intrinsically cordial character in his personal relationships—for example, his friendship with fellow artist Raymundo Colares who is depicted next to Antonio Manuel in the 1975 *Flan,* cynically entitled *Sabor doce para bocas amargas* (Sweet Taste for Bitter Mouths); or the intimate but explosive relationship he had with Pape, who appears wearing vampire fangs in one of the *Clandestina* (Clandestine) series, also from 1975. Both extremes of cordiality are equally present in his attitude about his own works as well as how he interacted with art institutions. In this sense, the *Urna quente* could be understood as a "cordial" object: the violent heartfelt blow that reveals that which is concealed and makes public what had previously been kept secret. Cordiality appears in his friendship with MAM director Niomar as well as in his irreverent naked display at an exhibition opening in protest against the 1970 Salon in the action *O corpo é a obra* (The Body Is the Work). Immediately following that action Antonio Manuel felt the need to discuss the event with someone who would be receptive; he visited Mário Pedrosa who, in turn, described the act as an "experimental exercise of liberty." Indeed, Antonio Manuel's habit of frequenting the houses and apartments of friends, such as Oiticica and Ivan Serpa, is testimony to the "cordiality" of his character. On one such occasion, not long after *O corpo é a obra,* Antonio Manuel and Oiticica—who had briefly returned to Rio before going back to New York as a Guggenheim fellowship recipient— arrived at Pedrosa's apartment to find that the critic had gone into hiding to avoid being arrested. Days later, Antonio Manuel and Pape assumed the responsibility of transporting Pedrosa from his hideout to the Chilean Embassy, where he would begin his second period of exile.[32]

During the 1970s, Antonio Manuel produced a very distinct series of *Flans* and *Urnas quentes.* The context in which these were produced is nevertheless quite distinct from that of the previous versions. This cannot be solely attributed to the demise of open conviviality following the AI-5 or more generally due to the crisis of the Left following the failure of the 1968 uprising. The *Flans* of the 1970s are fundamentally distinct from those of the late 1960s in that their production was based on a greater intimacy with the newspaper press itself. A student of Pape, Ivan Chagas Freitas became acquainted with Antonio Manuel and offered the artist unprecedented access to his father's *O DIA* newspaper printing workshops.

---

31   Sergio Buarque de Holanda (along with Gilberto Freyre and Caio Prado Junior) is among the most significant early contributors to the field of social sciences in Brazil. In *Raízes do Brasil,* first published in 1936, he debates the particularities of Brazilian society, such as the difficulty of separating the spheres of public and private life, which he described as characteristics of the "cordial man." See Sergio Buarque de Holanda, *Raízes do Brasil* (26th edition) (São Paulo: Compania das Letras, 2010).

32   Antonio Manuel, *Entrevista a Lúcia Carneiro e Ileana Pradilla.* Pedrosa had been exiled during the Vargas regime and only returned to Brazil in 1945, almost immediately becoming an advocate for abstraction particularly in light of the establishment of the São Paulo Biennial in 1951. See Asbury, "The Bienal de São Paulo: Between Nationalism and Internationalism," in *Espaço Aberto/Espaço Fechado: Sites for Sculpture in Modern Brazil,* ed. Penelope Curtis and Stephen Feeke (Leeds: The Henry Moore Institute, 2006), 72–83.

Antonio Manuel produced one or two *Flans* per week during his visits to the press over the course of a year. He would arrive with an already developed idea of what to do, bringing with him the necessary headlines and photographs, since the operation could involve as many as twelve newspaper employees. The process was indeed the same as that of producing a newspaper page, including molding and burning the flan. They were not merely appropriations although they sometimes contained material from an existing newspaper page. Later he would take this further, producing the plumb mold and printing actual paper sheets that could be mistaken for the newspaper itself, giving rise to another series entitled *Clandestinas* (Clandestines).

The last *Flan* to be produced was *Poema classificado* (Classified Poem) in 1975. It took the graphic format of a classified ads page and fragmented the poetic/descriptive sentence across its columns "corpo | grafico | 8colunas | massificadas | espaço cheio | redundante | ponto | final" (graphic | body | 8columns | popular | full space | redundant | final | stop) repeating it over twelve lines. At the top of the page ran the headline "Classified Poem," which is as ambivalent as the poem itself. While he was producing this strange newspaper page, Ivan's father (who also happed to be the governor of the state of Guanabara) walked in. Governor Chagas Freitas asked what was happening; moments later the whole operation came to an end.

One particular *Urna quente* produced in 1975 is distinct from all previous ones. After sealing the contents of the box, Antonio Manuel went to a notary office to register the fact that it would remain closed for an unspecified amount of time. The artist has joked about the fact that for a lawyer to state that something will happen "one day" is totally absurd, but in his mind he imagined thirty years to be an appropriate period of time.[33] He now confesses that this time elapsed too quickly and that he wishes to defer the opening of the box, perhaps indefinitely. Yet the cordial man has difficulties in keeping secrets, so while the notary's document is the visible compensation for that which is concealed, other boxes may still be produced and their contents revealed in its place. In fact, the artist now considers the *Urna quente* as a form of creative media—a language that he chooses to employ at different moments and in diverse contexts. In 2005, to mark the thirtieth anniversary of the sealing of that box, Antonio Manuel produced and destroyed an *Urna quente* that contained objects that registered his initial impressions of being in a divided city and feeling all around him the vestiges of the violence that erupted between communities that had once lived peacefully together.[34] The city was Nicosia and the division between Cypriote communities that took place in 1974 further evokes a sense of contemporaneity with that sealed box whose deferred revelation could now be understood in an altogether new context. The opening of the surrogate box in the presence of the mayor from the other part of the city evoked not so much a violent gesture but an effort toward reinstituting the intimacy between both sides.[35]

---

33   See Antonio Manuel, interview with Sheila Cabo and Rradial (Alexandre Vogler, Luís Andrade, and Ronald Duarte) in *Concinnitas* 5, UERJ, ART, Rio de Janeiro, 2003.
34   See Asbury, "Antonio Manuel: Occupations/Discoveries."
35   Ibid.

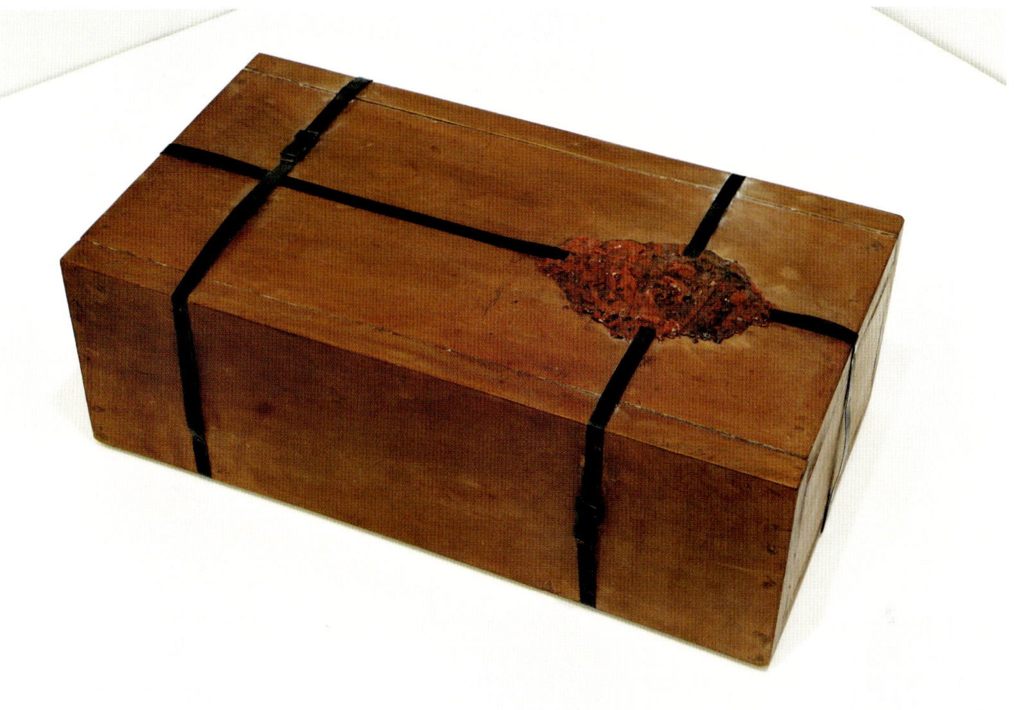

Urnas quente (Hot Ballot Box), 2004. Wood, sealing wax and tape, both 24 x 13 x 8 in. Courtesy the artist

Antonio Manuel has expressed the desire to reveal yet another secret relating to that "original" 1975 *Urna quente.* In 2004 he was invited by curator Lynn Zelevansky to participate in an exhibition at Los Angeles County Museum of Art entitled *Beyond Geometry: Experiments in Form, 1940s–1970s.* The exhibition was a welcome example of how artistic practices that shared common characteristics, despite being produced in diverse geopolitical regions and contexts, could be positively associated. Antonio Manuel was represented by his sealed and notarized 1975 *Urna quente.* At least this is what had been planned. Worried that the box might be violated due to the paranoid atmosphere in the United States during the George W. Bush administration, he decided it would be more prudent to produce a replica that was nearly identical in all of its details except for its contents.[36] Although this solution appeased his worries, it nevertheless caused new concerns. Not only did he feel uncomfortable with Zelevansky, for whom he had great respect, but he also found himself in the paradoxical position of being in possession of a fake of his own making. As an act of Brazilian cordiality—which reveals one's own flaws even as it proposes a practical solution to a problem—Antonio Manuel, the old political trickster, now brings this account to the public if not the contents themselves. The political context has indeed changed, yet if we consider, as the artist himself suggests, the *Urna quente* as a poetic language, this revelation has the potential of subjectively relating to both the preceding U.S. political administration as it does to more recent current affairs.

36   He admits no longer remembering what the original 1975 contents were. The artist in conversation with the author, Rio de Janeiro, April 20, 2011.

ANTONIO MANUEL

a arma fálica

ANTONIO MANUEL

a arma fálica

Acontece de fatos e fotos a fotonovela, que tem idade madura, 25 anos. Sai da gaveta tal qual *Urnas Quentes* - imagens-poemas hermeticamente fechadas, que precisam ser quebradas para descobrir seu código.

Em 1970, chamei a mim todas as energias criativas presentes, expondo-as NU ao público no MAM: *O corpo é a obra.*

Da página de jornal aos *flans*, tratava-se de captar a realidade e tornar possível a criação poética - síntese entre o verbal e o visual, *mise-en-scène* do trabalho que habita esta atmosfera criativa.

Em 1969, Hélio Oiticica viajava para Londres para fazer a sua exposição individual na Whitechapel. *Tendas, Parangolés e Éden* - embalagem da exportação de um espírito novo. Fui à Praça Mauá me despedir (Torquato Neto também foi no mesmo navio).

Com a fotonovela, pretendi trabalhar um novo meio de expressão, realizando na forma afetiva da parceria e no espírito do pensamento da arte, este trabalho. Havia a idéia e o argumento; a locação, eu já tinha estabelecido: A Praça Mauá e a casa do Oiticica, na rua Engenheiro Alfredo Duarte. Quanto ao cenário, foram utilizados os objetos da casa, com a participação do Hélio e de sua inseparável tevê prêto & branco.

As duas primeiras tomadas de cena, na Praça Mauá, eu fiz lembrando o seu embarque para Londres; mas também era o espaço da travessia do Atlântico, do além-mar. Consciente desse espaço e do sentimento de porto, quis vitalizar a sua nobreza e miséria diante de um país bárbaro, de torturas e crimes. A repressão política que se apresentava, obscura, nos atos torturosos da ditadura, nos levava à luta pelo "exercício experimental da liberdade", como chamou Mário Pedrosa. Não havia tostão no bolso, mas uma profunda vontade criativa, fazer da vida alegria e da arte, pensamento.

Nada foi mexido para atualizar a fotonovela. O argumento e os diálogos são os originais, como na época, registro de um clima experimental vivido no Rio de Janeiro. Apesar de o argumento ser uma ficção, hoje a realidade da vida e os limites da violência foram ultrapassados, e a vida, banalizada nesse espaço insuportável que ocupa hoje.

Que se curta esta fotonovela, despretenciosa e sincera, que germinou da vontade de fazer algo com alegria em parceria com Hélio Oiticica. Que ela, se possível, ajude a iluminar os sentidos e o espírito da vida.

Antonio Manuel
17 de setembro de 1995

a arma fálica

em missão de guerra o guru passou vários anos em
londres. como não foi possível levar sua mulher, que
sofria de um corrimento interminável, deixou-a
trancada em sua casa na gávea. neném, disputada a
tapa numa briga violenta, tinha sido mulher de
paulomarginal na época do estupro de sua mãe no
mangue, publicado na ocasião como crime passional.

antonio manuel   rio de janeiro 1970

em algum ano na década de 70...

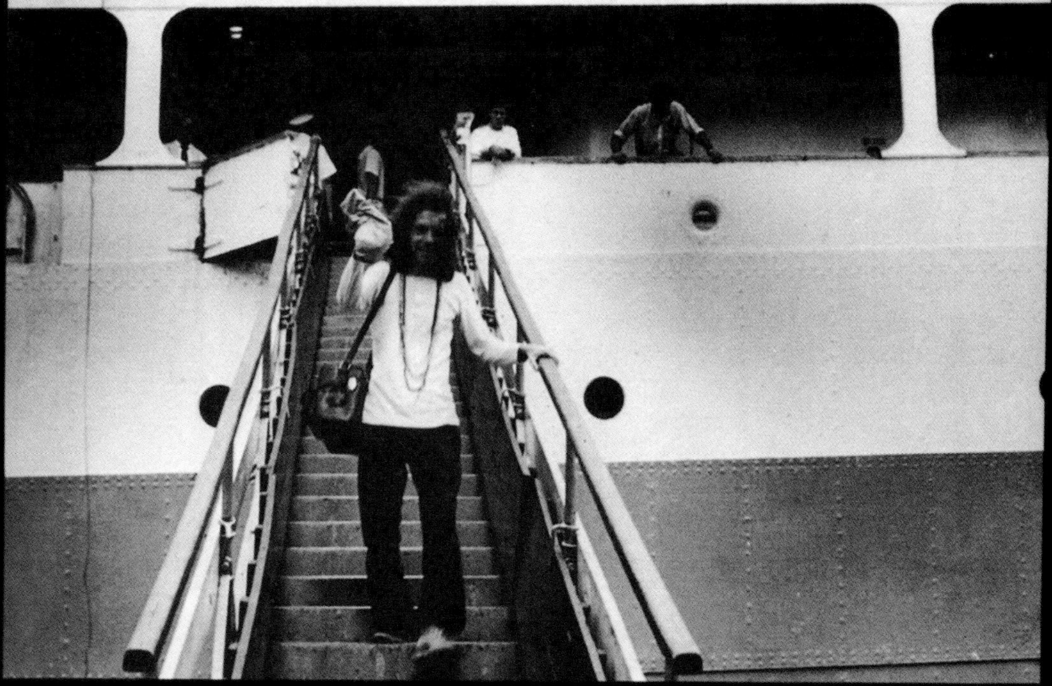

maravilha... maravilha... quantos profissionais... guilherme vai ficar louco.

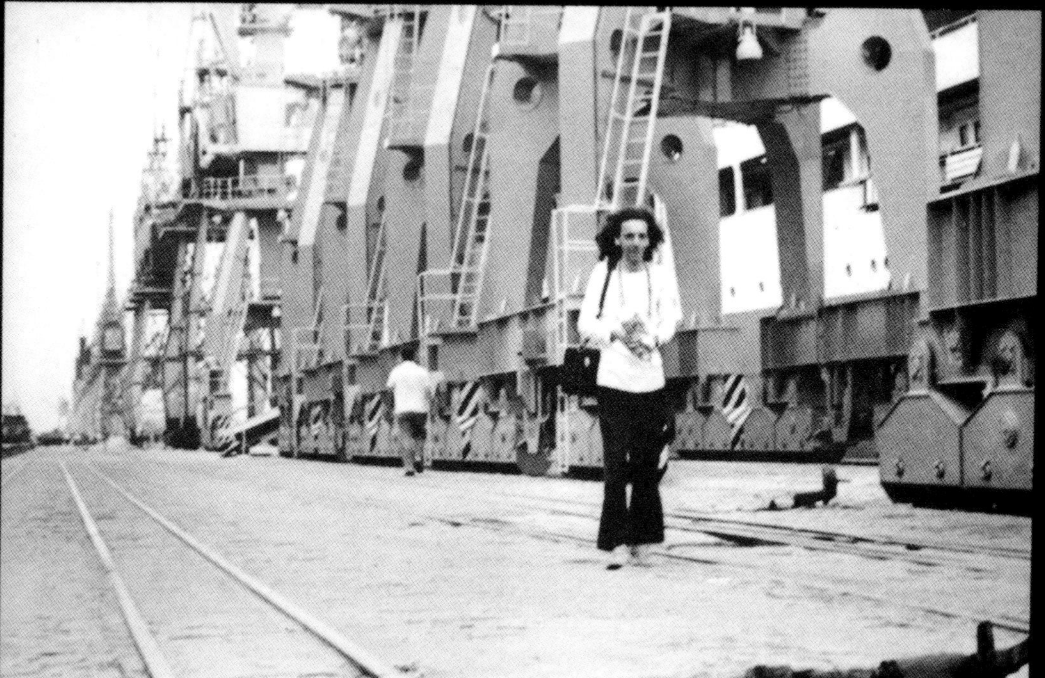

ninguém sabe que cheguei. diabo... que encomenda pesada pra esse tal de
ayela.

neném e paulomarginal estão ocupados chupando picolé.
felizes da vida.

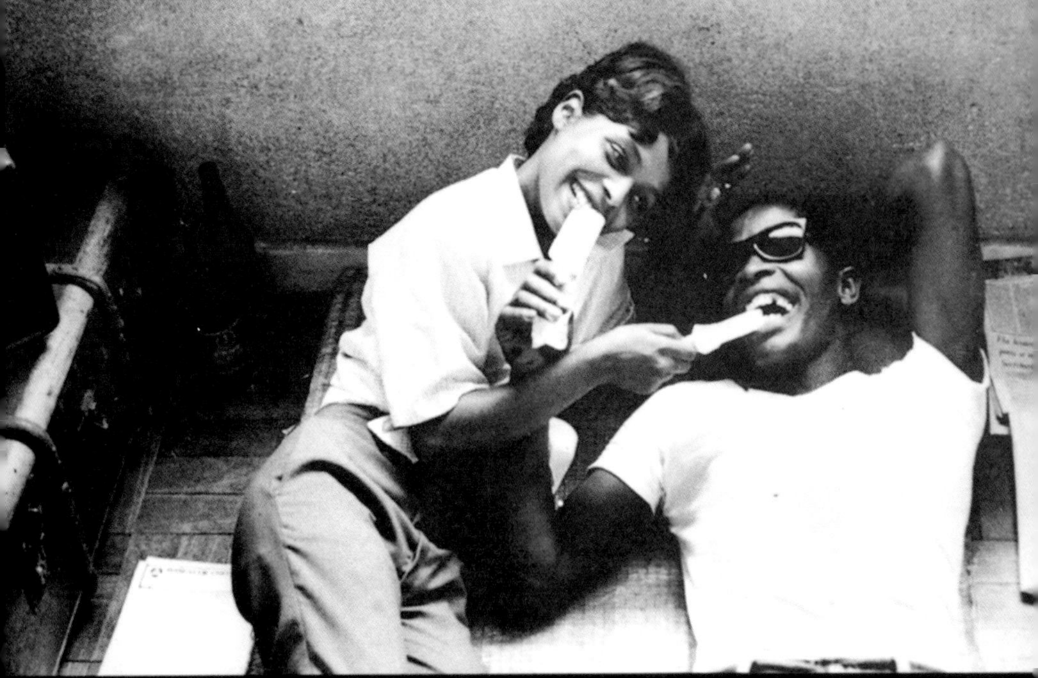

deixa dar uma mordidinha. legal... deixa.

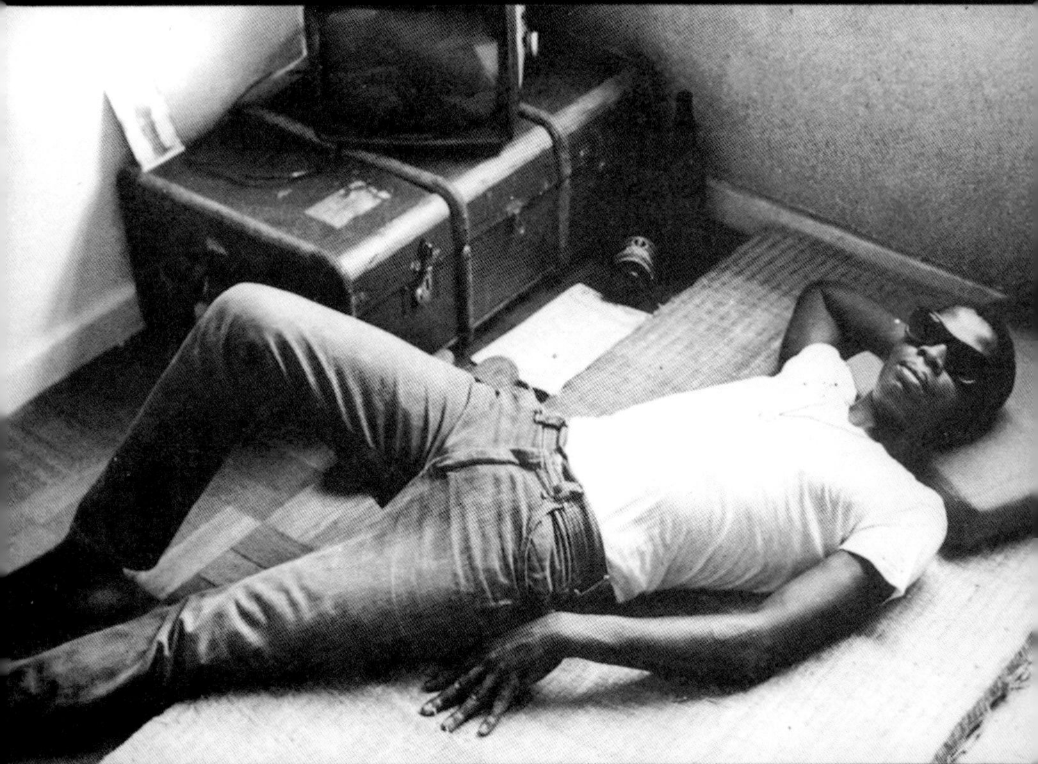

iiiihhhhhhhh... estão batendo na porta. logo agora no fim do picolé!

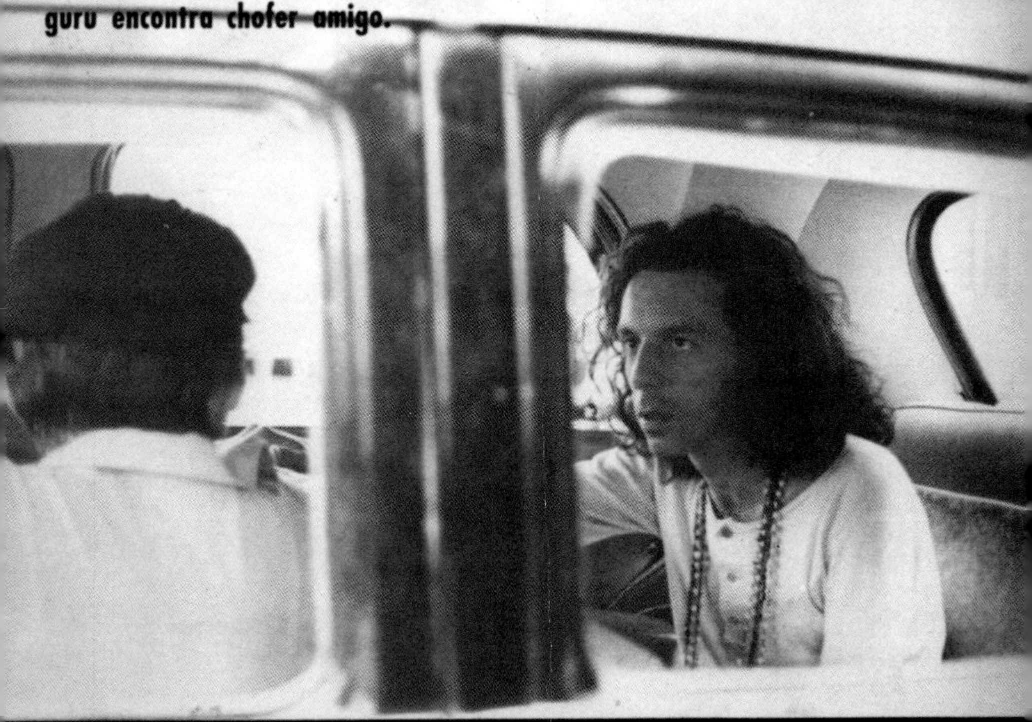

guru encontra chofer amigo.

guru, ainda bem que você voltou. neném está na maior onda com paulomarginal.

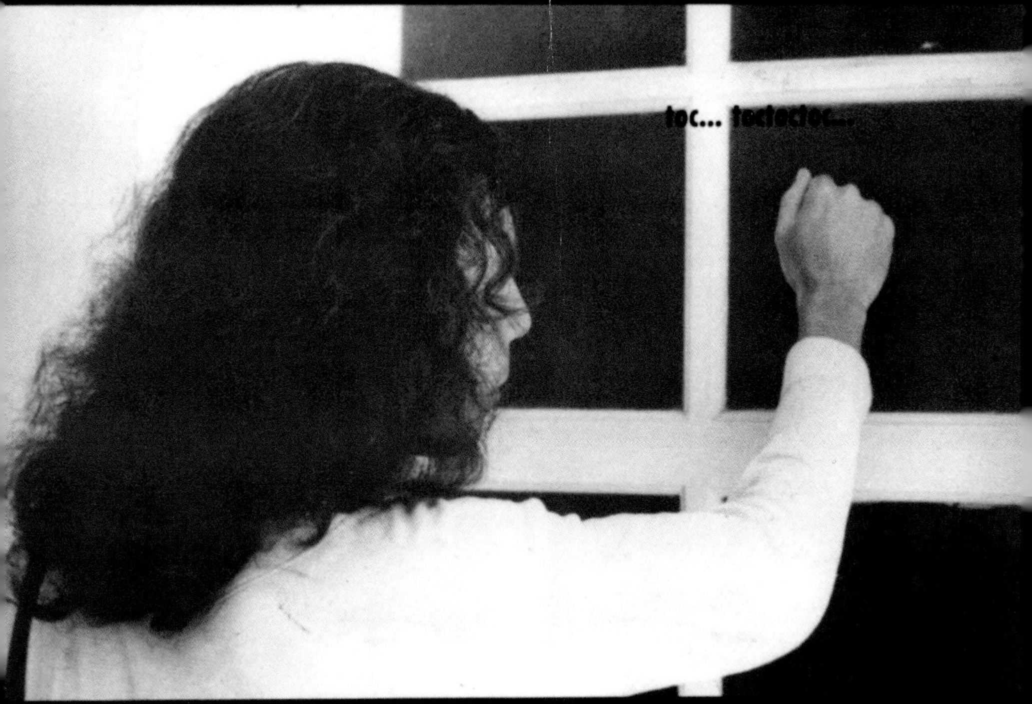

toc... toctoctoc...

argh... aquela piranhuda voltou a se encontrar com ele?
devia ter matado paulomarginal.

Vá ver nega! eu vou tirar um ronco. 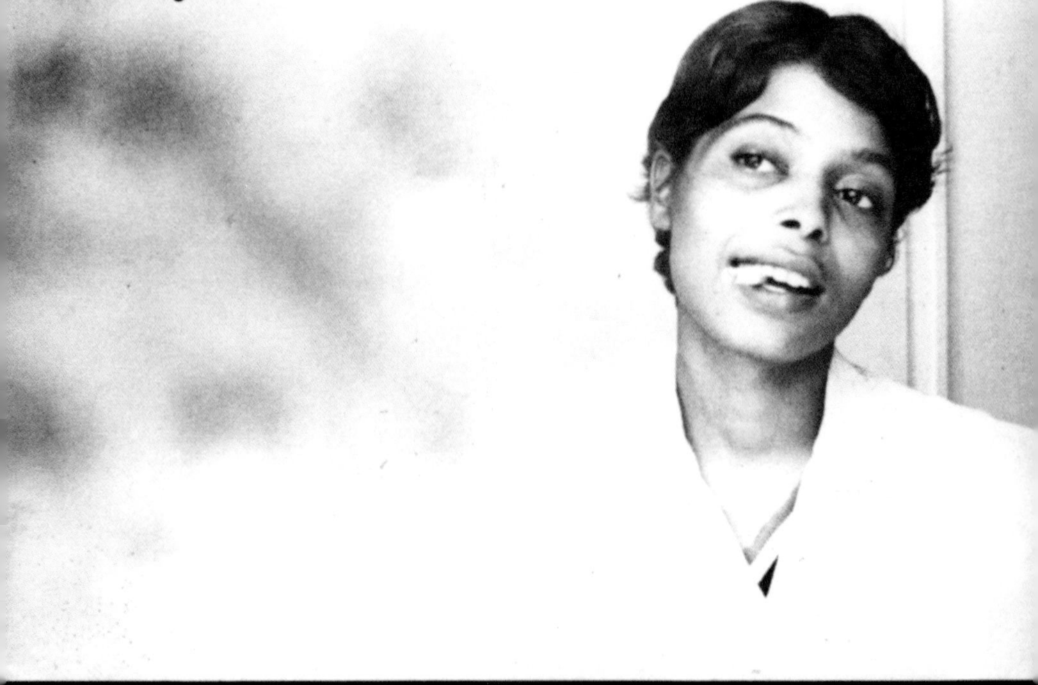
toc... toc... 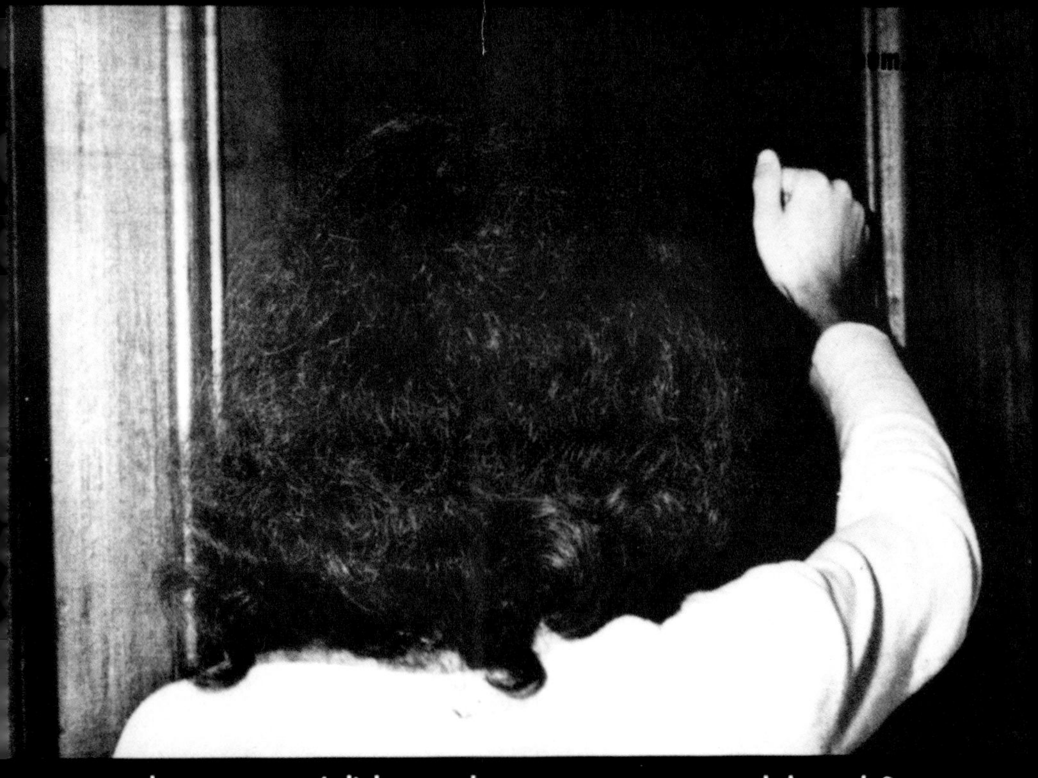
abra eşsa porta! diabo... onde vou encontrar esse tal de ayela?
e essa puta, por que não abre logo? humhumhumhum

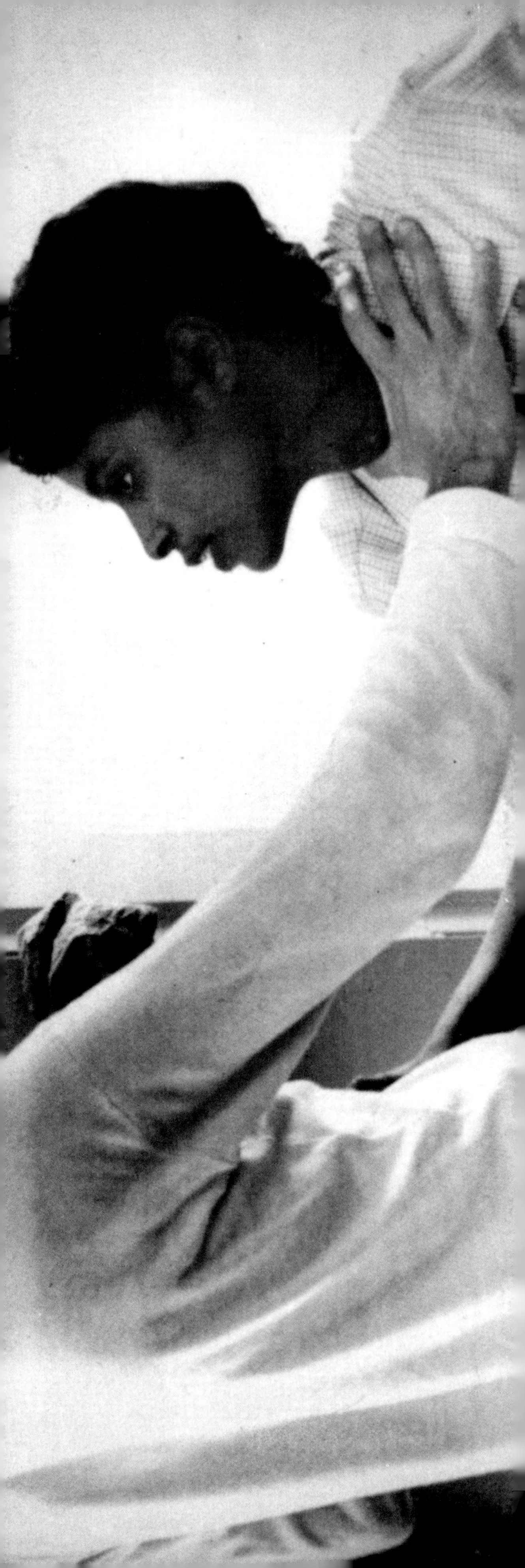

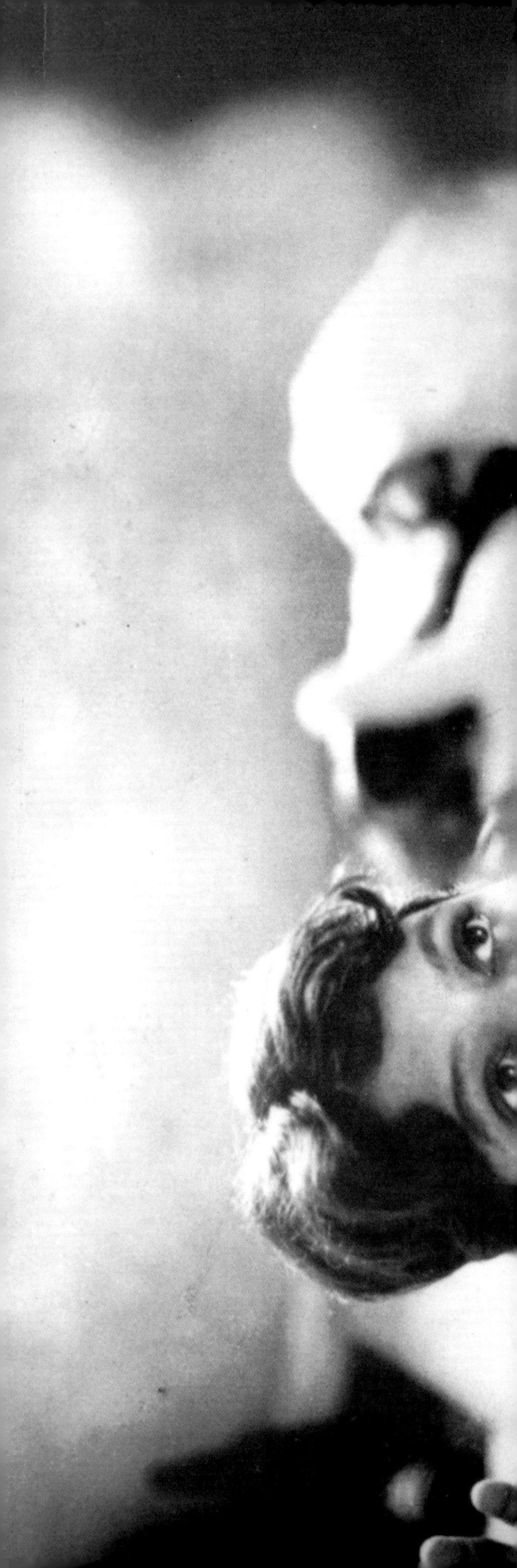

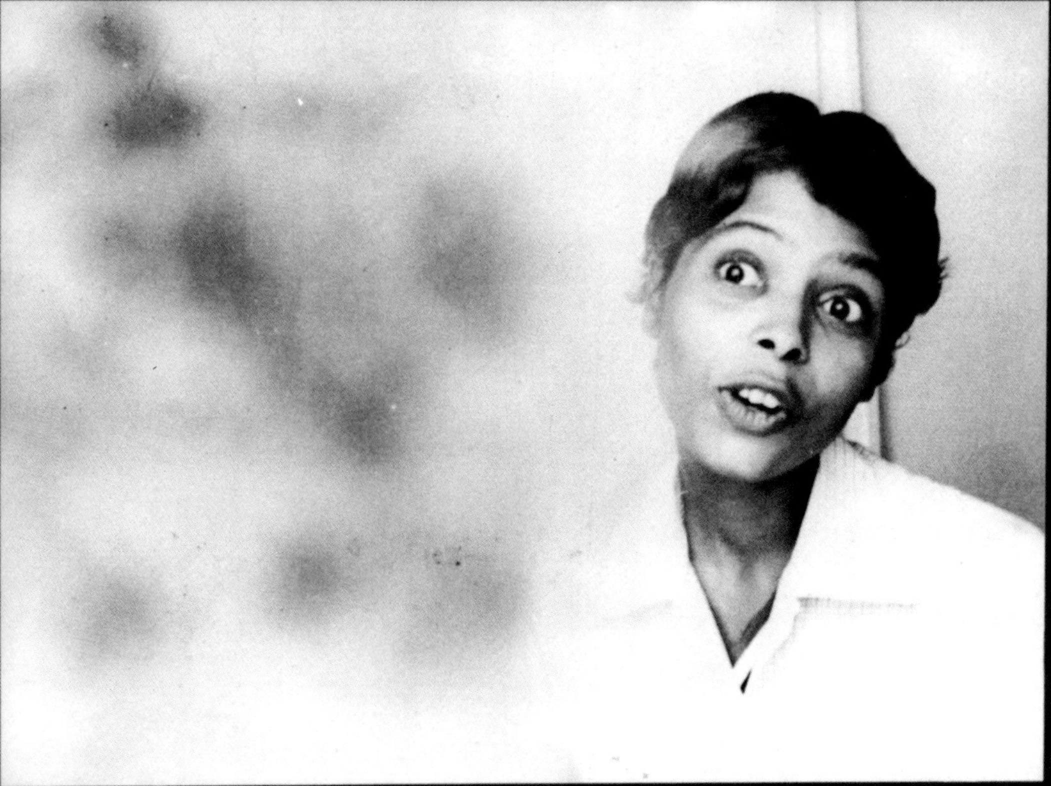

neném reconhece a voz de guru e fica apavorada. guguruzinho, você voltou meu benzinho!?

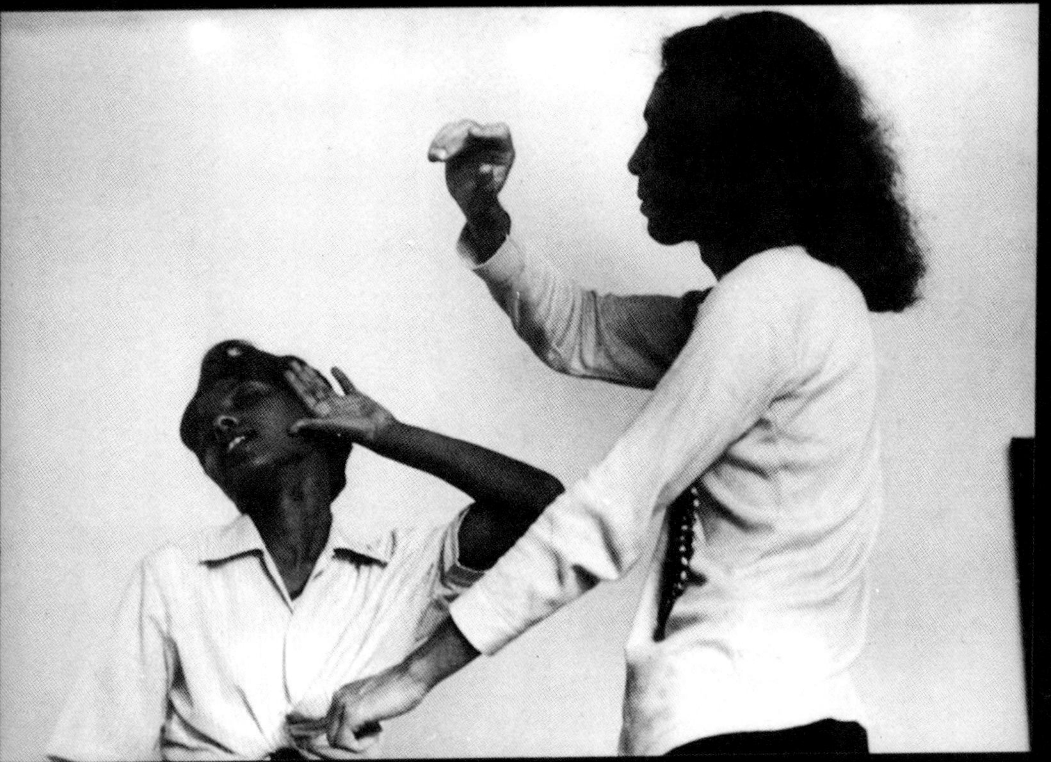

saia do meu caminho, sua puta!

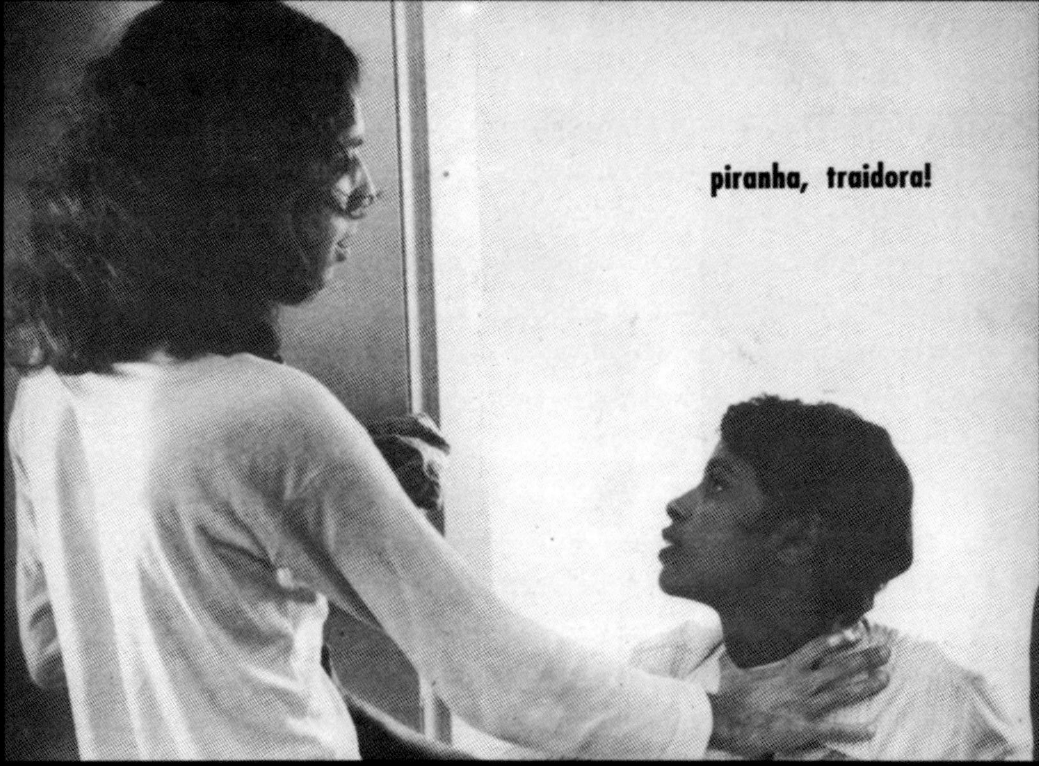

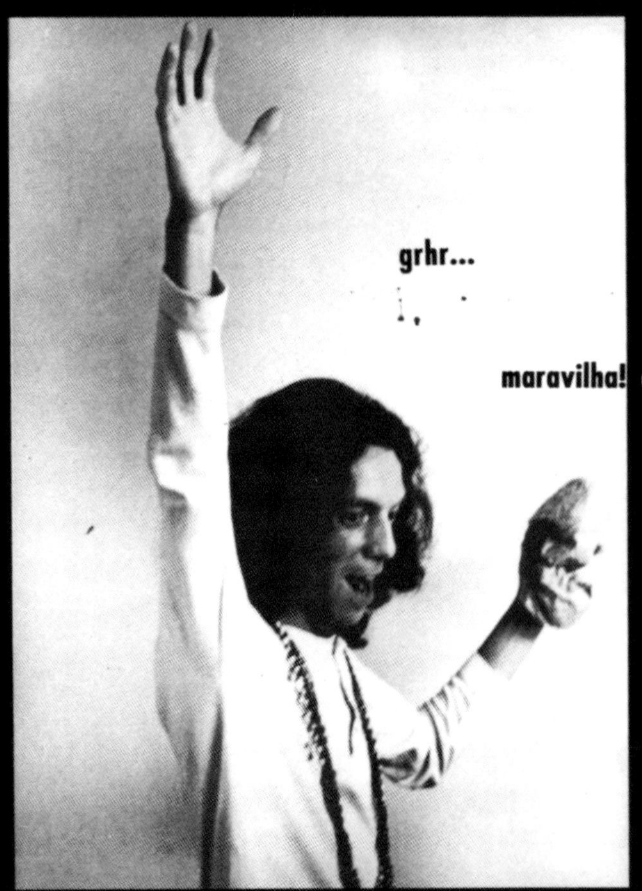

piranha, traidora!
oh...ah... pera aí. não pode entrar.
grhr...
maravilha! olha ele aí!

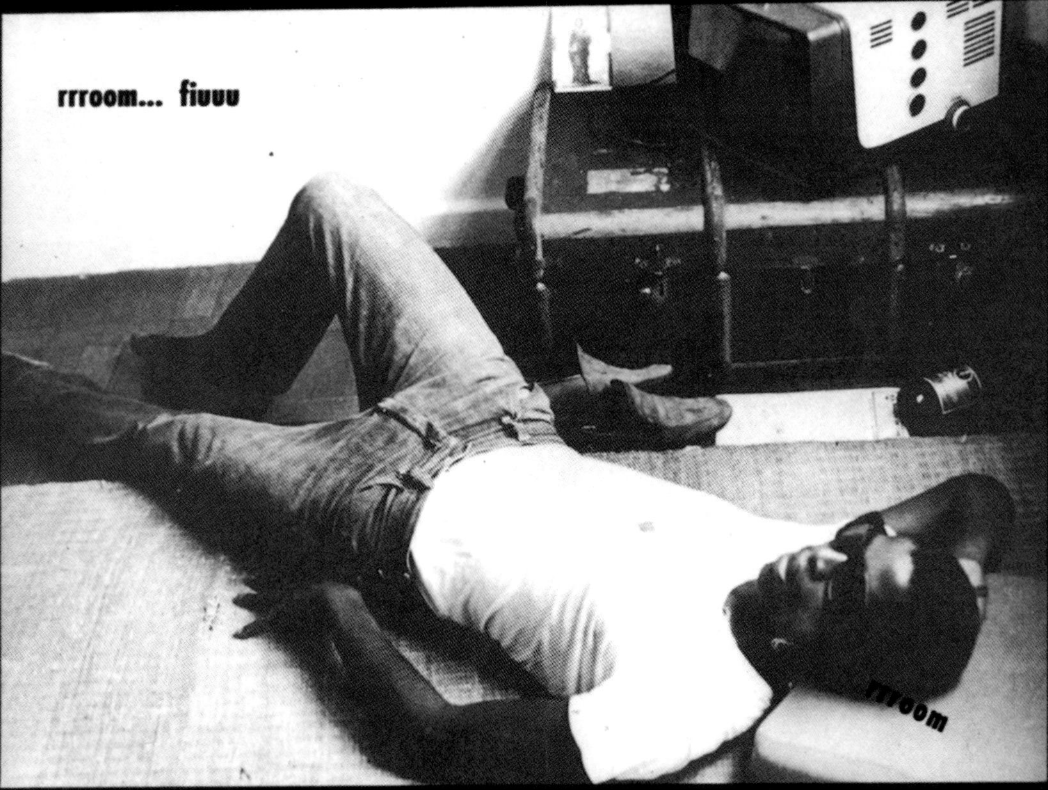

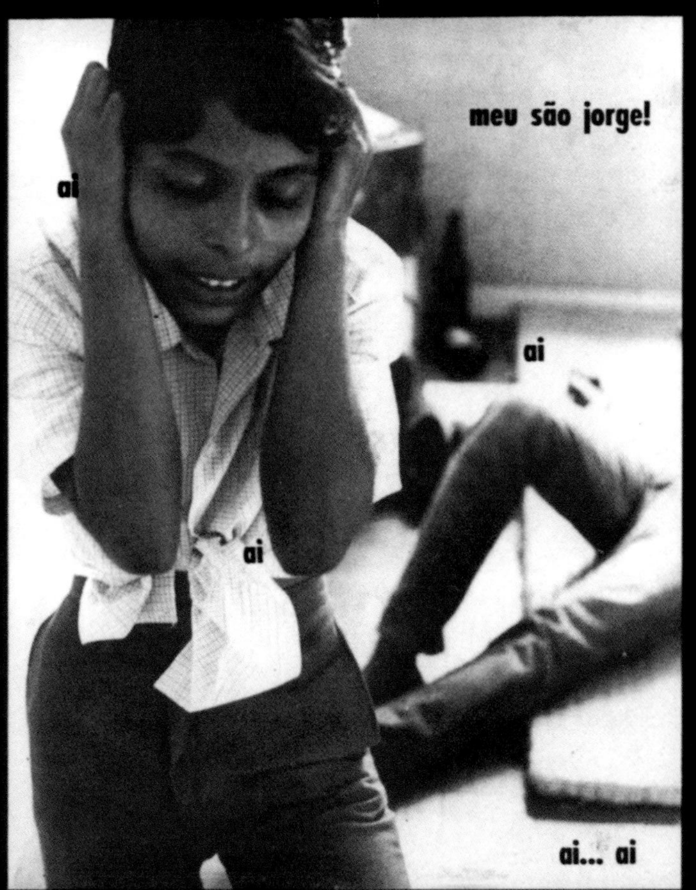
rrroom... fiuuu
rrroom
meu são jorge!
ai
ai
ai
ai
ai... ai

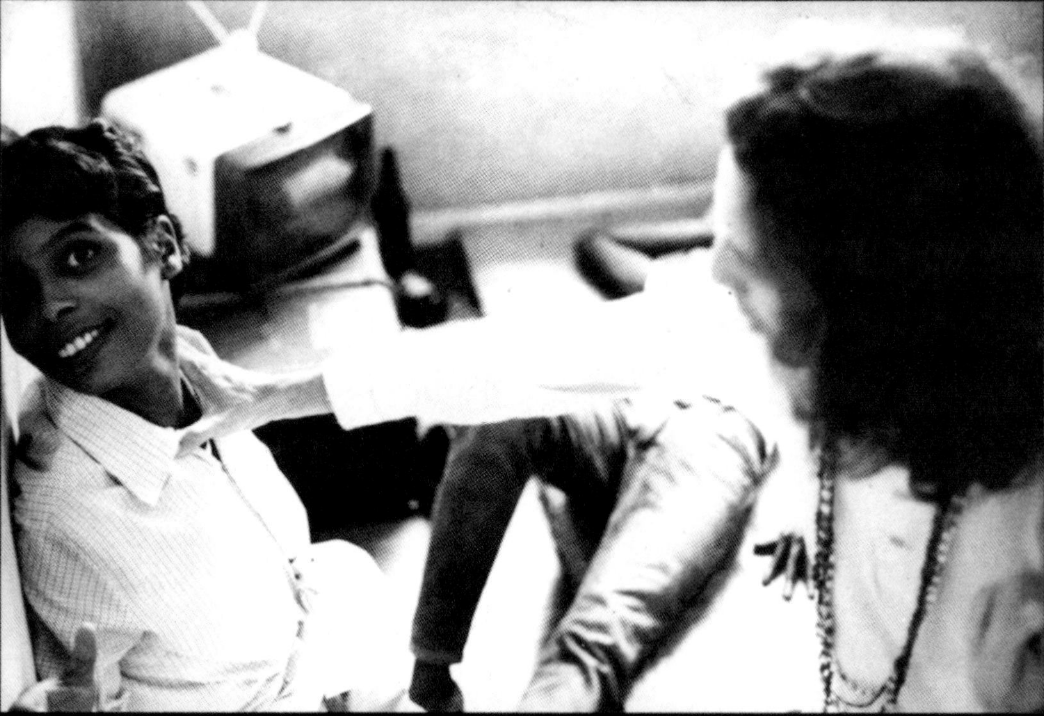

eu labutando em londres, e vocês aí pelos picolés da vida... vou te esganar...

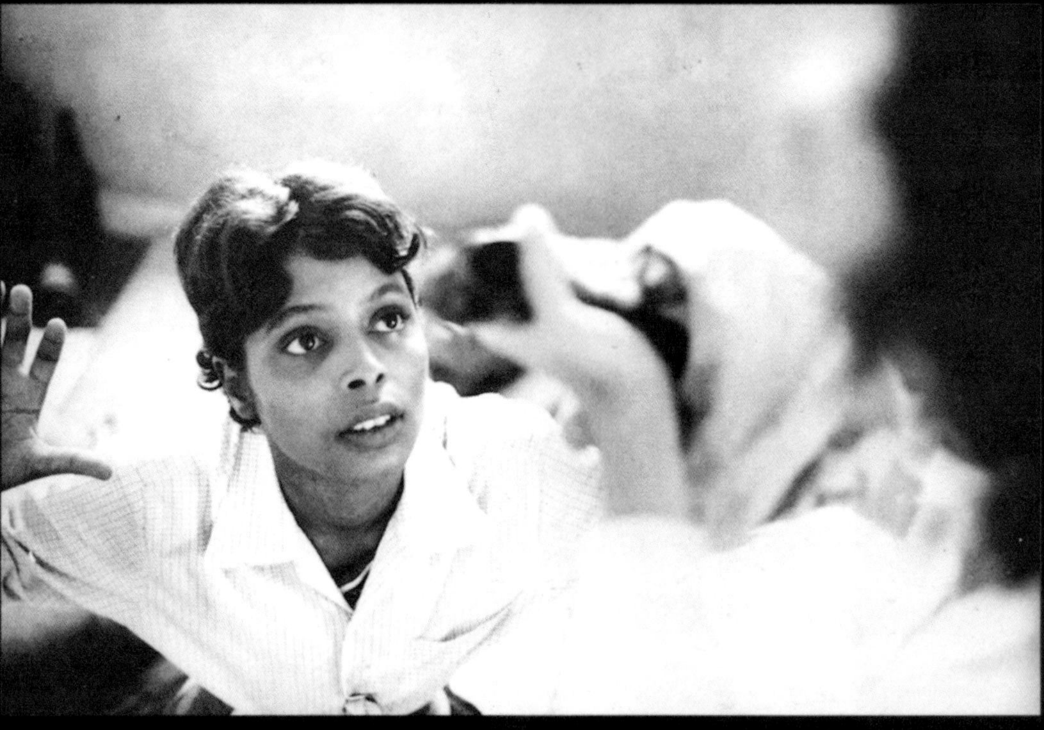

não grita não! vai acordar paulinho. ele sofre de insônia.

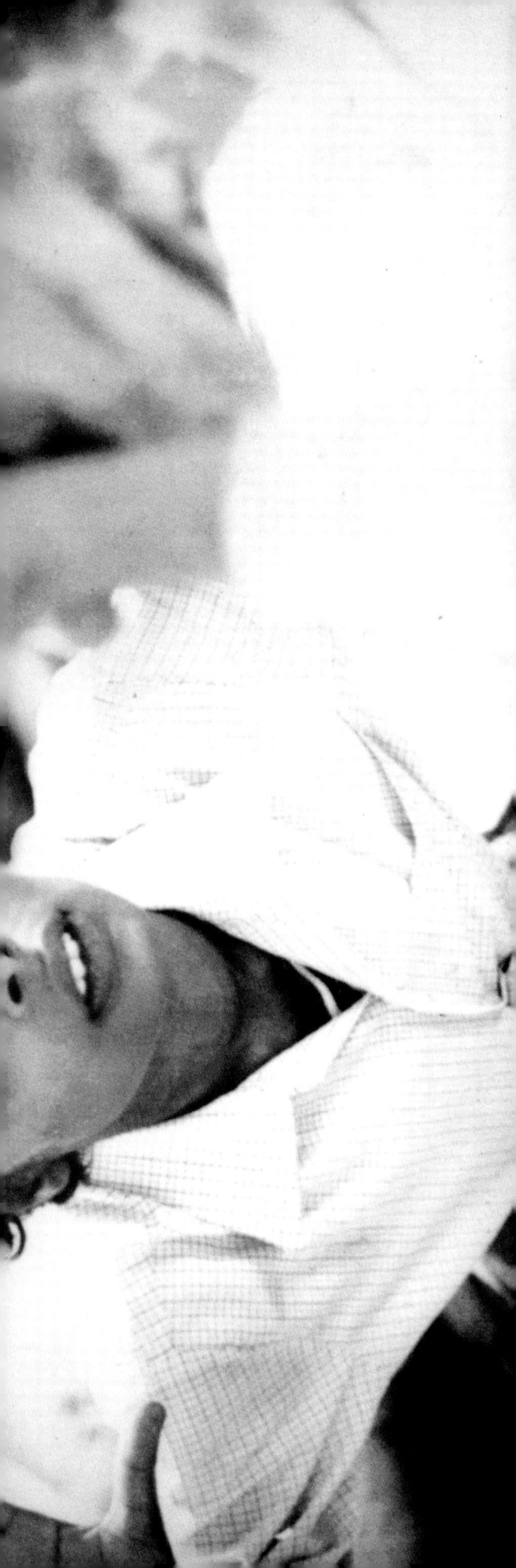

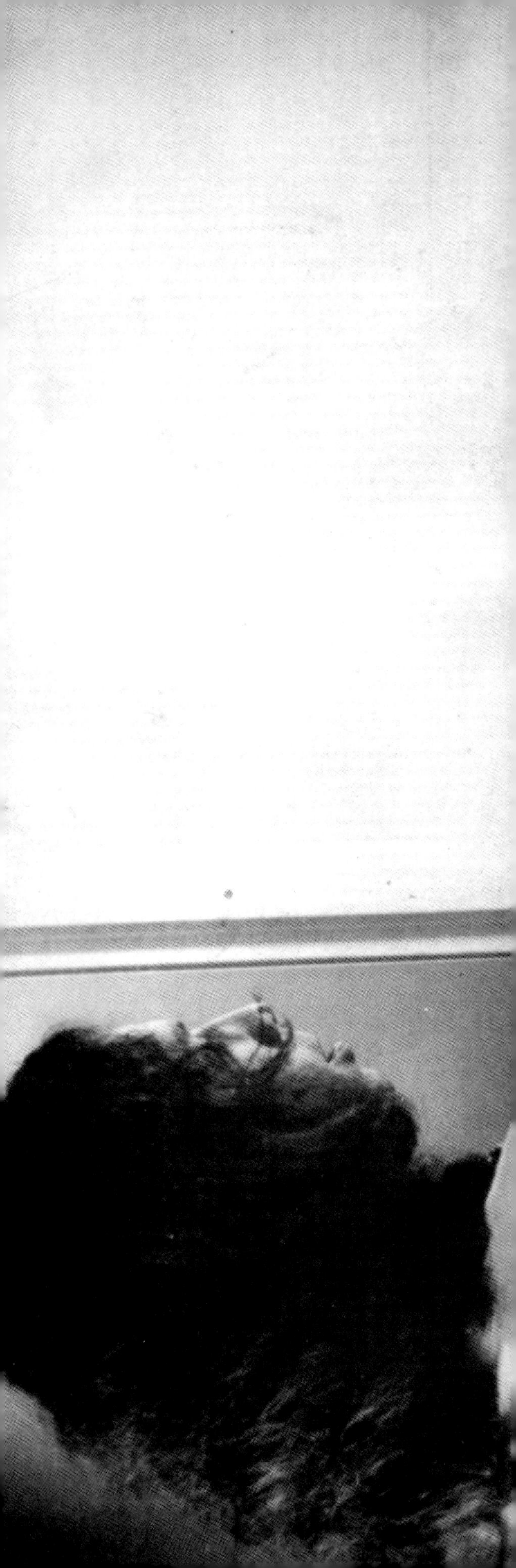

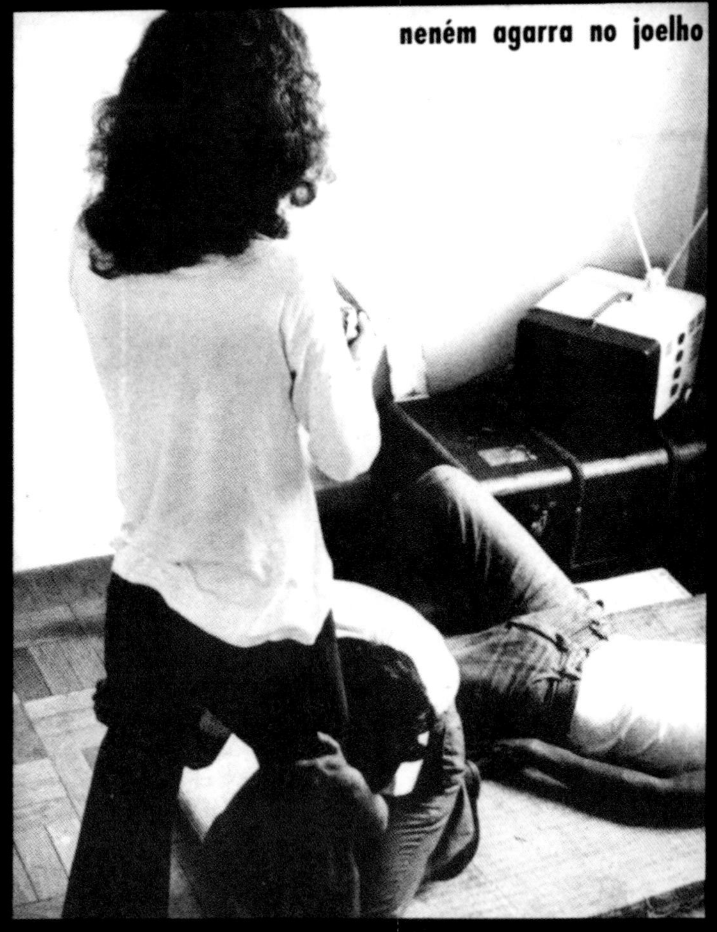
neném agarra no joelho implorando.
tome maracujina!
acorda patativa! não é sem tempo, 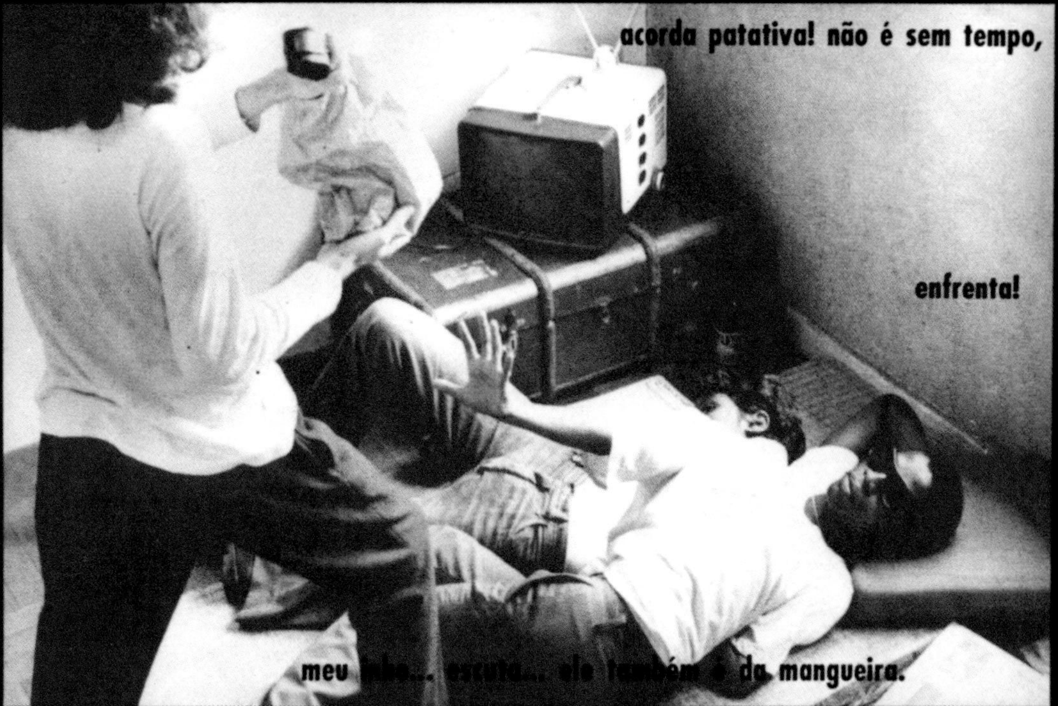
enfrenta!
meu bebo... escuta... ele também é da mangueira.

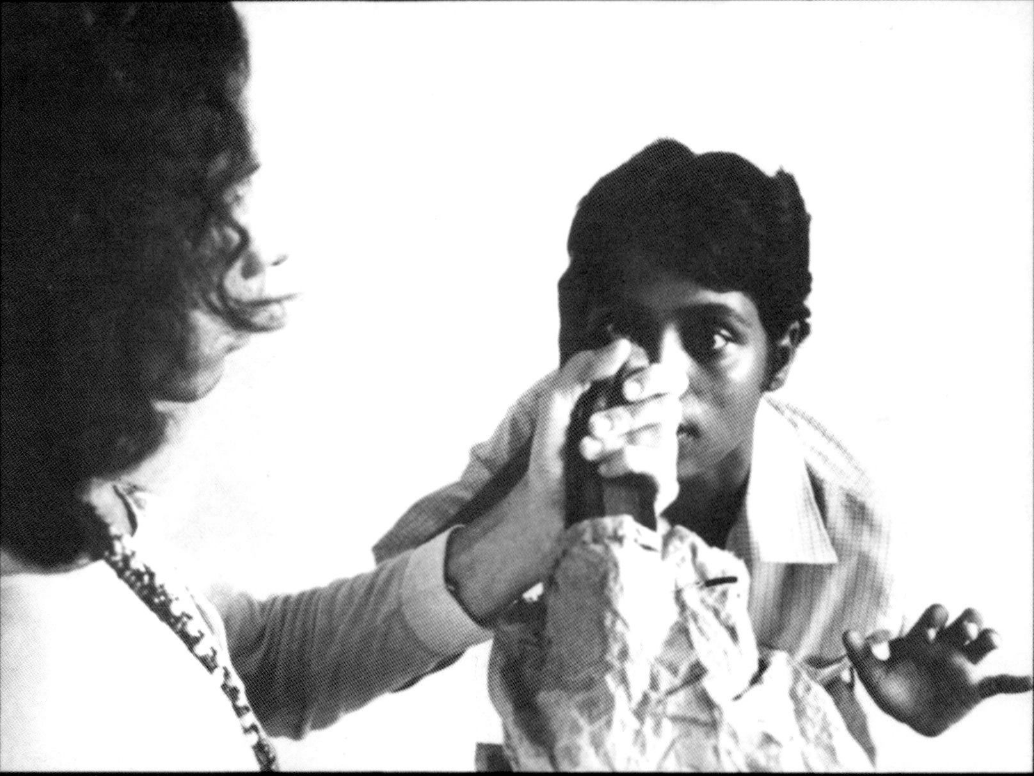

o que é isso? uma caceta?

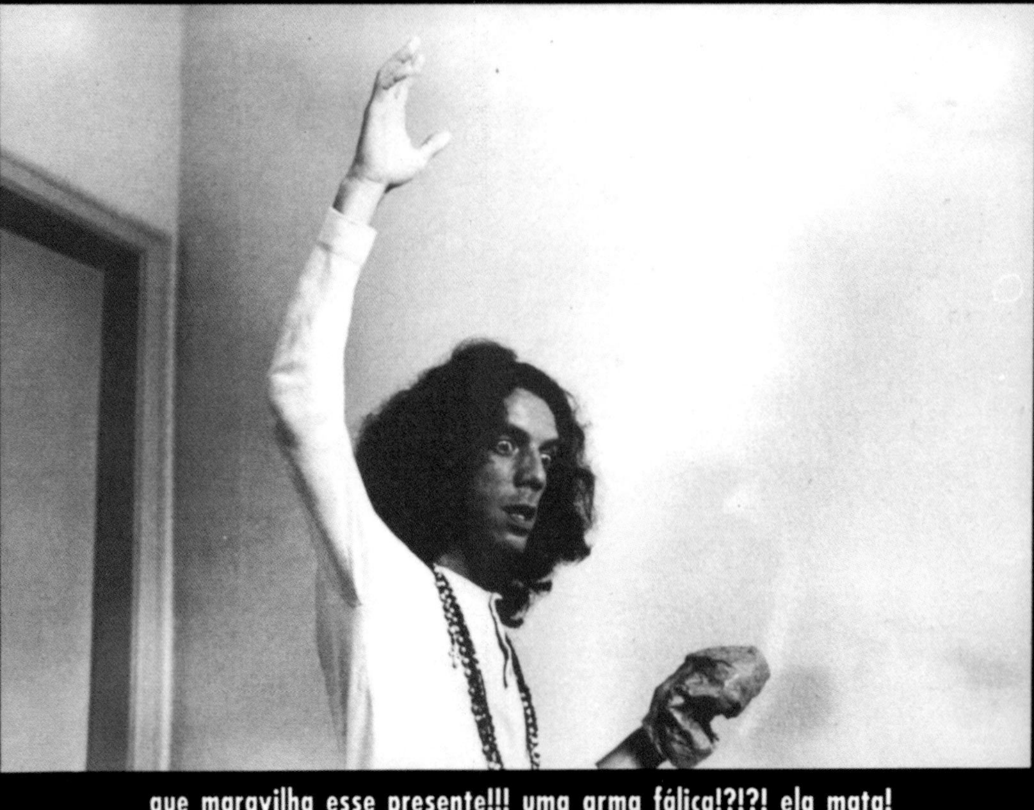

que maravilha esse presente!!! uma arma fálica!?!?! ela mata!
vou matá-lo... agrhmrrrrrrr.

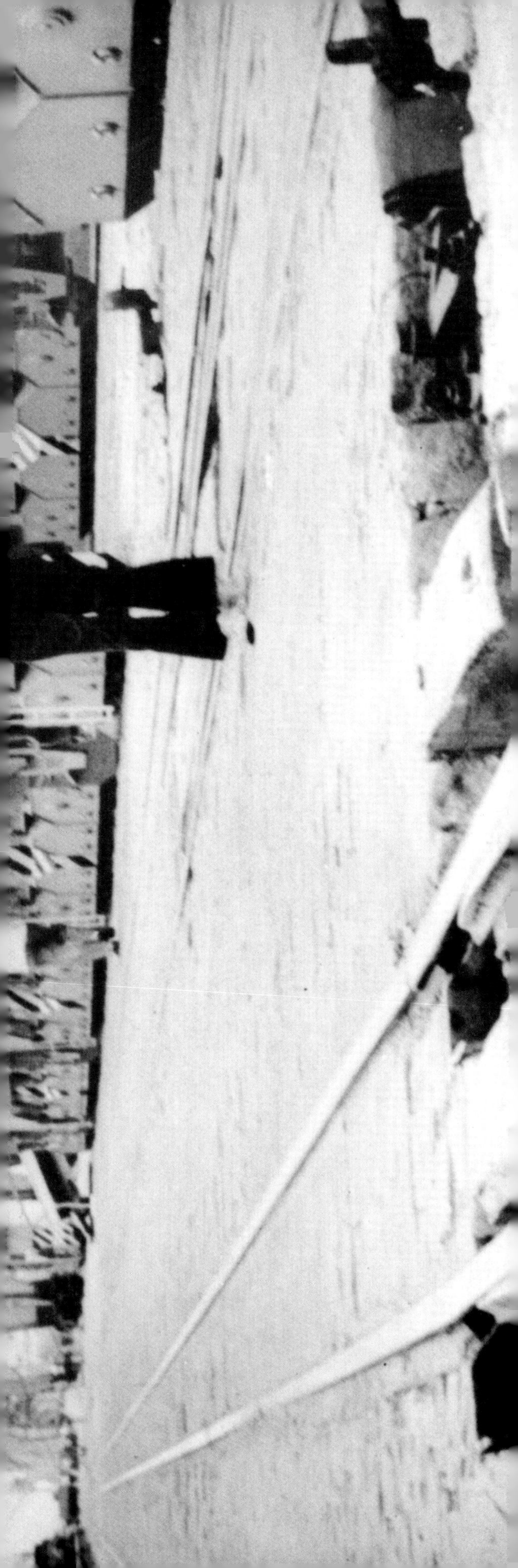

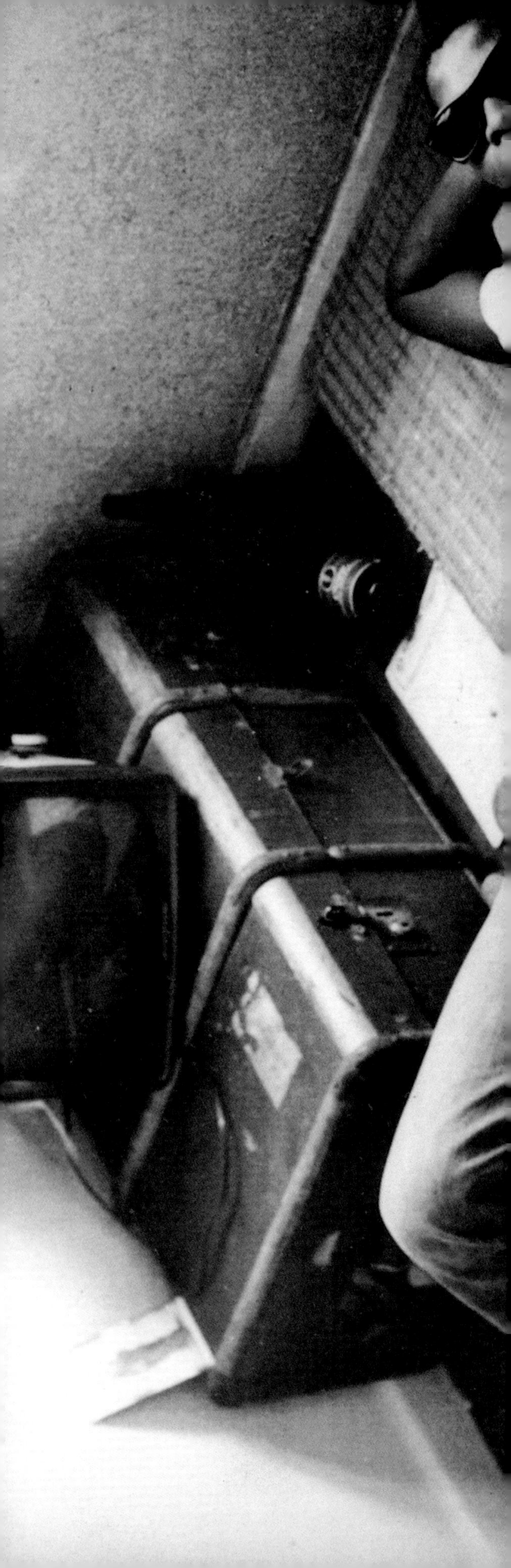

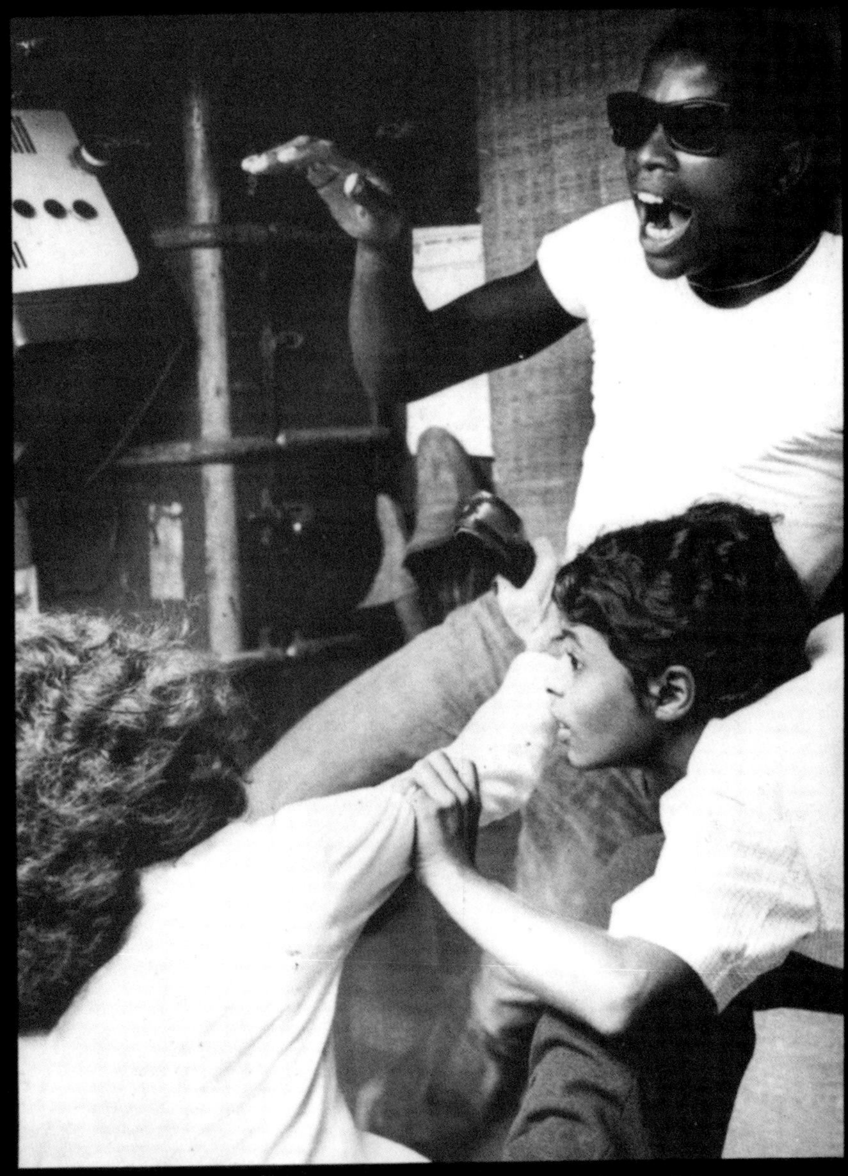

me matou... NÃO! essa arma era pro tal de ayela!...
guilherme mandou pra mim. tava esperando chegar...

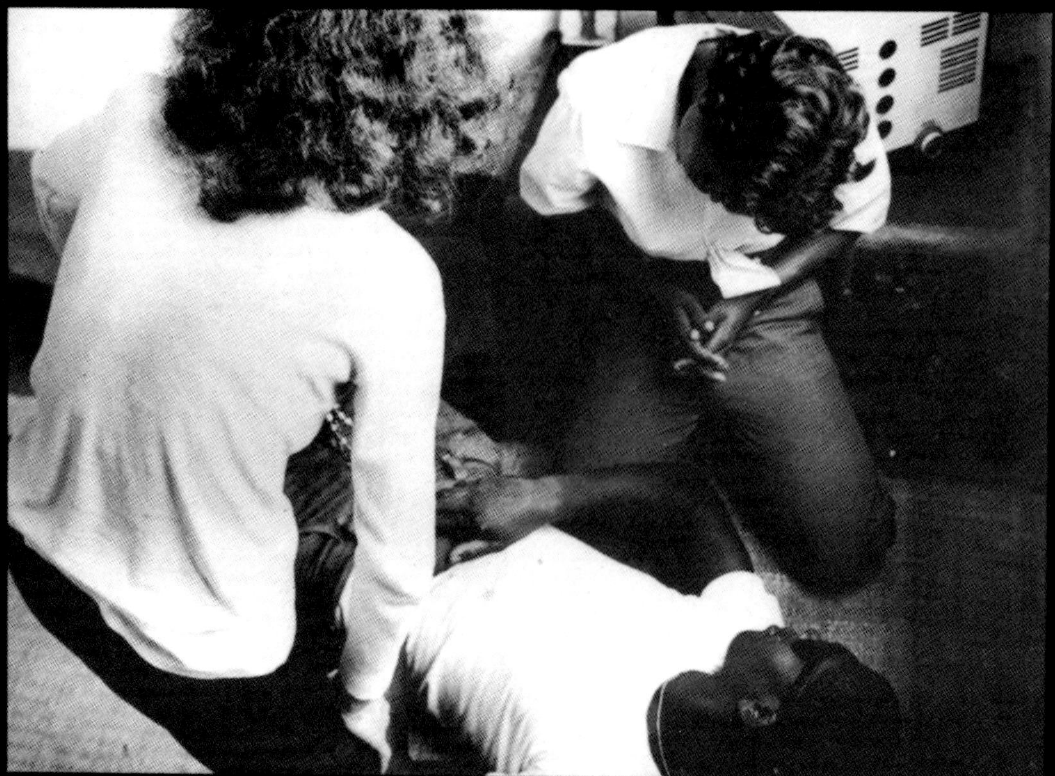

viu? matou paulomarginal. tá morto. mortinho.

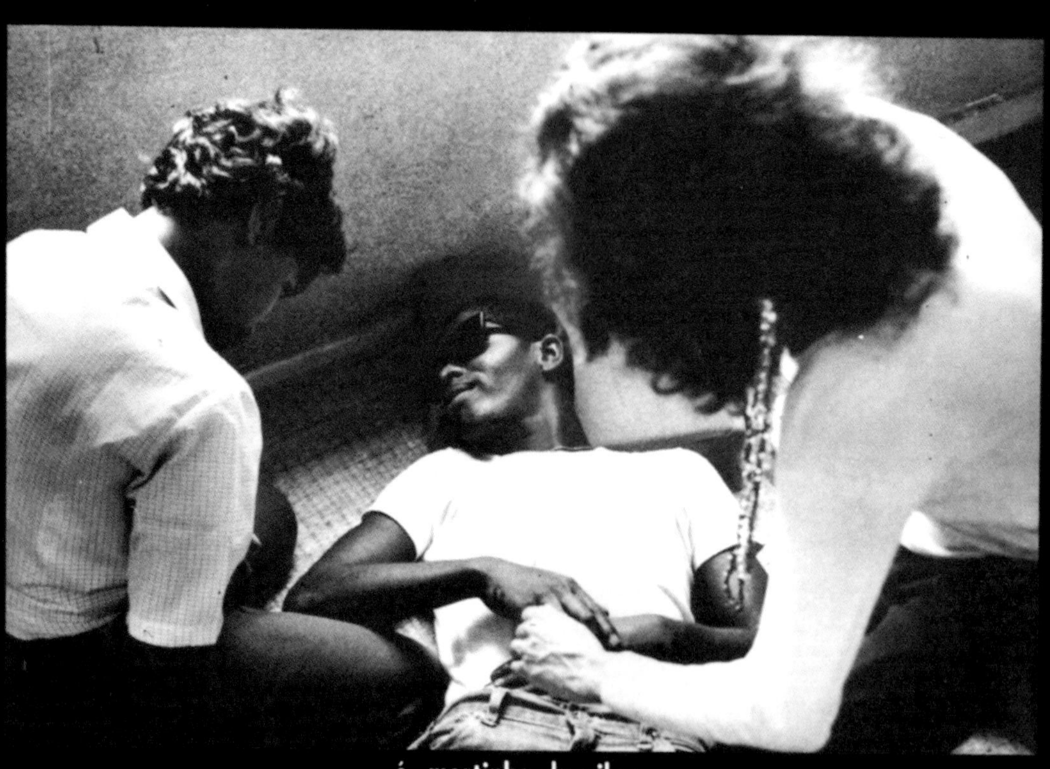

é, mortinho da silva.

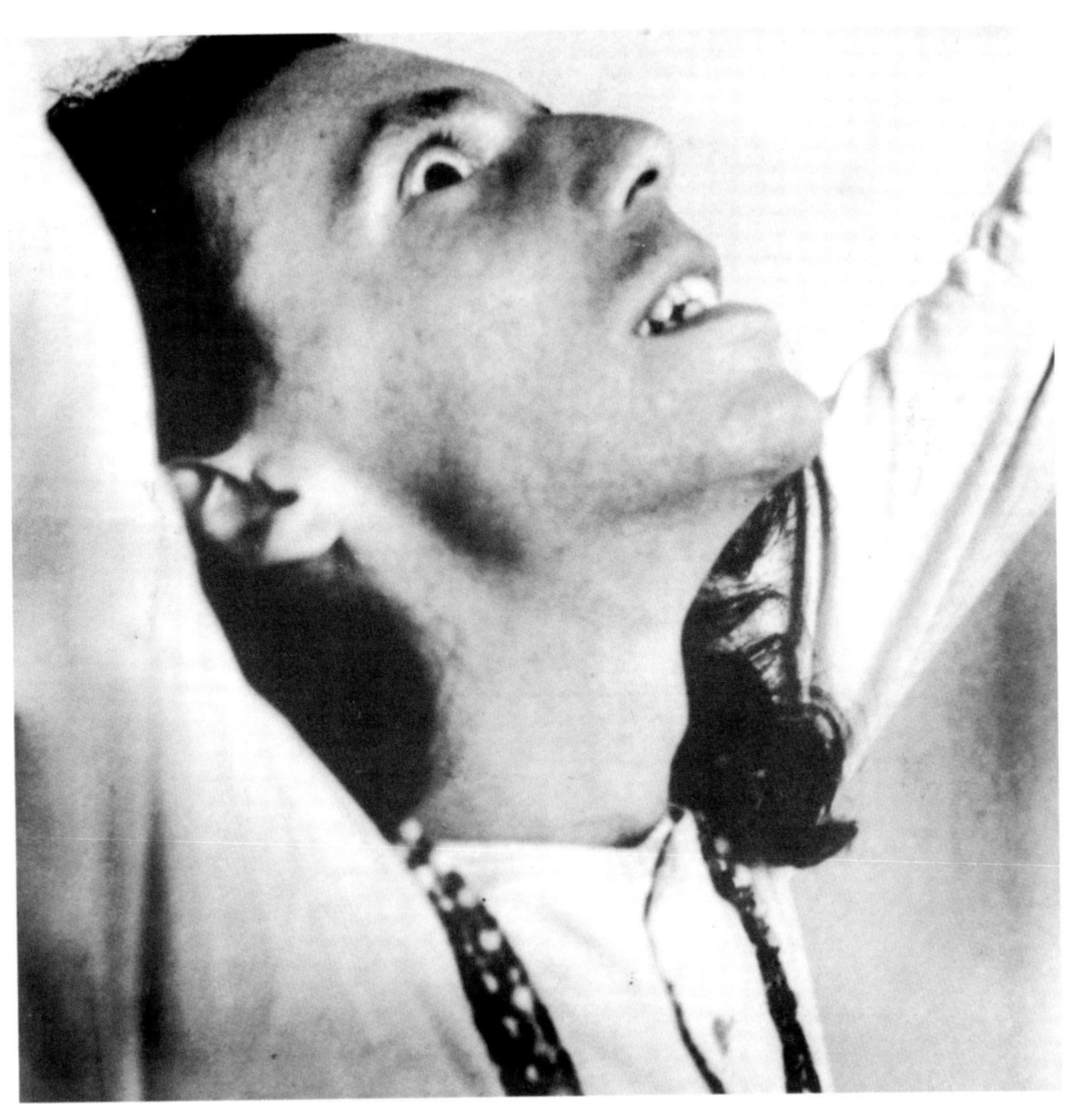

FICHA TÉCNICA

Criação e realização: Antonio Manuel
Fotografia: Kiko
Diálogos: Antonio Manuel, com colaboração de Lygia Pape
Projeto Gráfico: Luciano Figueiredo

E APRESENTANDO

Hélio Oiticica: *guru*
Tineca: *neném*
Paulo: *paulomarginal*

Rio de Janeiro, 1970
Proibida a reprodução integral ou parcial sem autorização do autor.
Direitos autorais: Antonio Manuel S. Oliveira

AGRADECIMENTOS

Agradeço a Lygia Pape que colaborou na produção e nos diálogos, e que, 25 anos depois, lembrou a existência deste trabalho. A Eva Doris Rosental, Claudia Saldanha e Reynaldo Roels Jr., do RioArte, que tornaram realidade esta publicação de 1.500 exemplares. A Luciano Figueiredo, por sua dedicação ao projeto gráfico. Aos amigos Vladimir Elias, Hugo Denizart e Alex Varela. A Roberta, Claudio e Cesar Oiticica, Eduardo Clark e seu primo Kiko, autor das fotos. A Vicente de Mello, que fez as reproduções. E finalmente a Paulo e Tineca, as estrelas da fotonovelajuntamente com Hélio Oiticica.

PREFEITO DO RIO DE JANEIRO
Cesar Maia

SECRETÁRIA MUNICIPAL DE CULTURA
Helena Severo

INSTITUTO MUNICIPAL DE ARTE E CULTURA-RIOARTE
Eva Doris Rosental
Presidente
Maria Julia Vieira Pinheiro
Diretora de Projetos
Claudia Saldanha
Diretora da Divisão de Artes Visuais

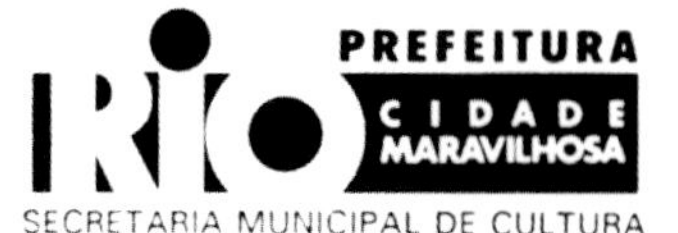

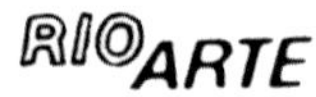

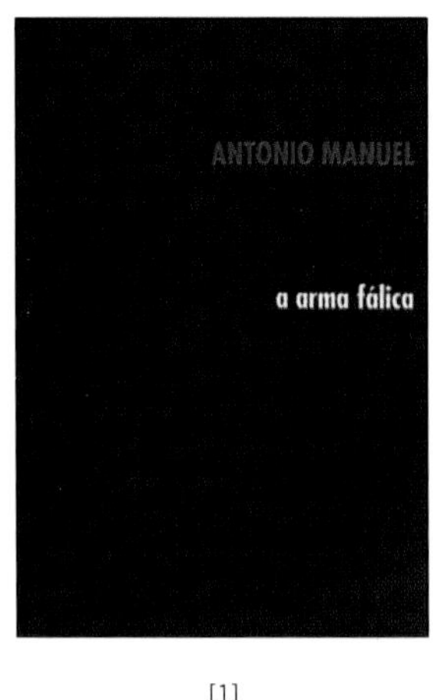

[1]

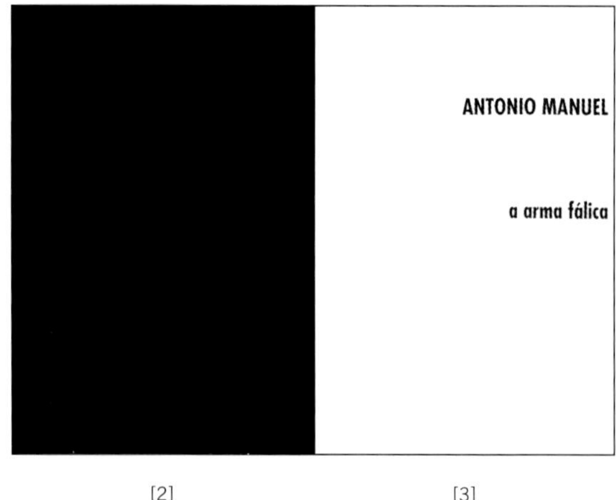

[2]   [3]

[1] + [3]

ANTONIO MANUEL
A PHALLIC WEAPON

[4]   [5]

[5]

The *fotonovela* happens from facts and photos, which is at the mature age of 25. Coming out of the drawer is *Urnas quentes* (Hot Ballot Boxes) – the hermetically sealed poem-images, which must be broken in order to discover its code.

In 1970, I summoned all my present creative energies, exposing them NAKED to the public at MAM: *O corpo é a obra* (The Body Is the Work).

From the newspaper page to the *Flans,* it was about capturing reality and making poetic creation possible – a synthesis between the verbal and the visual, a *mise-en-scène* of the work that inhabits this creative atmosphere.

In 1969, Hélio Oiticica traveled to London to make his solo exhibition at Whitechapel. *Tendas, Parangolés e Éden* (Tents, Parangolés and Eden)[1] – the export packaging of a new spirit. I went to Praça Mauá to say goodbye (Torquato Neto also went on the same ship).

With the photo-novella, I wanted to work on a new means of expression, carrying out this work in the affective form of partnership and in the spirit of thinking about art. There was the idea and argument; the location, I had already established it: Praça Mauá and Oiticica's house on Rua Engenheiro Alfredo Duarte. As for the scenario, we used household objects, with Hélio's participation and his inseparable Black & White TV.

I did the first two scene takes in Praça Mauá recalling his departure for London; but there was also the space of crossing the Atlantic, beyond the sea. Aware of this space and port feeling, I wanted to vitalize his nobility and misery in the face of a barbarous, torturing, criminal country. The political repression that was happening, hidden, in the dictatorship's torturous actions, brought us to fight for "the experimental exercise of freedom," as Mário Pedrosa called it. Without a cent, but a profound creative will to make joy from life and thought from art.

Nothing has been changed to update the *fotonovela.* The argument and dialogues are original, like at the time, a record of a lived experimental climate in Rio de Janeiro. Despite the argument being fiction, nowadays the reality of life and the limits of violence have been surpassed, and life, trivialized in the unbearable space it occupies today.

Enjoy this *fotonovela,* unpretentious and sincere, that sprouted from the will to do something delightful in partnership with Hélio Oiticica. Let it, if possible, help to illuminate the senses and the spirit of life.

Antonio Manuel
September 17, 1995

1   Editors' note: Hélio Oiticica named the show the *Whitechapel Experiment.*

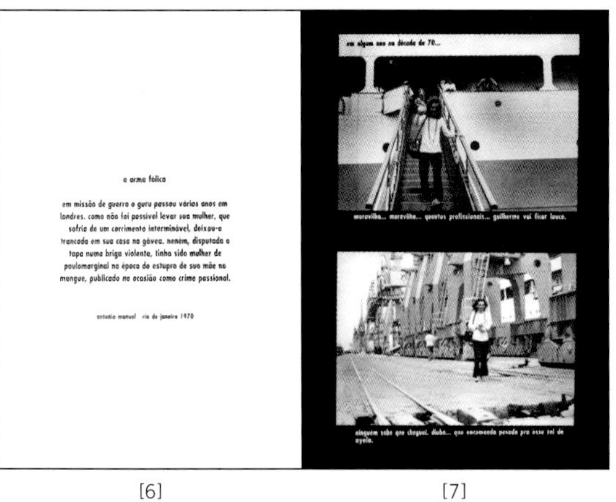

[6]   [7]

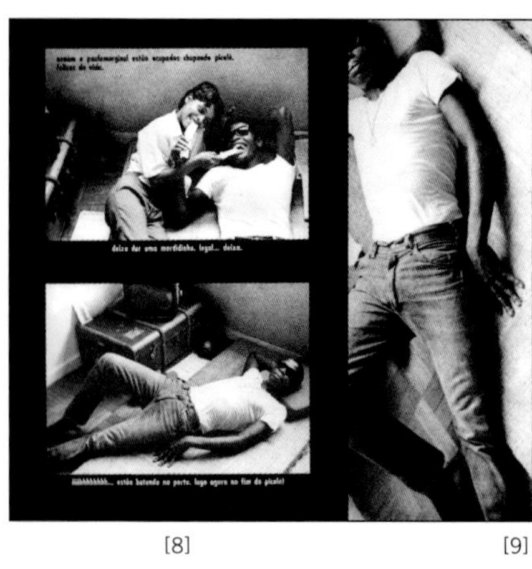

[8]   [9]

[6]
a phallic weapon

the guru spent several years in london on a war mission.
since it was not possible to bring his wife, who suffered
from an interminable vaginal discharge, he left her locked
up in their home in gávea. neném, disputed over by fists
in a violent brawl, had been married to paulomarginal
at the time of her mother's rape in mangue, published in
the newspapers as a crime of passion.

antonio manuel   rio de janeiro   1970

[7]
in some year in the 70s …
wonderful… wonderful… so many workers… guilherme
will go nuts.
nobody knows I have arrived. damn it… what a tall order
for this ayela guy.

[8]
neném and paulomarginal are busy sucking on a
popsicle. as happy as can be.
let me have a little bite. alright… she does.
aaahhhhhh … someone's knocking on the door. just
when i'm finishing my popsicle!

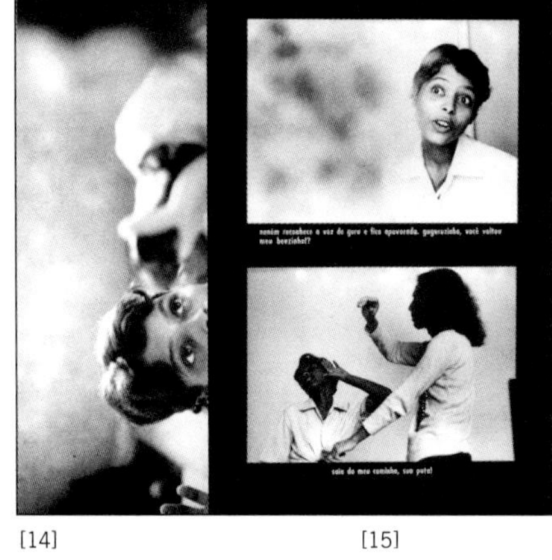

[14]   [15]

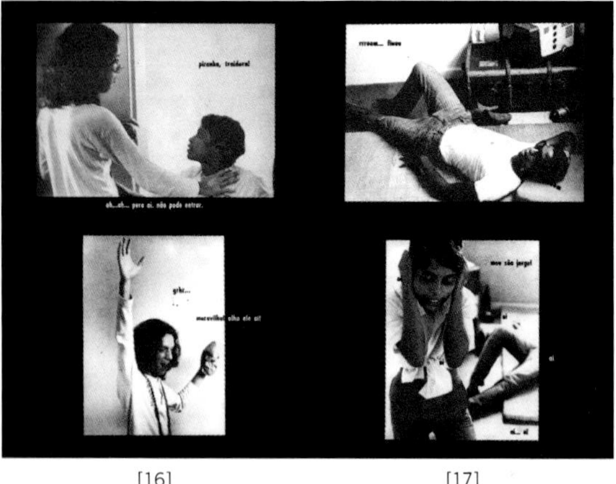

[16]   [17]

[15]
neném recognizes guru's voice and gets really scared.
guguruzinho, have you come back, my sweet?
get out of my way, you whore!

[16]
slut, traitor!
oh … ah … hold on. you can't enter.
grrr …
wonderful. look at him there!

[17]
zzzzzz… zzzzz
zzzzzz
oh oh oh oh
oh my god! oh… oh

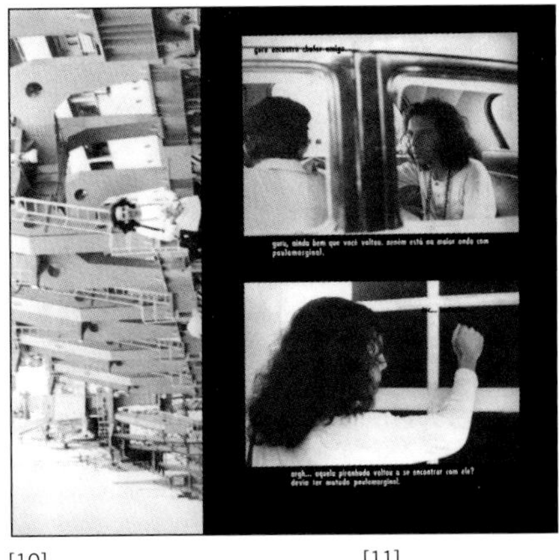

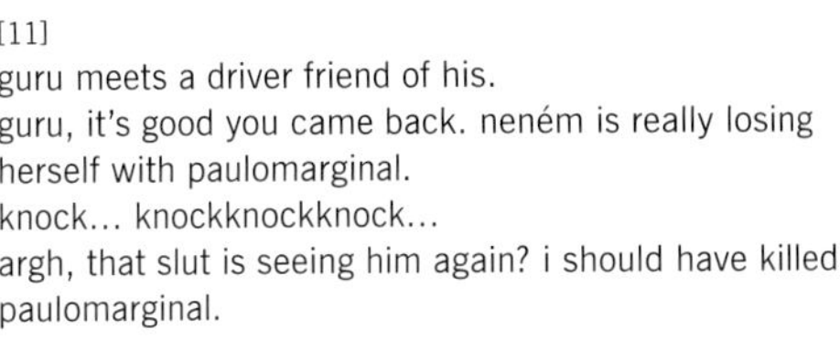

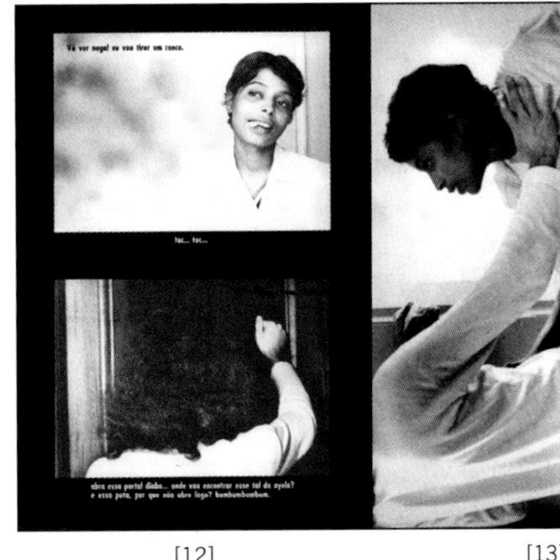

[10]   [11]   [12]   [13]

[11]
guru meets a driver friend of his.
guru, it's good you came back. neném is really losing
herself with paulomarginal.
knock… knockknockknock…
argh, that slut is seeing him again? i should have killed
paulomarginal.

[12]
go check it out, nega! i'm going to take a nap.
knock… knock…
boom… boom… boom…
open the door! goddammit… where am i going to find
this ayela guy? and this whore, why won't she open the
door? boomboomboomboom

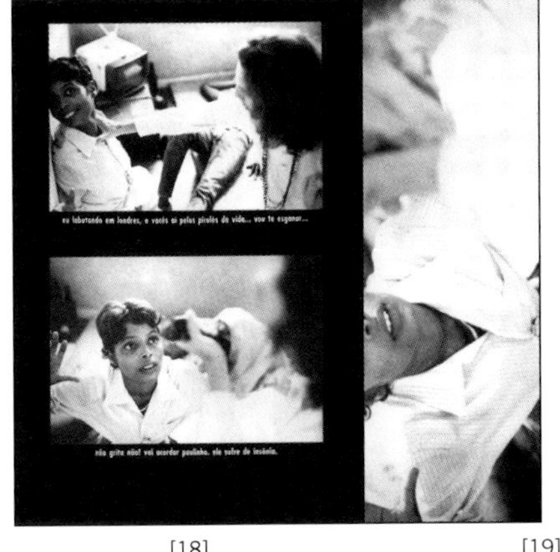

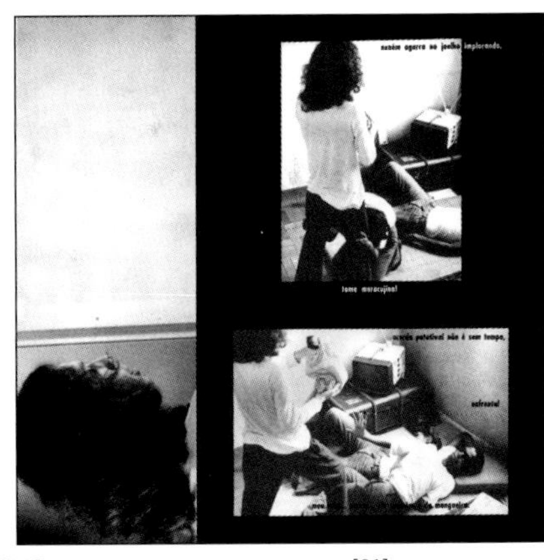

[18]   [19]   [20]   [21]

[18]
while i'm working hard in london, the two of you are here
playing with popsicles … i'm going to strangle you …
don't scream! you are going to wake up paulinho. he has
insomnia.

[21]
neném is now on her knees, begging.
take a chill pill!
wake up, dumbass. useless, face it!
honey … listen … he is also from mangueira.

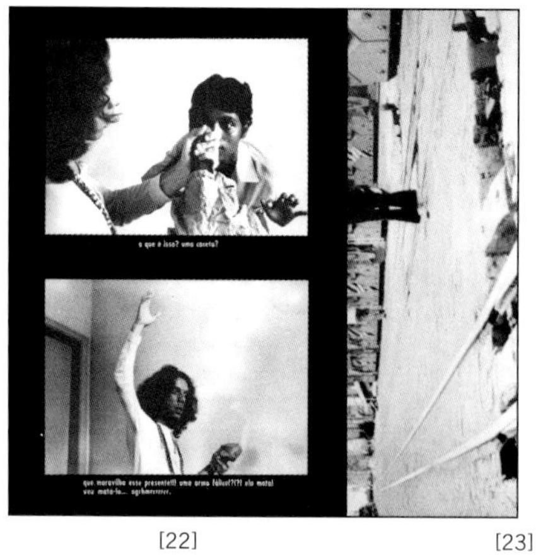

[22]

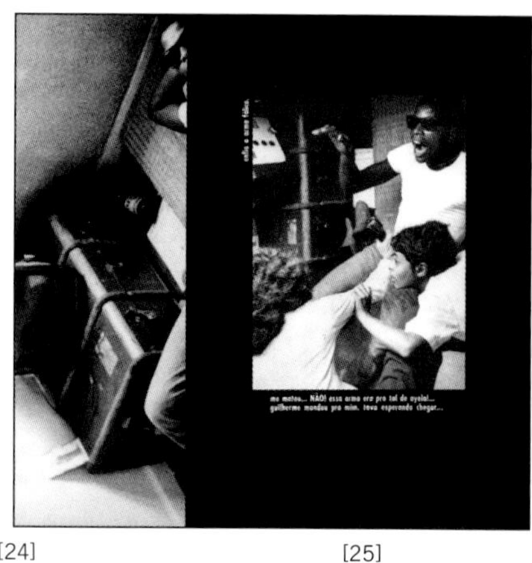

[23]

[24]

[25]

[22]
what is this? a dick?
what a cool gift!!! a phallic weapon?!?! it kills!
i am going to kill you… arghhhhhhhh

[25]
slips the phallic weapon on.
it killed me … NO! this weapon was for that ayela guy!
… guillherme sent it to me. i was waiting for it.

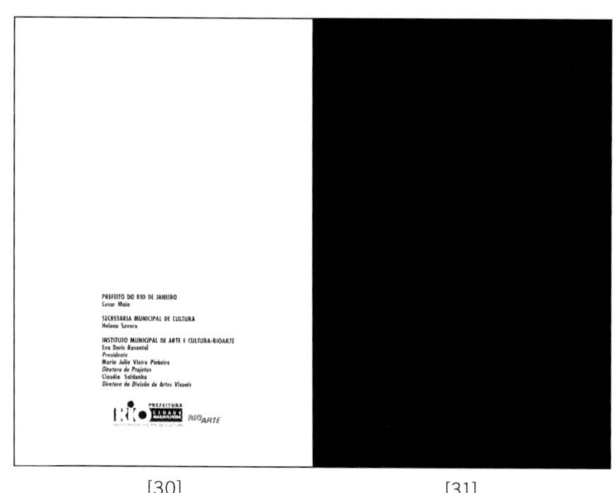

[30]

[31]

[32]

[30]
MAYOR OF RIO DE JANEIRO
Cesar Maia

MUNICIPAL SECRETARY OF CULTURE
Helena Severo

RIOARTE MUNICIPAL ART AND CULTURAL INSTITUTE
Eva Doris Rosental
President
Maria Julia Vieira Pinheiro
Project Director
Claudia Saldanha
Visual Arts Division Director

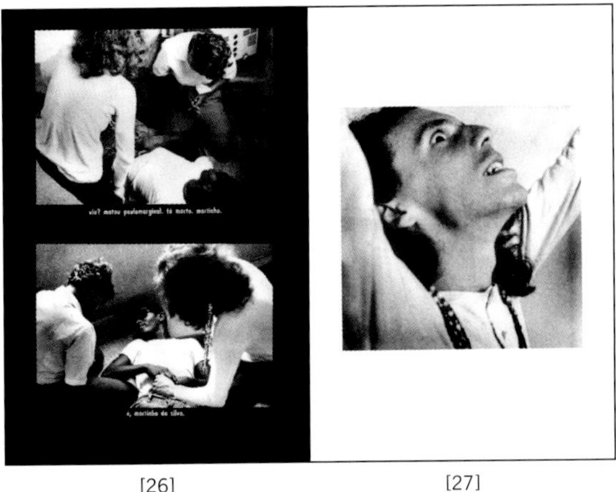

[26]   [27]

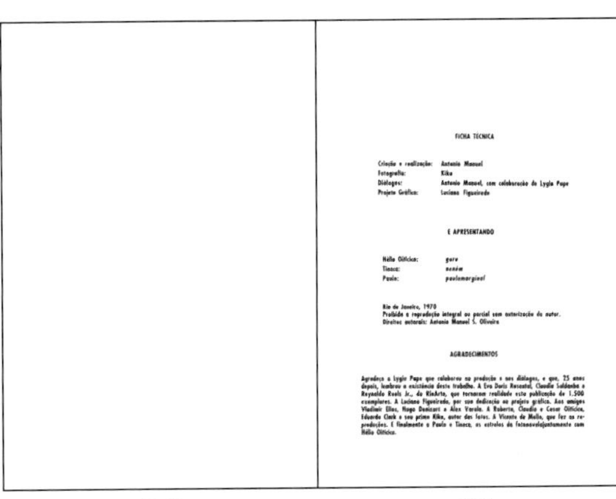

[28]   [29]

[26]
see? you killed paulomarginal. he's dead. really dead.
yep, dead as a doornail.

[29]
TECHNICAL SPECIFICATIONS

Concept and design: Antonio Manuel
Photography: Kiko
Dialogues: Antonio Manuel,
                     in collaboration with Lygia Pape
Graphic design: Luciano Figueiredo

AND PRESENTING ...

Hélio Oiticica: *guru*
Tineca: *neném*
Paulo: *paulomarginal*

Rio de Janeiro, 1970
Reproduction in whole or in part is prohibited without
permission of the author.
Copyright: Antonio Manuel S. Oliveira

ACKNOWLEDGMENTS

I would like to thank Lygia Pape, who collaborated in the
production and dialogues, and who, 25 years later, recalled the
existence of this work. To Eva Doris and Claudia Saldanha
and Reynaldo Roels Jr, from RioArte, who made the publication
of 1,500 copies come true. To Luciano Figueiredo, for his
dedication to the graphic design. To my friends Vladimir Elias,
Hugo Denizart and Alex Varela. To Roberta, Claudio and Cesar
Oiticica, Eduardo Clark and his cousin Kiko, the photographer.
To Vicente de Mello, who made the reproductions. And finally
to Paulo and Tineca, the co-stars of the *fotonovela* together
with Hélio Oiticica.

A PHALLIC WEAPON:
A *FOTONOVELA* IN 24 POSES

GABRIELA RANGEL

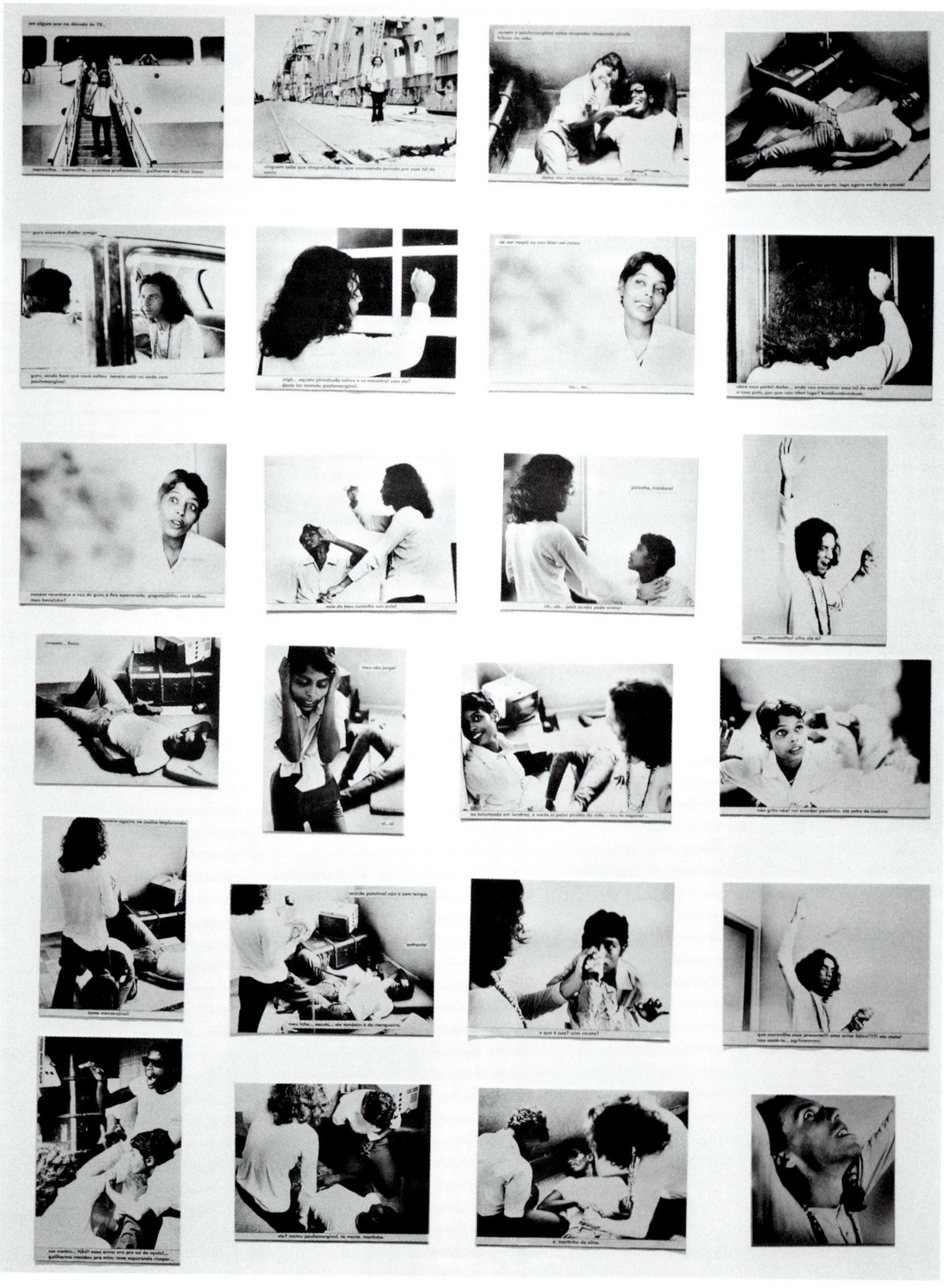

A arma fálica (A Phallic Weapon), 1970. *Fotonovela* maquette with gelatin silver prints mounted on board, 56 x 44 in. Courtesy the artist and Gilberto Chateaubriand Collection, Museu de Arte Moderna, Rio de Janeiro

A REVOLUTION WITH(OUT) A GURU

Sometime in 1970, Antonio Manuel staged *A arma fálica* (The Phallic Weapon), a black-and-white *fotonovela* that starred Hélio Oiticica, who played the role of Guru, and featured untrained actors identified by its author as Tineca and Paulo. According to Antonio Manuel, the name "Guru" for the main character conveyed an orientalist drive of the period: "a pseudonym that reveals the spirit of the age (macrobiotic, vegetarian, yoga, Hare Krishna)," which in Brazil coexisted "with repression and an urban atmosphere of marginality."[1] As in the artist's later filmic experiences such as *Loucura & Cultura* (Madness & Culture), 1973, and *Semi Ótica* (Semi Otics/Optics), 1975, he worked in collaboration with friends, and friends of friends, to produce works with meager resources. With a level of intensity similar to the risk-taking, collaborative spirit to be found in the neo-avant-garde of New York's SoHo neighborhood, the absence of an art market as well as an increasing politicization of artists in Brazil contributed to nurturing a collective, spontaneous and dazzling energy that proved an innovative force for the visual arts during the 1970s.[2] This resulted in strong yet unassuming creative exchanges between artists from different disciplines and backgrounds as well as eventual collaborators from the metropolitan shantytowns (favelas) with no access to culture. Referring to the conditions of production of the time, Manuel has stated: "there was no money but a profound creative will, to make life happy, and art, thought."[3] *A arma fálica* was conceived as a photographic fiction meant to be published in the *Carioca* tabloid *O Pasquim,* active since 1969. However, the original plan could not be completed until 1995.

It is no accident that Antonio Manuel intended to publish his provocative *fotonovela* in *O Pasquim,* a satiric publication focused on film, pop music, soccer, violence, feminism, sex and mass culture.[4] Founded by leftist journalists and graphic designers from the southern bank of Rio de Janeiro, it acted as a powerful magnet for attracting a number of important artists aligned with the opposition against the civil/military dictatorship that took over the country when leftist President João Goulard was ousted in 1964. Caetano Veloso, despite his growing popularity, was briefly forced into exile and from London he published his chronicles and an interview in *O Pasquim.*[5] Notably, the newspaper included contributions

---

I would like to thank Natalie Bunnell for her research assistance.

1   Antonio Manuel interviewed by the author via email, June 15, 2011.

2   In the United States, the Vietnam War provoked critical responses from many artists. By contrast, in Brazil the 1964 coup d'état was the political factor that triggered a virulent reaction from intellectuals and the art community.

3   Antonio Manuel interviewed by the author, June 15, 2011. Translation: Alexandra García.

4   See José Luiz Braga (Brasilia: Universidade de Brasilia, 1991). Its title meaning literally "pasquinade," *O Pasquim* was a weekly lampoon newspaper edited in Rio de Janeiro by Jaguar (Sérgio Jaguaribe), Sérgio Cabral, Tarso de Castro, Carlos Prósperi, Claudius, Luiz Carlos Maciel and Ziraldo. In spite of its independent structure and artisanal production, the newspaper's coverage was national, eventually enjoying massive distribution (100,000 copies.) Established after the AI-5, *O Pasquim* reached the peak of its popularity during the worst years of censorship (*anos de chumbo*). Due to its irreverent humor and popular bent combined with a subtle political critique, many of its publishers were briefly sent to jail. However, the tabloid managed to survive until the dictatorship was dismantled.

5   In 1968, two weeks after the AI-5 was implemented, Caetano and Gilberto Gil were arrested and charged with disrespecting the national anthem and flag.

by Oiticica, Ferreira Gullar, Vinícius de Moraes, Odete Lara, Carlos Diegues, Glauber Rocha, as well as many figures associated with the Tropicalista circle.[6] It also included large sections dedicated to emerging pop singers such as Maria Bethânia, Gal Costa and Gilberto Gil. *O Pasquim* was a unique amalgam of mass entertainment with a calculated policy of political acrimony and satiric wit. Although the language was ambivalent the message was clear: *O Pasquim* aimed its abrasive critique of political repression, and paired it with fake morality. Yet in 1970 some of its publishers were sent to jail when the magazine's seventy-second issue was cancelled as it was being printed. After the incident, a military "reviewer" occupied a permanent position in the newspaper's editorial room in order to proofread the content before it went out to the public.[7]

Curiously enough, Antonio Manuel conceived his *fotonovela* shortly after the implementation of the Ato Institucional No. 5 (AI-5), a legal corpus implemented unconstitutionally in 1968 that eroded civil liberties along with educational autonomy and artistic experimentation. The AI-5 not only frustrated the aspirations of a generation that came of age after the advent of bossa nova, modern architecture, Concrete and Neoconcrete art, Theatre of the Oppressed and Cinema Novo, but forced leading Brazilian artists, academics and intellectuals to flee the country and take refuge in different parts of Europe and the Americas. Among them was Mário Pedrosa: the most influential art critic in Brazil and a Trotskyist intellectual who had co-founded the Partido Trabalhista Brasilero (PTB).[8] In this context, *O Pasquim* became one of the few alternative press ventures to bridge the exile and local scenes at the time of a nascent national cultural industry in Brazil that accompanied the so-called economic miracle.[9]

Regrettably, AI-5 arrived at the end of the 1960s—the very moment of the effervescence of diverse countercultural movements and dissidence articulated by new mindsets in the visuals arts, experimental theater, film, pop music and the social sciences. Despite the dictatorship "a relative left-wing cultural hegemony" was maintained until the implementation of AI-5, which sparked a witch hunt against musicians and theater directors, especially targeting those associated to Tropicalismo.[10] Frederico Morais argues that the "political unconsciousness" unleashed by Tropicalismo was a creative explosion with a clear revolutionary meaning rather than a Dionysian catharsis.[11] The military attacks directed against the university proved that the idea of the revolution had already spread quickly among the

---

6   Tropicália (or Tropicalismo) was a short-lived cultural movement (1967–69) in the visual arts, music and theater in Brazil that merged high-art and Pop tactics. It reacted against the ideas of teleological progress. Its name originated from a *penetrable* made by Oiticica.

7   Braga, *O Pasquim e os anos 70*, 36–37.

8   At the end of the 1960s, Mario Pedrosa was the president of the Associação Brasileira de Críticos de Arte, and in 1972 the *New York Review of Books* published an open letter addressed to General Emilio Garrastazu Médici, President of Brazil, in which a number of international artists and intellectuals, including Pablo Picasso, Alexander Calder, Yve-Alain Bois, Carlos Cruz Diez and Max Bill demanded Pedrosa's freedom. Aracy Amaral has documented the influential effect of Pedrosa's ethical/political position during the worst years of the Brazilian dictatorship for Antonio Manuel's generation in Aracy Amaral, *Arte para quê? A preocupação social na arte brasileira, 1930–1970* (Sao Paulo: Studio Nobel, 2003), 331–333.

9   The *O Globo* TV network's license to operate was granted in 1957. Nonetheless, it did not begin operation until 1965, eventually becoming a huge conglomerate with technical support received by U.S. Time-Life group, thanks to its ties to the military regime.

10   Tania Pellegrini and Sabrina Wilson, "Brazil in the 1970s: Literature and Politics," in *Latin American Perspectives* 21, no. 1 (Winter 1994): 59. Critic Roberto Schwartz originally developed the idea.

11   Amaral, *Arte para quê?*, 334.

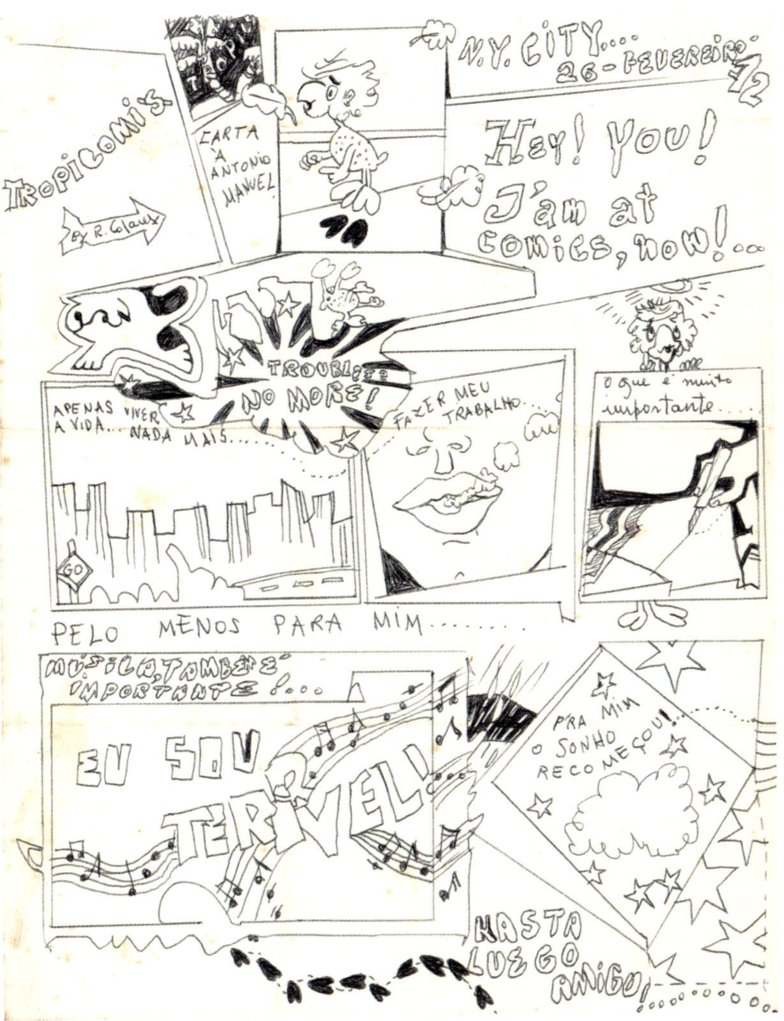

Raymundo Colares, *Tropicomix (Carta à Antonio Manuel)* (Tropicomix [Letter to Antonio Manuel]), February 1972. Ink on paper, 7.9 x 8.1 in. Courtesy Terezinha Colares and Antonio Manuel

country's youth. For Edgar Morin, the end of the 1960s was marked in Europe and in the Western Hemisphere by a general crisis in which the university proved inadequate and anachronistic to the demands of new demographic realities and professional necessities:

> Osmosis occurs between the libertarian existential exigency of some and the planetary politicization of others. For those and others, it is said that the university is at the same time the strongest bastion of bourgeois society (that which makes up the cadres) and its weakest link, since the students are its majority and can there spread the spirit of the revolution.[12]

12   Claude Lefort, Cornelius Castoriadis, Edgar Morin, ed., *Mai 68 La Brèche* (Paris: Fayard, 1988), 17. Translation: Damian Kraus

The repression and censorship prevalent in Brazil is a well-documented fact that informed Antonio Manuel's early works as well as works by Antonio Dias, Cildo Meireles and Carlos Zílio. (Zílio became a militant activist who pursued political action as an "unconventional new form of artistic practice."[13]) On a broader scale, South America in the 1970s became a site of confrontation where an entire generation of angry and rebellious middle-class students endured excruciating conditions of censorship (and self-censorship) imposed by the state apparatus. Obliquely (or even directly) supported by Cold War United States foreign policies, the new authoritarian regimes that took power between the 1960s and '70s in Uruguay, Argentina, Bolivia and Chile, pursued an anti-communist regional inoculation against the virus of the Cuban revolution, promoting, instead, the ideology of progress and developmentalism favored by local elites.

Arte hoje, histórias verídicas (Art Today, True Stories), 1976, a 16mm, black-and-white documentary written and directed by Manuel, summarizes the unconventional spirit of political contestation, experimental independence and communality that characterized the Brazilian artistic milieu of the years that followed the AI-5. Moreover, *Arte hoje* tackles the innovative vigor that began to crystallize in 1967, in the form of an amorphous "state."[14] A pivotal figure from the Neoconcrete generation, Hélio Oiticica was instrumental in involving artists whose work engaged with the international tenets of Pop and realism to participate in the influential exhibition *Nova Objetividade Brasileira* (New Brazilian Objectivity.)[15] More importantly, he identified a shift from an organized way of thinking to a "no unity of thought" nurtured by years of aesthetic debates between Brazilian poets, critics, architects, filmmakers and artists. Oiticica's commitment to making experimental art in an underdeveloped country connected his participatory strategies to the aspirations of a nascent generation, making him a central figure (even a guru). Significantly, Oiticica was represented in *Arte Hoje* through some of the photographic sequences of *A arma fálica*. As Manuel recalls, Oiticica's trip to London inspired *A arma fálica's* plot: "Inviting Hélio to be the leading actor of the *fotonovela* came out of our living together, being that his departure for London inspired the subject matter in *arma fálica*."[16] The *fotonovela* was shot during an interlude Oiticica spent in his hometown. Shortly after, he moved to New York were he spent several years in self-imposed exile.

13   Milton Machado, "Power to the Imagination: Art in the 1970s and Other Brazilian Miracles," (paper presented at *International Perspectives on Brazilian Sculpture,* Henry Moore Institute, March 10, 2006), 2.
14   See Hélio Oiticica, "General Scheme of the New Objectivity," in *Hélio Oiticica* (Rotterdam: Witte de With, 1992), 110–119. For Oiticica the new "state" (a non-organized plurality of artistic tendencies) merged poignant questions discussed by the Neoconcrete and Concrete local avant-gardes with broader issues of mass culture, political engagement and participation.
15   According to Aracy Amaral, Hélio Oiticica, Ferreira Gullar, Mário Pedrosa and Waldemar Cordeiro were among the few who understood the shift.
16   Antonio Manuel interviewed by the author, June 15, 2011. Author's translation.

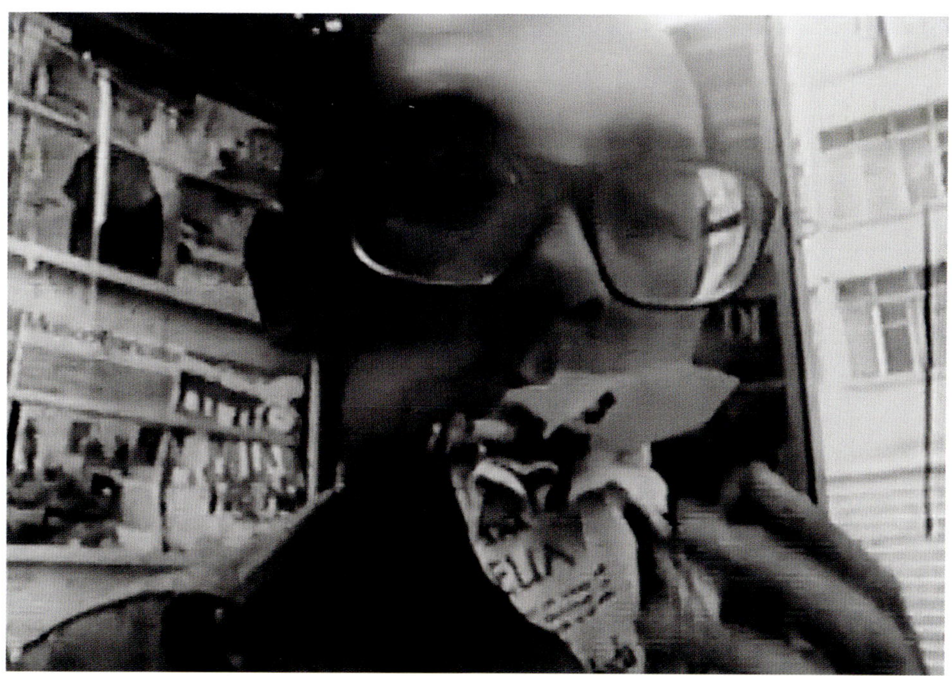

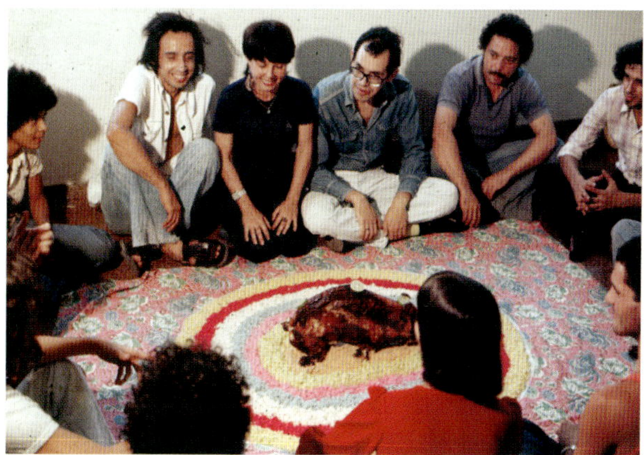

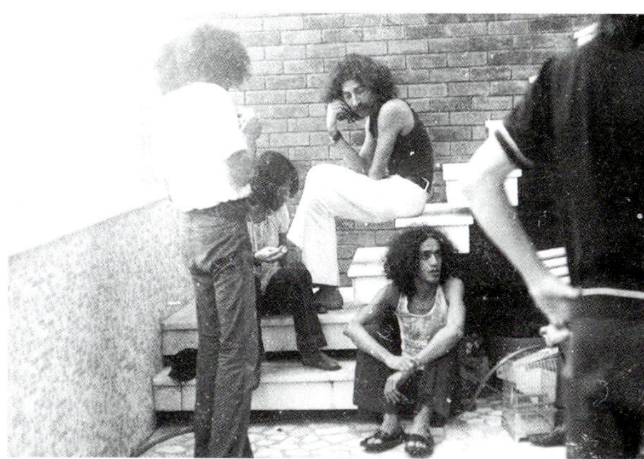

Top: Still from *Arte hoje, Histórias verídicas* (Art Today, True Stories), 1976. B&W with sound and color photographs, 14 minutes, 16mm. Courtesy the artist

Middle: Production image of *Arte hoje, Histórias verídicas* (Art Today, True Stories), 1976. B&W with sound and color photographs, 14 minutes, 16mm. Courtesy the artist

Bottom: Production image of *Loucura & Cultura* (Madness & Culture) with, left to right sitting on stairs: Dedé, Paulinho Lima, and Caetano Veloso, 1973. B&W with sound, 10 minutes, 35 mm. Courtesy the artist

MISE-EN-PAGE

In the 1960s Antonio Manuel was a devoted partner (and precocious collaborator) of more established artists such as Ivan Serpa, Oiticica, Lygia Pape (founder of the *Frente* Neoconcrete group) and Rogério Duarte, a graphic designer and intellectual associated with Cinema Novo. Antonio Manuel often visited Mário Pedrosa. During his formative years he made a living in advertising while attending workshops at Museu de Arte Moderna de Rio de Janeiro (MAM RJ); he also regularly visited Serpa's studio and audited several classes at the university. Described by Paulo Venancio Filho as the "only heterodox legatee of Neoconcretism,"[17] he participated in art salons and local biennials organized for emerging artists in different Brazilian cities; his work received an award at the prestigious *Bienal de São Paulo* and was selected for the international pavilion at the *Bienniale di Venezia.* He quickly became an eminent member of the lively nucleus of artists, writers and intellectuals who were looking for alternative forms of expression amid rapid sociopolitical change.

A arma fálica remained a dormant project in the artist's drawer for twenty-five years until the Instituto Municipal de Arte e Cultura (RioArte) published it in 1995 under the expert graphic direction of Luciano Figueiredo. Antonio Manuel's *fotonovela* coincided with the beginnings of Cinema Marginal or Udigrudi, with text written in collaboration with Pape.[18] The photographic fiction begins with a prologue that gives an epic, surreal undertone to the story:

> the guru spent several years in london on a war mission. since it was not
> possible to bring his wife, who suffered from an interminable vaginal discharge,
> he left her locked up in their home in gávea. neném, disputed over by fists in
> a violent brawl, had been married to paulomarginal at the time of her mother's
> rape in mangue, published in the newspapers as a crime of passion.[19]

The main character Guru, played by Oiticica, depicts a *malandro* who arrives on a ship from London unannounced.[20] Guru is told by a cabbie that his wife Neném is having an affair with Paulomarginal, a thug from Mangueira. Fulfilling a formulaic (and predictable) solution to the conflict, the protagonist kills his wife's lover. However, the melodramatic mode intrinsic to the genre has a unique Oedipal twist as the murder is committed with an unusual object that the reader never sees and which Guru has brought from London to be delivered to someone named Ayela. With a "phallic weapon" the betrayed husband literally beats Paulomarginal's sexual member, instantly killing him. An important aspect to be considered within this type of "hard-boiled" narrative is the physical feature of the actress

17   Paulo Venancio Filho argues that Manuel inherited the legacy of Neoconcretism by confronting its crisis. See Paulo Venancio Filho, "Act and Fact," in *Antonio Manuel Fatos,* Banco do Brasil, São Paulo, 2007. p. 127

18   At age 22, Rogério Sganzarla completed what is considered the first marginal film: the feature-length film *Bandido da Luz Vermelha* (1968). After Cinema Novo, independent films in Brazil became more urban and allegorical in terms of 1920s modernist aesthetics, reflecting fragmentary discourses that expressed a crisis of representation. *Udigrudi* was a phonetic adaption of the English word "underground". Cinema Novo's Marxist metaphor of hunger manifested itself through garbage. See Robert Stamm and Ismail Xavier, "Recent Brazilian Cinema: Allegory/Metacinema/Carnival," *Film Quarterly* 41, no. 3, (Spring 1988): 16.

19   Translated by Mari Hayman. The original text in Portuguese reads: *em missão de guerra o guru passou vários anos em londres. como não foi possivel levar sua mulher, que sofría de um corrimento interminável, deixou-a trancada em sua casa na gávea. neném, disputada a tapa numa briga violenta, tinha sido mulher de paulomarginal na época do estupro de sua mãe no mangue, publicado no ocasião como crime pasional.*

20   A *malandro* is a streetwise rogue, who must subsist amid adverse conditions. The *malandro* was a prototypical figure in Brazilian pop music, film, and theater during the dictatorship.

cast for Neném's role—a petite tomboy who challenges dominant views on gender by confronting the stereotypical representation of an unfaithful woman from the margins. Despite the violent and crude tone of the captions, the action is hyperbolic and parodic, transforming the *fotonovela*'s formulaic conventions into a subversive fiction peppered with autobiographic elements, dark humor and artsy inside jokes. The graphic unfolding of some of the photographic frames reinforced Antonio Manuel's unconventional approach to the genre through the use of quarter-page enlarged reproductions printed horizontally in which some dramatic situations were highlighted, creating an interruption or a pause in the reading.

Notably, the poses construed an artificial look due to the use of high-contrast black-and-white photography and many high and low-angle shots. With its small crew, modest budget and without any art direction, it was necessary to be pragmatic and film in locations around Rio. Praça Mauá was chosen as the spot where the ship from London was anchored while Guru and Neném's home was represented by Oiticica's real home on Rua Engenheiro Alfredo Duarte.[21] The remaining cast—the taxi driver, Neném and her lover Paulomarginal—consisted of friends and friends of friends recruited by Manuel from the San Carlos favela and the Jardim Botanico neighborhood. Conspicuously, Tineca also wore a *Parangolé* during one of the samba gatherings organized by Oiticica in the Mangueira favela.

Antonio Manuel's initial aim to stage a chronological storyline in twenty-four poses suggests the artist's intention to explore a self-reflexive visual economy in which the principle of motion in film (twenty-four images per second) would wrap and contain an entire story.[22] This idea is also linked to the conceptual strategy developed later for the piece *Exposição de Antonio Manuel — De 0 à 24 horas* (Exhibition of Antonio Manuel — From 0 to 24 Hours), 1973, a *mise-en-page* of an exhibition of censored works meant to be presented at MAM, but published instead in *O Jornal.* In fact, *Exposição de Antonio Manuel — De 0 à 24 horas* was thought to last twenty-four hours—the regular circulation time of a newspaper.[23] It is also significant that *A arma fálica* was Antonio Manuel's inaugural approach to film, a medium that allowed him to expand the notion of montage: "the *fotonovela* was the first step for making movies, which would be produced."[24]

Years before, he had developed a body of work using both the process of production and the semiotic properties of newspapers in which he explored different facets of montage techniques through printing. With *A arma fálica* he wanted to further his explorations of montage and photo mechanical processes using a popular genre with no aesthetic lineage:

21   The photographer is credited as Kiko, Marcos Lins Andrade, Lygia Clark's nephew and Eduardo Clark's cousin.
22   This principle is associated with the "persistence of vision." The artist's original plan changed when the *fotonovela* was finally published in 1995.
23   Frederico Morais coined the expression *mise-en-page* to describe Manuel's work. See Frederico Morais, "Frutos do Espaço: A virtualidade de imagem," in *Antonio Manuel* (Rio de Janeiro: Funarte, 1980), 35–36.
24   Antonio Manuel interviewed by the author, June 15, 2011. Translation: Alexandra García.

"He intended to work a new means of expression in an economic and graphic way ... He was interested in the montage and the rhythm of photographs taken, while at the same time he wanted to make a graphic non-verbal object with continuity and movement."[25] Another relevant aspect is the sequential structure of the *fotonovela,* which is similar to the spatial narrativity of the comic, also linked to what Antonio Manuel has defined as the constructive aspect of film through measured planes.[26]

The *fotonovela* or *photo-roman* is a subgenre that originated in Italy and became very popular in Latin America (particularly in Brazil). In adapting classical Western literature for mass audiences, it has been considered a degraded literary form since its inception.[27] By the 1960s it was a commodity appropriated in France by filmmakers and writers, who tested its creative potentiality by transferring its stylistic or conceptual properties into experimental writing and cinema. *Photo-roman* was the foundation of Chris Marker's *La Jetée* (1962, released in 1964), an influential avant-garde film consisting of motionless images. Rosalind Krauss has pointed out that Marker's paradoxical operation:

> Is the fact that Marker never repeated this formula what makes us so clear about the fact that, however unprecedented, the work did not constitute a new medium for him? And does his refusal to acknowledge it thus as a "medium"— like a language he could develop and continue to speak—make us reevaluate the very condition of the still within the filmic unreeling of *La Jetée,* suggesting that Marker's recourse to motionless images was never intended as a rupture with cinematic grammar as we know it, but rather as a way, precisely, of filming the 'final' image we would see at the moment of our own deaths, an image whose approach we can narrate cinematically but whose occurrence we can only produce as an explosively static "still"?[28]

Obviously, Antonio Manuel did not invent or create a new medium nor he repeated his formula. Rather, he extracted a radical foundation for documentary photography deprived of the presentation of facts or evidences but through the use of fiction—the kind of fiction made to entertain without causing any harm. By depicting marginality through a *fotonovela,* perhaps he was interrogating the role of documentary photography, its legitimacy and accuracy within the realm of violence or political repression.

---

25 Ibid.

26 Antonio Manuel interviewed by Lúcia Carneiro and Ileana Pradilla, trans., Lya Valeria Grizzo Serignolli, available for download at http://www.pharosart.org/AntonioManuel.htm, accessed August 2, 2011.

27 By the 1970s the *fotonovela* was already a popular genre in Brazil and Latin America.

28 Rosalind Krauss, "'And Then Turn Away': An Essay on James Coleman," *October* 81 (Summer 1997): 7.

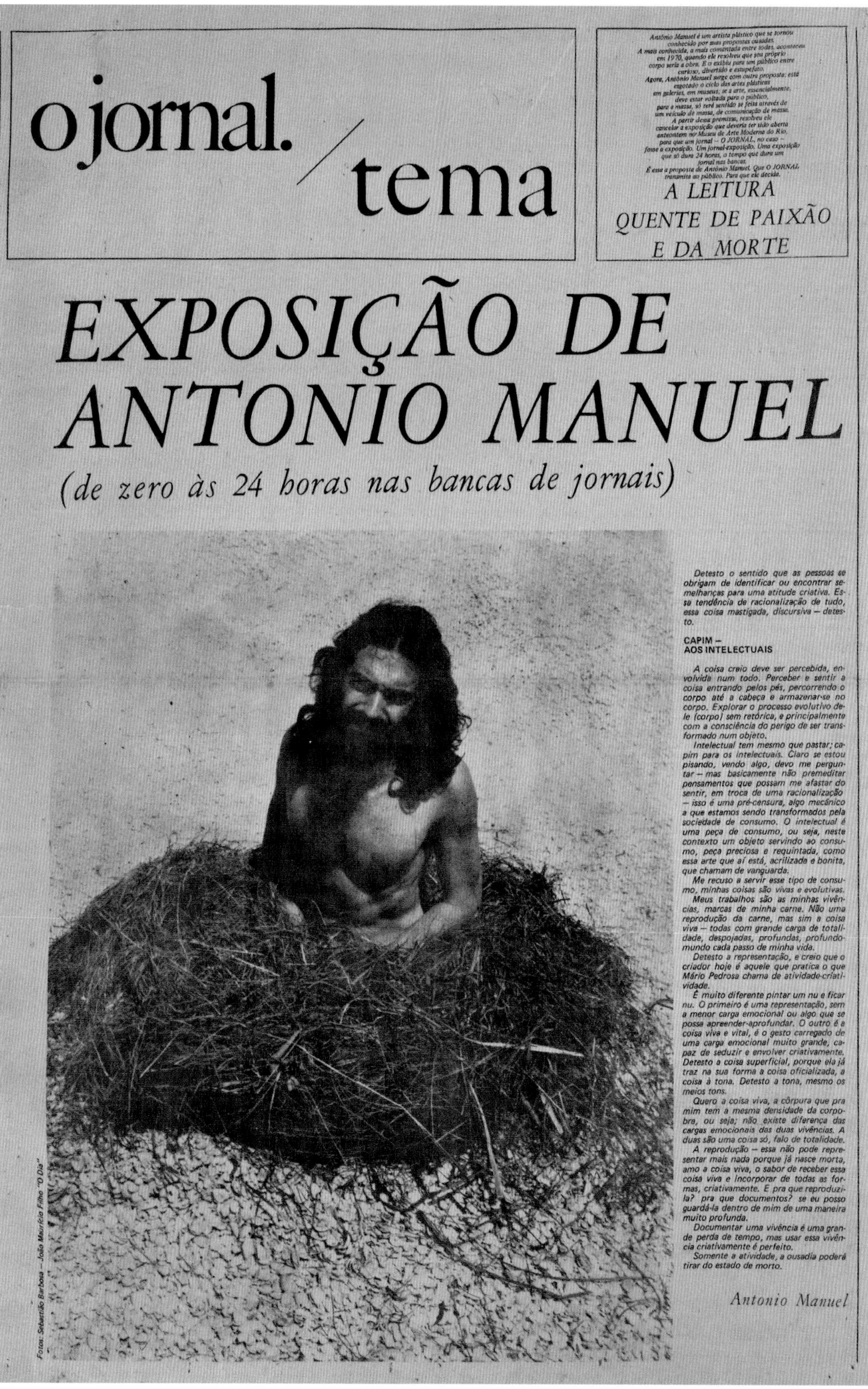

Exposição Antonio Manuel – De 0 a 24 horas (Exhibition of Antonio Manuel – From 0 to 24 Hours), 1973. Newspaper, 22 x 15 in. Courtesy the artist

ANTONIO MANUEL'S EXERCITATION

JUDITH RODENBECK

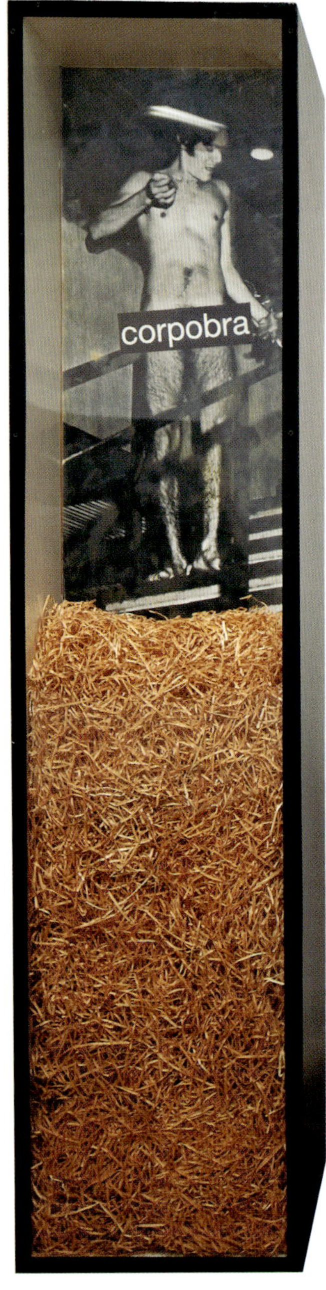

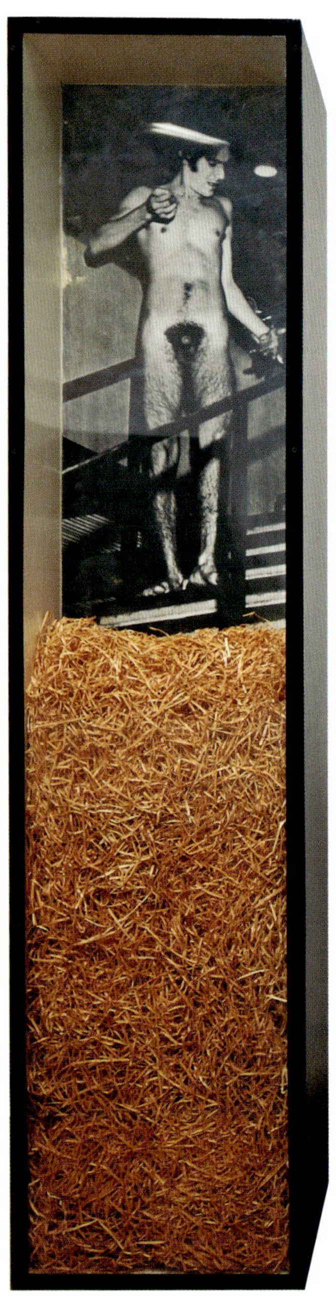

Corpobra (Bodywork), 1970. Wood, straw, photograph, acrylic and rope, 79 x 19 x 18.5 in. Courtesy the artist

For politically engaged Brazilians the *anos de chumbo,* the "leaden years" between 1970 and 1974, were especially fraught. While right-wing military dictatorship over the country lasted for over two decades (from the coup d'état in 1964 until 1985), this period saw the declaration of a national state of emergency, the suspension of *habeas corpus* and the massing of power in the hands of an authoritarian military elite in the name of a security state. These juridical moves, in turn, resulted in the imprisonment and torture of dissidents, censorship of the media and the arts, hundreds of targeted assassinations, kidnappings and disappearances, the stultification of the working and middle class in favor of a corporatist elite and the de facto exile—whether internal or external, juridical or self-imposed—of many of Brazil's most important cultural workers. Among the best known were the critic Mário Pedrosa, poet Ferreira Gullar, musicians Gilberto Gil and Caetano Veloso, artist Lygia Clark (who spent the worst years in Paris) and Hélio Oiticica (who had been living in London since 1968 and by late 1970 had relocated to New York).[1]

Antonio Manuel's engagements with body art and with performance practices more broadly during these "leaden years" form a small, tightly configured set, ranging from monomorphic works such as *O corpo é a obra* (The Body Is the Work), 1970, a deceptively simple action that crosses the embodied with the conceptual, to complex redeployments of photographic documentation in proliferating quasi-guerilla print projects addressed to the twenty-four-hour cycle of the sensationalist (yet censored) news. In 1968 Antonio Manuel inaugurated these explorations with the series *Urnas quentes* (Hot Ballot Boxes), sealed crates containing "hot" news imagery and fragments of hortatory language; at their initial unveiling these boxes were smashed open by viewers—a performative fate that became part of their conception as works, adding the unpredictable element of a viewer engagement in which affective force prompted physical action.[2] "There was great violence and voracity concerning this work," recalls Antonio Manuel. "The work was completed with this action, this gesture."[3]

This "voracity" along with an "urgent dialectic of hiding and revealing," as Guy Brett has put it, are characteristic of Antonio Manuel's artistic practice during the "leaden years;" in the face of political repression and an official clamp-down on artistic freedom, Antonio Manuel's explorations of bodily and social experience yielded a tensile practice that, as Brett observes, "reached its purest, most rebellious form" in a singular act of 1970.[4] That year, Antonio Manuel's submission to the Salão Nacional de Arte Moderna at Museu de Arte Moderna in Rio de Janeiro was a Duchampian piece called *O corpo é a obra,* in which the artist proposed to present his own body as an artwork. Rejection by the Salon

1   According to the correspondence between Oiticica and Clark, both artists received exhibition funding from Itamaraty (Brazil's Ministry of Foreign Affairs). See Ed. Luciano Figueiredo, *Lygia Clark Hélio Oiticica, Cartas (1964–1974)* (Rio de Janeiro: Editora UFRJ, 1996).

2   For more on the *Urnas quentes* see Michael Asbury, *"Flans, Urnas quentes* and the Radicalism of a Cordial Man," in this catalogue.

3   "Antonio Manuel: Interview with Lúcia Carneiro and Ileana Pradilla," trans. Lya Valeria Grizzo Serignolli, in *Antonio Manuel,* ed. Michael Asbury and Garo Keheyan (Nicosia, Cyprus: Pharos Centre for Contemporary Art, 2005), 135; interview originally published in *Serie Palavra do Artista* (Rio de Janeiro: Lacerda Editores, 1999).

4   Guy Brett, "States of Fear and Freedom," in *Fatos: Antonio Manuel* (São Paolo: Centro Cultural do Banco do Brasil; Rio de Janeiro: Organização Metrópolis, Produções Culturais, 2007), 135.

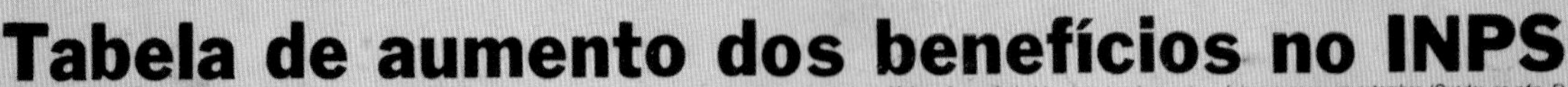

Tabela de aumento dos benefícios no INPS

Percentuais de acréscimos em decorrência dos novos níveis do salário- mínimo — 16 por cento até maio de 1972 — Majoração será devida a contar de agosto próximo e paga em setembro (Quadro na pág. 5)

CONFLITOS E MORTES NA ARGENTINA

Campora assume em clima de guerra — Violentos incidentes nas ruas de Buenos Aires marcaram a cerimônia de posse do Presidente peronista — Anunciou que restabelecerá relações com Cuba (P. 13)

Confusão no MAM

PINTOR MOSTRA POS - ARTE

Fundador: CHAGAS FREITAS Diretor: OTHON PAULINO

O DIA

O JORNAL DE MAIOR CIRCULAÇÃO DO PAÍS

GB e RJ **50** CENTAVOS

Redação e Administração: Rua Riachuelo, 359. Tel.: 222-7751 — Telex 386

ANO XXII   Rio de Janeiro, sábado, 26 de maio de 1973   Nº 7.692

Bandido milionário esconde o tesouro

Faz fortuna assaltando bancos — Levou a Polícia ao local onde enterrou saco com metralhadora e revólveres — Está realizado e la para o exterior — Lindas garotas e carros do ano nos melhores hotéis — Mulher comparsa é o "fino" no gati'ho — Garante que vai fugir —————— (PAGINA 5)

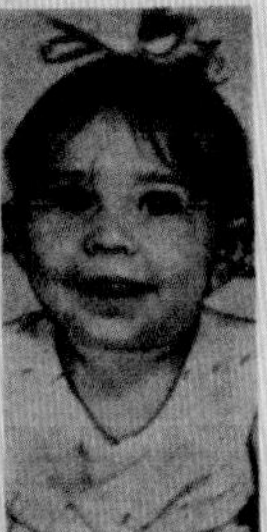

Alvo fatídico

Maria das Graças Lemos treinava tiro ao alvo no quintal de sua residência, com um rifle calibre 22, tentando acertar em uma lata. Vários tiros foram dados, mas um deles foi atingir a menina Mônica, de dois anos e meio, que passeava com a babá pelo quintal da casa vizinha. A criança morreu no hospital e, sua mãe, Eleutéria Dias, em prantos, está pedindo justiça —————— (Página 7)

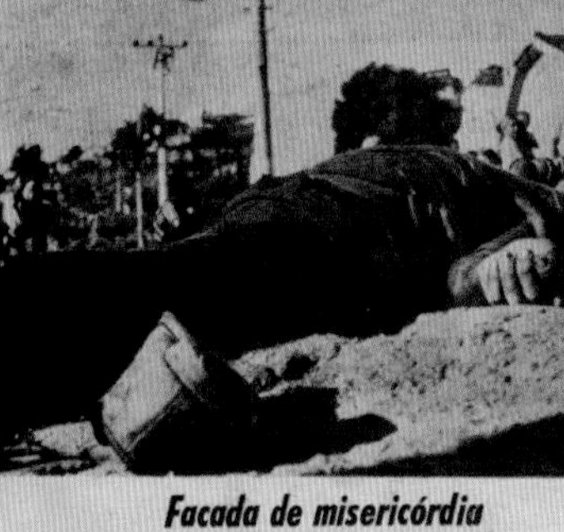

Facada de misericórdia

José Raimundo, birosqueiro do Morro do Adeus, foi, ontem, assassinado por dois inimigos, quando, pela manhã, chegava a casa, trazendo o pão e o leite para os filhos. Ao perceber os assassinos, ainda sacou o 38 e travou tiroteio. Recebeu três balaços e caiu numa poça de sangue. Um dos matadores, cheio de ódio, aproximou-se do homem agonizante e, com uma peixeira, desferiu-lhe profundo golpe no coração —————— (Página 6)

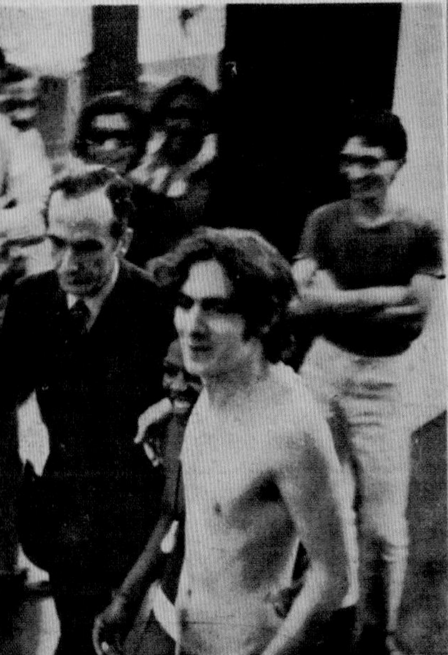

pintor não pinta — estremeceu e entrou em transe — pintar é velho — agora o negócio é mostrar a coisa viva — quase põe fogo no museu de arte moderna — o bode preto fedia — o mato estava podre — duas velhotas desmaiaram.

Bala de rifle matou menor

CHIQUINHO CONTRA A BOLÍVIA

Luís Pereira saiu machucado ontem, pode até ser cortado, e Zagalo já escalou o Pastor para a partida de amanhã — Piazza é o novo capitão da Seleção Brasileira — Cinco nomes do banco vão ser escolhidos hoje — Técnico e observadores concordam: treino de ontem foi melhor do que o primeiro —————— (Na página 16)

Sambista achou 65 milhões e devolveu

A passista da Unidos de São Carlos ganha apenas Cr$ 500 por mês — Encontrou a fortuna no interior de um táxi — Dinheiro pertência a um congressista estrangeiro — Aplausos de diplomatas (PAGINA 5)

Confusão no MAM: Pintor mostra pós-arte (Confusion at MAM: Painter Shows Post-Art), 1973. Newspaper, 22 x 15 in. Courtesy the artist prompted what is probably Antonio Manuel's most notorious action, an intervention into the opening of the Salon itself when, stripped naked, Antonio Manuel inserted the rejected work, live, into the space of the Salon. This action brought the immediate attention of the police and resulted in the closing of the exhibition to the public on its first full day. Antonio Manuel, already known for projects strongly critical of Brazil's political situation, went into hiding; the critic Mário Pedrosa, who was harboring him, declared Antonio Manuel's action an "experimental exercise of freedom"[5]—a ringing phrase that would come to stand for the most vital Brazilian art of this moment.

Performative actions, so crucial to vanguard artistic practices since the 1960s, necessarily foreground the body in both its liveness and its *livedness,* that is, not just its sentient electricity and rudimentary phenomenologies but its status *also* as marked site, as construction, as axiomatic structure.[6] These logics of identity, whether as sensorial percept or institutional concept, evoke the very grounds of the body's materiality and its construction (as meat and metaphor), of its autonomy and its subjection. The simplicity of Antonio Manuel's action in *O corpo é a obra* presents a lively youthful arrogance (the hale body and attractive physique), to be sure—in this regard the action appears as a *jouissant* deployment of the playful international idiom of popism, a view supported by documentary photographs showing the laughing artist accompanied by the beaming woman who had spontaneously joined his liberatory gesture. Yet seen under the expansive view of an unfolding critical logic, *O corpo* has the strange effect, not unlike that of the anamorphic death's head that hovers like a curse before the two figures of authority in Holbein's famous *Ambassadors,* 1533, of revealing the contours and ultimate limits of power. Hélio Oiticica's notes from October 11, 1971, contain this fragment: "the *experimental exercitation* [sic] *of liberty* evoked by Mário Pedrosa does not consist in the 'production of works,' but in the 'initiative of taking hold of *the experimental.*'"[7] The deliberate neologism "exercitation" is piquant, posing Antonio Manuel's piece as both exercise and excitation, both careful preparatory sketch and flamboyant gestural provocation, a dual life as both design and stain. Antonio Manuel, in a later newspaper-based artwork, *Clandestinas* (Clandestines), 1973, would also mine the potential of such wordplay by incorporating documentation from *O corpo é a obra* and dubbing the piece "post-art," ironizing that nomenclature with the double-entendre of "posing": "Confusão no MAM: Pintor mostra pós-arte" (Confusion at MAM: Painter Demonstrates Post-Art or Painter Demonstrates Posing).

Antonio Manuel's *O corpo é a obra* literally names itself as body art—a reading Antonio Manuel would encourage yet complicate with *O bode* (The Goat), 1972, in which he presented a (scape)goat as an artwork[8] —thus aligning with a genre of performance that

---

5   Mário Pedrosa, "Excerpts from a statement about *O corpo é a obra,* May 1970," in *Antonio Manuel* (Porto: Museu de Arte Contemporânea de Serralves, 2000), 56. Later in that essay Pedrosa says, "Through your attitude, you have splendidly posited the ethical problem, which is fundamental in the art of today."

6   I appropriate these terms from Rosalind Krauss's essay, "Sculpture in the Expanded Field," *October* 8 (Spring 1979): 30–44. The constraints of her 1979 argument are well known, especially to artists and critics working through the logics of identity and interpellation evoked here, but in their "expansive" possibilities her terms can be generative. Arguably, Brazilian Neoconcretism expanded phenomenology along these lines.

7   Box 0210/71, 16, Itaú Cultural, Programa Hélio Oiticica, http://www.itaucultural.org.br/aplicexternas/enciclopedia/ho/detalhe/docs/dsp_imagem.cfm?name=Normal/0210.71%20p16%20tradu%C3%A7ao%20-%20777.gif, accessed August 29, 2011.

8   Of the goat Antonio Manuel says: "I related it to body-art [a word play with bode-art]. It was shown almost as a magnet, because the goat, in Quimbanda, has the connotation of an element which absorbs negativity. It is an animal which embodied the bad vibes that were around at that time." "Interview with Lúcia Carneiro and Ileana Pradilla," 132–133. See Claudia Calirman's detailed discussion in her essay, "Antonio Manuel: The Politics of Irreverence," in this catalogue. Antonio Manuel's poetic, indeed linguistic, inclusion of the signifying animal may recall contemporaneous works by Jannis Kounellis and others associated with Arte Povera; but Antonio Manuel's gesture, semiotically complex and explicitly antiheroic, has much more in common with the biotic aspects of Marcel Broodthaers's witty oeuvre.

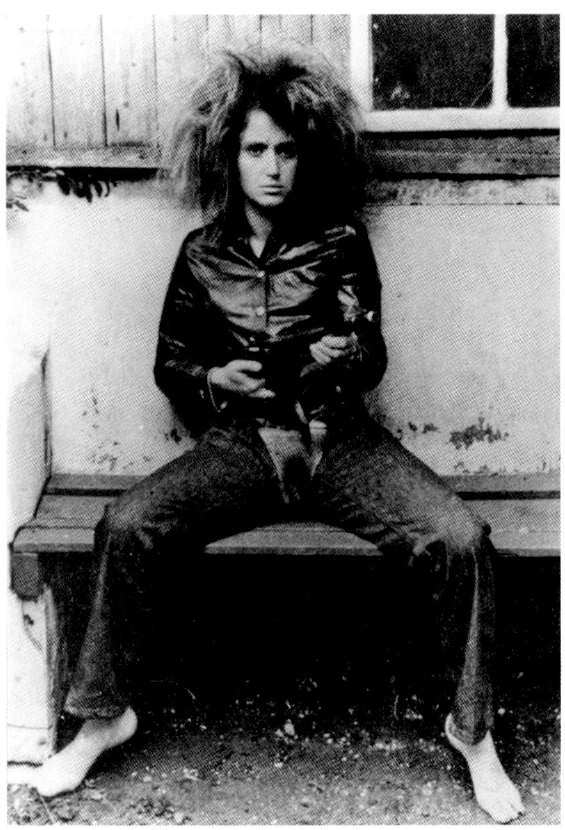

VALIE EXPORT with photography by Peter Hassmann,
Action Pants: Genital Panic, 1969. Screenprint (set of 6),
26.4 x 19.6 in. each. Courtesy VALIE EXPORT

literally incorporates the body, whether as fact, problem, or metaphor. The canon of body
art typically ranges from the "living sculptures" of Piero Manzoni or Gilbert and George to
the public interventions of VALIE EXPORT or Vito Acconci, while its strategies range from
feats of endurance and masochism, at one extreme, to the more abstract and photo-
conceptual (Dennis Oppenheim's work in this genre straddled these possibilities). *O corpo*
resonates directly with that other well-known "nude gallery opening" piece, the 1977
Imponderabilia of Marina Abramovic and Ulay, in which the artists presented gallerygoers
with the conundrum of their two nude bodies tightly framing a gallery entrance in such a
way that "viewers" would have to face one of them as they passed into the gallery. But
Imponderabilia is a cool endurance work of refined dramaturgical classicism (in both the
theatrical and sociological senses), while Antonio Manuel's action is messy, its confronta-
tions not "imponderable" but directly, if multiply, articulated (socially, politically, formally).
In this regard it may share more in spirit with two performative outliers in the genre of
body art, one nominally "cinematic" and the other nominally "sculptural": the "expanded
cinema" of VALIE EXPORT's 1969 infamous *Action Pants: Genital Panic,* a feminist action

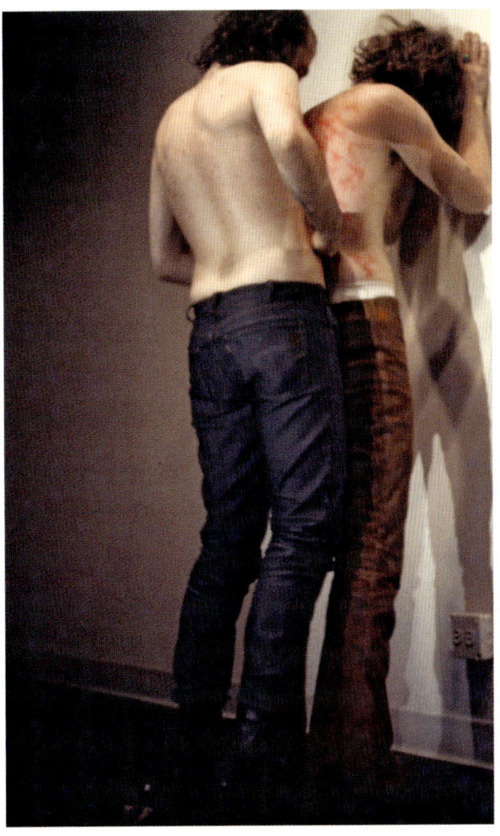 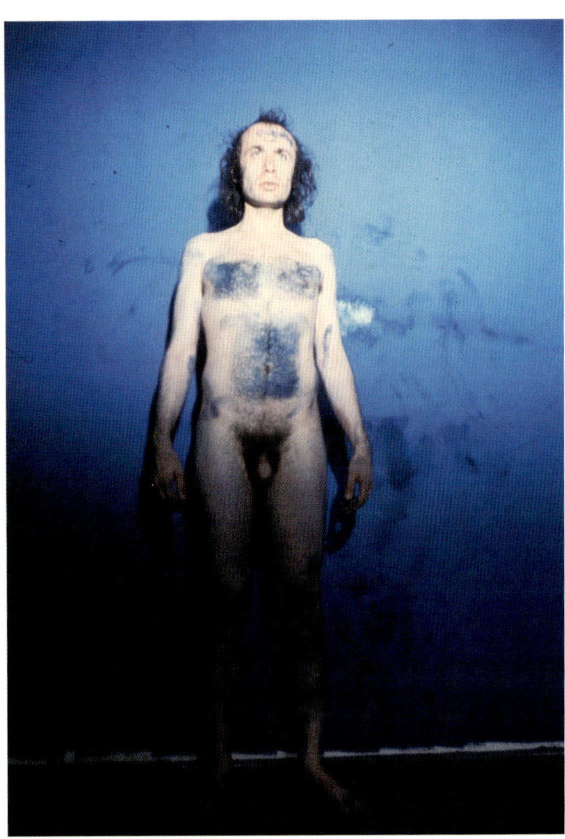

Left: Vito Acconci with Kathy Dillon and Dennis Oppenheim in the performance *Applications,* 1970, at the Art Institute of Chicago. Super-8 film, color, silent, 20 minutes. Courtesy Vito Acconci

Right: Vito Acconci in the photographed activity *RUN-OFF,* July 1970. Photograph by Bernadette Mayer. Courtesy Vito Acconci

that confronted viewers at an art-house cinema with the very real female genitalia of the artist and the recoding of the artist as readymade accomplished by Bruce Nauman's 1966–1967/1970 photograph *Self Portrait of the Artist as a Fountain,* a self-conscious evocation of Marcel Duchamp's infamous sculpture.

The death's head Antonio Manuel's action inserted into that Salon opening, and arguably inserted into the canon of body art, may well be the outlaw skull of Duchamp—and herein lies the ethical imperative of Antonio Manuel's gesture: in Rio de Janeiro in 1970 the readymade is recoded as the body itself.[9] *Wanted Rose Sélavy/Duchamp psico-grafado,* 1975, thus declares one of Antonio Manuel's extraordinary *Flans,* a series of works executed upon the raised papier-mâché matrix of an intermedial newspaper printing mechanism. Antonio Manuel's *Wanted,* a "non-print" (as his colleague Hélio Oiticica dubbed the flans) or "pre-journalism," is a work of singular analytic economy and condensation, graphically citing and extending Duchamp's play with the readymade and with gender while indicating, too, the "psychographic" aspects of the sensationalist marketing of both art and news (a steady subject for Antonio Manuel).[10] Where the boldface headline

9 For more on ethical imperatives in performance art see Peggy Phelan, *Unmarked: The Politics of Performance* (London: Routledge, 1993).
10 In notes from April 22, 1973, described as "remake of a text made in London in 1968," Hélio Oiticica calls these "não-gravura, não-poster, não-serigrafia" (non-printing, non-poster, non-serigraphy), the print in a pre-journalistic state (which he translates as "pre-stage news-print"), the day-to-day tragicomic. Flans enclosed in Antonio Manuel's *Hot Ballot Boxes* present "day's iniquities/gray Lynotyped day/misery's copy desk/neither letter nor message" See Hélio Oiticica, "Antonio Manuel's Hot Urns," *Antonio Manuel* (Porto: Museu de Arte Contemporânea de Serralves, 2000), 50; see also Box 0210/71, 27–30, Itaú Cultural, Programa Hélio Oiticica, http://www.itaucultural.org.br/aplicexternas/enciclopedia/ho/index.cfm?fuseaction=documentos&cod=777&tipo=2, accessed August 29, 2011.

screams in black, "Wanted," above that register, in the space normally occupied by the name of the newspaper, one can make out the words "Duchamp psicografado" impressed into the thick paper. And below the header, in the graphic space allotted to photography, a strange, head-like mask appears: a constrasty, nearly black image of Duchamp's *Fountain,* but inverted in such a way that the infamous readymade reclaims its functional orientation as urinal (seen from slightly above, as it would be by a user) while suggesting, through the gestalt of its assembly—protruding lateral flanges for ears, inverted-pear shape, with drainage holes in the rough spaces of nose and mouth—a mugshot. Duchamp's *Fountain* has been "wanted," of course, since 1917, when it was submitted to the Society of Independent Artists in New York for exhibition, rejected from that unjuried show and then misplaced. The "original" *Fountain* exists only through the medium of an ironized photo-journalism: as the photograph and accompanying reportage published in the Dada magazine, *The Blind Man.* This readymade, a signal gesture of twentieth-century vanguard "anti-art," accomplished a singular goal within aesthetics: to demonstrate that the work of art is discursive (and the "artworld" institutional); it accomplished this via the nominalist act of disappearance and reportage.[11]

Rereading *O corpo é a obra* through the Duchampian gesture produces a fountain of meanings. The same can be said of the later deployment of *O corpo*'s imagery in printed and constructed works such as the interactive vitrine *Corpobra* (Bodywork), 1970, or the newsprint interventions of the *Clandestinas,* both of which performatively implicate the viewer in defying censorship.[12] Consider: the extra-juridical nature of *O corpo é a obra,* given its follow-on from the rejection of the eponymous piece; the police action to shut down not just Antonio Manuel's piece (in any event already completed) but the entire proceedings of the exhibition, that is, the repression of the very condition of possibility of Antonio Manuel's work. If anything, Antonio Manuel's body was *not,* in this instance, "the work" being named. The concept of "bare life," most prominently associated with the work of Giorgio Agamben, might seem at one and the same time both a perversely inappropriate and an overly literal rubric through which to approach Antonio Manuel's *O corpo;* yet *O corpo é a obra* was occasion for a much larger institutional demonstration: of the pervasiveness of state authority, both as it applied in the immediate situation (closing the gallery, Antonio Manuel going into hiding) and as it was already being deployed in the larger arena of Brazilian governance, i.e., in the nakedness of those imprisoned and tortured by the ruling junta and the disappearance of actual bodies. And if Antonio Manuel's exercise made the body directly visible among the complacent suits of the cultural elite, it pointedly clarified the degree to which that cultural elite was itself subject to sovereign power.[13] It is precisely *this* juxtaposition—between pop and politics—that gives Antonio Manuel's singular action such force.[14] As an action, *O corpo é a obra* turns the internationally current genre of body art on its head, revealing the institutional limitations of the very category it was presumed to inhabit,

---

11   See Arthur Danto, "The Artworld," *Journal of Philosophy* 61 (October 1964): 571–584.

12   For extended descriptions of these works see Claudia Calirman's essay in this catalogue.

13   See Giorgio Agamben, *Homo Sacer: Sovereign Power and Bare Life,* trans. Daniel Heller-Roazen (Stanford: Stanford University Press, 1998).

14   Antonio Manuel notes that for many works from this period, "The agents of dictatorship themselves gave such works political connotations, often without the knowledge of the artist." "Interview with Lúcia Carneiro and Ileana Pradilla," 119. On the revision of Pop in Brazil by what critics dubbed an "ethical attitude," see Clarival Valladares, "Atualidade das Artes Plásticas," *Introdução à Realidade Brasileira* (Rio de Janeiro: Editôra Cadernos Brasileiros S/A, 1968), 111–146.

for inasmuch as Antonio Manuel's art intervention poses the very matter of the "body" as "work," it reveals the broader political, juridical and even carceral circumstances not just of art's institutions and its public but of the body's production. Instantly suppressed, Antonio Manuel's work lays bare the mechanisms of suppression, whether internal to the art system (self-censorship) or imposed by the police/authorities. Yet the very fact of its having taken place, of its joyful acknowledgement by another (the woman who joined the artist in his exercise) and of the work being such a threat that not just the work (or the artist) but the entire Salon needed suppression indicates a small space of possibility. A demonstration of the limits of authority: in that lies the "exercitation" of freedom.

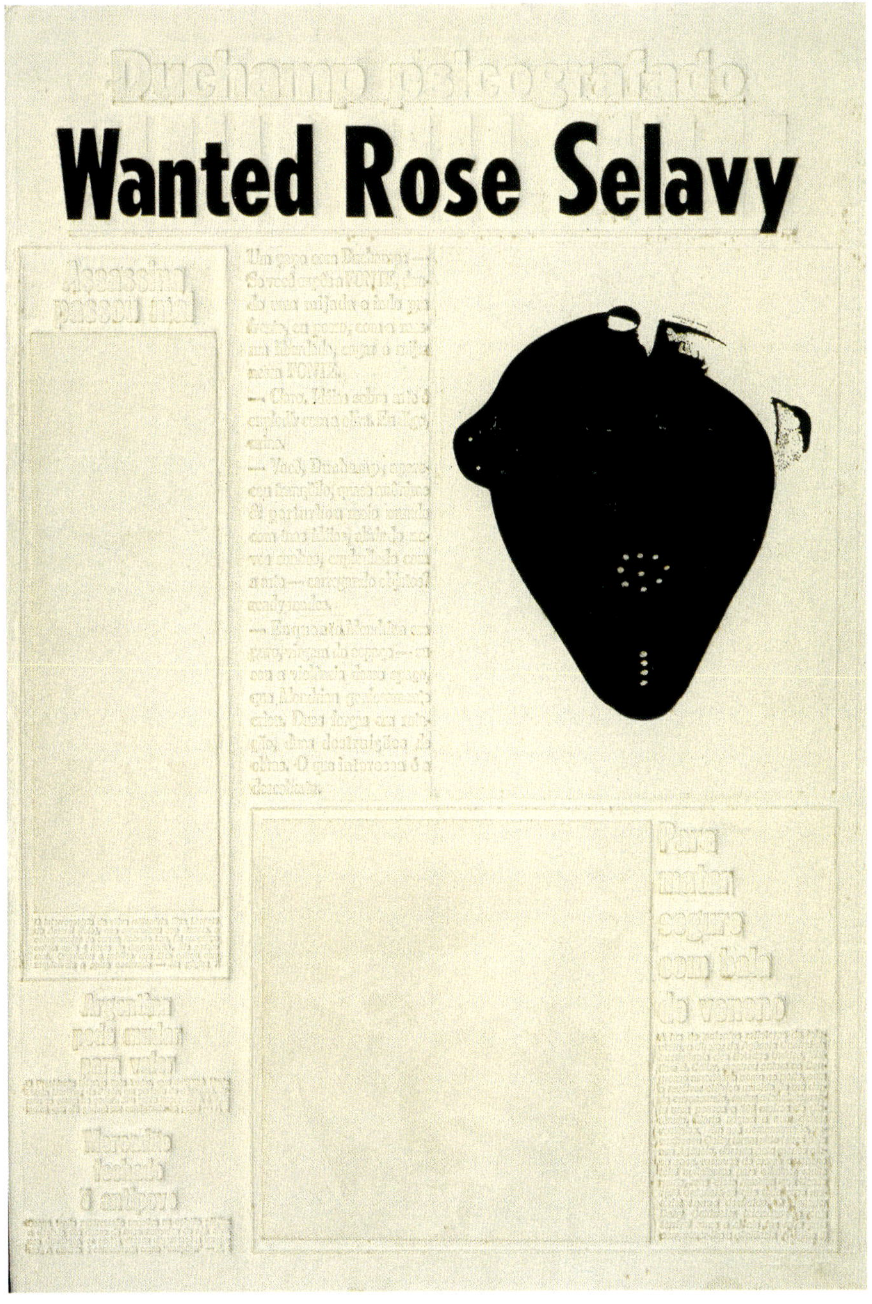

Wanted: Rose Selavy, 1975. From the *Flan* series, ink on papier-mâché stereotype mold, 22 x 15 in. Courtesy the artist

INTERVIEW

ANTONIO MANUEL WITH BEVERLY ADAMS

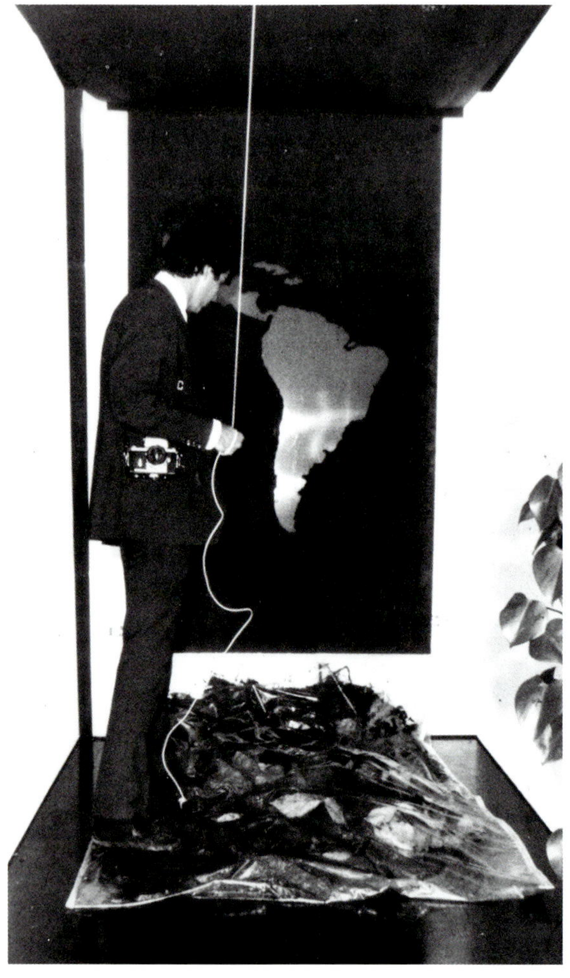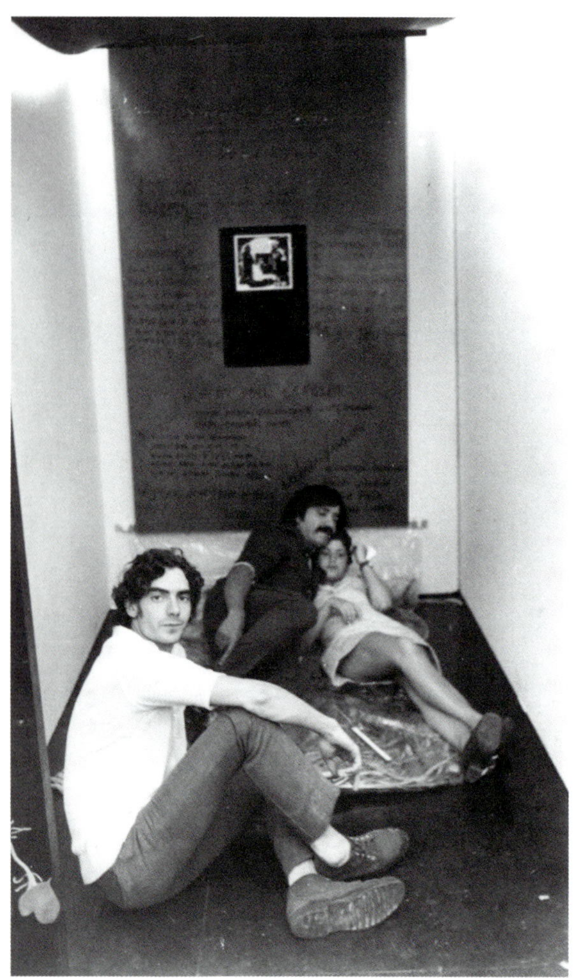

Left: Installation of *Soy loco por ti* (I'm Crazy for You), 1969, at the Salaõ de Bússola. Courtesy the artist

Right: Antonio Manuel sitting with friends in the installation of *Tropicologia*, 1969, at the Salaõ de Bússola. Courtesy the artist

BEVERLY ADAMS: Antonio, you came of age artistically in the 1960s when the Brazilian artistic experimentation was at its height and the military dictatorship was consolidating its power. How did these naturally opposing forces impact your work and your process? How was this beginning important for you?

ANTONIO MANUEL: Hélio Oiticica's *Parangolés,* Lygia Pape's *Livro da criação* (Book of Creation) and Lygia Clark's sensorial experiences all came about in the 1960s, and it's right about this moment in Brazilian art history that I started experimenting with newspapers and objects. I met Hélio Oiticica and Lygia Pape at Museu de Arte Moderna (MAM) in Rio de Janeiro, and we became friends and started doing art experiments on a daily basis. I was Hélio's partner for his *Parangolé P22, Cape 18, Nirvana,* and Lygia's partner for filmmaking. There was a very violent and repressive political climate because of the military dictatorship. Ethics thus became one of our work tools, together with an experimental outlook on life and art. The work of art that I feel best captures the repressive and experimental context is my series called *Urnas quentes* (Hot Ballot Boxes), which was presented for the first time in the *Apocalipopótese* (Apocalypopothesis), a collective exhibition held in 1968.[1] The work consisted of 20 wooden boxes that the public had to break open in order to discover what was inside. It was like a hermetically sealed poem revealed upon opening. It's rather strange to think that this was the same year that the dictatorship passed the Ato institucional no. 5 (Institutional Act No. 5 (AI-5)), doing away with personal liberties, closing down the national congress, forbidding everything, including the freedom to vote. Everything was shut down when the AI-5 came into place, and this is when the *Urnas quentes* were created.

BA: Freedom and experimentation are central to your work, but in Urnas quentes you incite people to be violent in order to discover your work. Did you realize how much effort it would take – an act of violence – in order to break open the boxes?

AM: Yes, the *Urnas quentes* require a certain amount of force in order to break into them. It's an ambiguous work in the sense that you have to resort to violence in order to see what's inside and discover the internal code.

It's the language of the work itself using force to find a poem. In the *Urnas quentes,* the poems were written with paint and brush in a loose style with sayings like: "Hunger," "Down with the Dictatorship," "Freedom to the People." This was also interesting. After the exhibition we saw graffiti in the streets, which started showing up little by little with these same kinds of expressions of revolt.

---

1   The exhibition *Apocalipopótese,* was held at Aterro do Flamengo, Rio de Janeiro, in 1968 and organized by Hélio Oiticica and Rogério Duarte as a collective art experience within Frederico Morais's *Arte no Aterro: um mês de arte pública* (Art at Aterro: A Month of Public Art).

BA: Did you use *Urnas quentes* to incite people to think about the violence in their daily lives?

AM: Yes, exactly, because a certain effort really was necessary, just like with anything in life, things need this effort in order to get going, to advance conceptually, as knowledge. So it is like life itself, but we are talking about the experience of art. The sealed object evokes longing and solicits physical movement in order to open it. *Urnas quentes* were an attempt to expand this knowledge or, in sum, spark curiosity about breaking the box and how this could be done physically, about the poetics hermetically sealed within the box. This is why the series was a language, like life itself.

BA: *Apocalipopótesis,* was held outside of an institutional setting, Aterro do Flamengo, yet despite censorship, many institutions were exhibiting works that were contentious and critical of the mounting repression. Could you talk about your participation in *O Salão da Bússola* (The Compass Salon) in 1969?

AM: *O Salão da Bússola* was important; vanguard and radical art in diversity of materials was featured in the exhibition. It was at about that time that Mário Pedrosa organized an international boycott of the *X Bienal de São Paulo.* Most of the Brazilian artists joined the boycott, except for one or two. The American artists, organized by Gordon Matta-Clark, didn't send work to the Biennial either. Some of the Brazilian artists already had their work ready for the Biennial and they sent it to *O Salão da Bússola.*

I showed three pieces of work, *Soy loco por ti* (I'm Crazy for You), a map of Latin America spilling blood, together with a transparent plastic map containing greenery. People could lie down on it.

The second piece was called *Corpura,* a kind of banana and palm leaf curtain that lifted, revealing a dense and brilliant red color. The third piece of work was a panel with a *Flan* in the middle. I wrote whatever came into mind on the panel, in homage to my friends who were in exile abroad.

Soy loco por ti started a whole controversy between two art critics; on the one hand, Mário Schenberg vigorously defended the work, saying that it was creative and very carioca. On the other, Walmir Ayala attacked it saying it was pessimistic. Thanks to this discussion, *Soy loco por ti* the jury gave it a prize.

BA: It is amazing that there was such strong works in the salon given the fact that the jury included a general and a priest.

AM: The story involved a general, a priest, an advertising specialist and an artist. While the artwork was being selected, the jury came under heavy political pressure, receiving anonymous phone calls and threats of violence. The art critic, Jayme Maurício, was threatened like this over the telephone – they said that he would suffer the consequences if he selected certain pieces of art. Jayme Maurício got scared and quit the jury. With all this tension, the salon promoter called me to tell me that he was afraid of going through with *O Salão da Bússola,* and he asked me to remove some of my work that had been selected by the jury. I gave him a counter proposal; basically that I would take my work out of the show in exchange for an air ticket abroad and two-thousand dollars. I felt like leaving Brazil and breathing fresh air. So then the promoter told me he would call a meeting at his office the next day and give me their response. We scheduled a meeting the following day at MAM. He showed up with a general and a priest and we all went to look at the work. The authorities said that there was no problem whatsoever with the work and that it could all be shown. This is why no deal was made, because the work was displayed in the exhibition and ended up getting awarded by the jury.

BA: But you had other problems with censorship.

AM: I ran into trouble at the *Bienal da Bahia* in 1968. The army removed my work, a four-meter diptych on violence and the student movement at that time. They removed the work and, to this day, never returned it to me. The French critic, Pierre Restany, also a friend of mine, told me years later that he had heard that this work that had been removed from the biennial by the army and burned. The state government of Bahia and the Biennial directors never, at any point, tried to justify their removing the work and its disappearance. A few years ago, the newspaper *O Globo* ran a series of reports saying that in Bahia the army bruned a number of documents, and I believe that this was the case with artwork as well.

On the opening day of the *Bienal da Bahia* I saw the police turn off the lights and close the exhibit. There were a lot of people at the door, all nervously chattering among themselves. What made things worse was that the next day in the *Jornal da Bahia* they published a photo of material considered as subversive that was found in some young students' apartment. At this time, Fernando Gabeira, an investigative journalist for the *Jornal do Brasil* requested financial aid for the student movement and I gave them 50 silk-screen lithographs of Che Guevara. One of them was found right in that apartment in Bahia during the Biennial.

I was then advised by friends in Bahia to leave immediately for Rio de Janeiro. I preferred taking the bus. An artist-friend, Wanda Pimentel, could smell danger in the air and went with me to the bus station. She was worried about my safety because of the situation. That's how it occurred to me to write a short account of what was happening and put it in a matchbox. I sat in the front rows and I thought that if anything happened, I could leave the matchbox on the seat or discretely throw it out the window. This thought followed me all the way to Rio de Janeiro, with me clutching to my matchbox. If anyone were to take me off the bus, I would discretely get rid of the matchbox. During the dictatorship, the police went aboard buses, into restaurants, apartments, houses and on streets with black hoods and "disappeared" people.

For me the matchbox with its message inside is quite similar to the *Urnas quentes.*

BA: Did you want to leave the country?

AM: Yes, I felt like I was suffocating, my friends were all abroad.[2] I exchanged correspondence with Hélio Oiticica, telling him I was thinking of going to London. I had been selected to participate in the [VI] *Biennale de Paris* at this time, but I couldn't send my work because the Brazilian government wouldn't let me. In 1969, the army invaded the MAM in Rio de Janeiro and closed the Brazilian exhibit.

BA: With *Urnas quentes* you offer the experience of discovery and revolt to the public and offer them a chance to intervene in the work. In other works of the same period you use your own body as something experimental and confrontational.

AM: The work is an experiment, a discovery. There's a rationale winding naturally between these two ideas, communicating with each other as a dialectics. Years ago when I was young, the idea was to break with the rules of the art game; museums, galleries and all other kinds of official rules. We were being experimental and our interest, for example, in breaking with criteria for judging artwork, was to open new spaces and make new forms of communication possible. Ethics and aesthetics are at stake in this sense, and a whole creative experience is incorporated into this way of thinking.

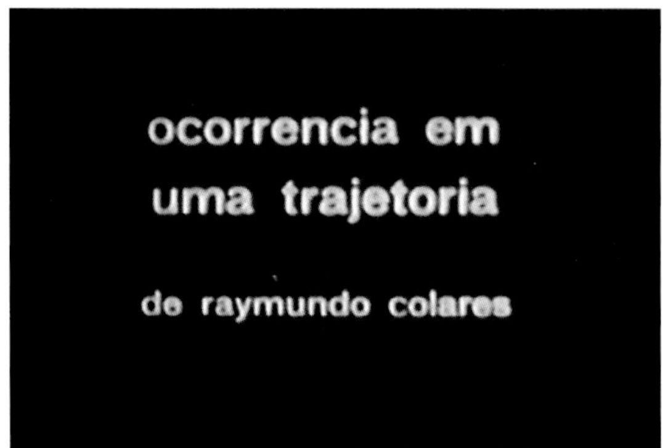

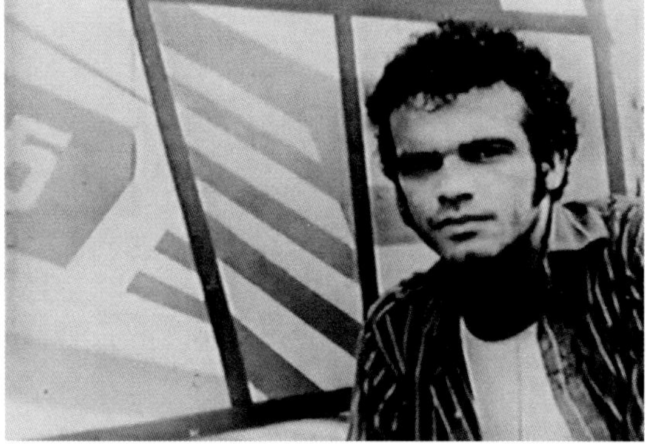

Stills from *Arte hoje, Histórias verídicas* (Art Today, True Stories), directed by Antonio Manuel, 1976. B&W with sound and color photographs, 14 minutes, 16mm. Courtesy the artist

   2   During this time Antonio Manuel associated and collaborated with artists who remained in Brazil, such as Raymundo Colares.

BA: In 1970 at the *Salão Nacional de Arte Moderna* (National Modern Art Salon) held at MAM in Rio de Janeiro, you showed up despite having been rejected by the jury, as your proposal – the naked artist as the work of art. And you did it in a way that it was a serious and direct confrontation with the museum, with the Salon as an institution.

AM: *O corpo é a obra* (The Body Is the Work) was a confrontation with institutions. The initial idea, when I registered myself as the work of art, was to question the subjective criteria used for choosing and judging artwork. In order to participate in the salon, the artist had to fill out a registration form and submit the work of art to a panel. This is how it worked; either they accepted you or they didn't. As a work of art I was refused. Yet on the official inauguration day, I decided to go ahead with the work. I invited a model from the *Escola de Belas Artes,* who was at the museum, to go with me. Vera [Pedrosa] and I, totally naked, walked among the artwork, together with authorities, artists, and the general public. *O corpo é a obra,* was a way of stripping down in order to oppose the political, aesthetic and social system. The work was disassociated from the jury, outside of the salon, independent, just as it had been created. And it was quite a scandal.

BA: Immediately after the opening at MAM, you went to visit the art critic, Mário Pedrosa. Pedrosa was a key intellectual voice during this period both in terms of his critical work with art, and – as a founder of the *Partido Trabalhista Brasileiro* (Brazilian Labor Party) – in terms of his political engagement.

AM: Mário Pedrosa was a very important person in my life. After *O corpo é a obra* was over at MAM, I went to his place with some friends, still in the heat of the action, and we spent most of the night there talking. Hugo Denizart had a recorder and recorded the whole conversation. As a result, the text was released with all of Mario's commentary on *O corpo é a obra,* in which he said what I was doing was "an experimental exercise of freedom."

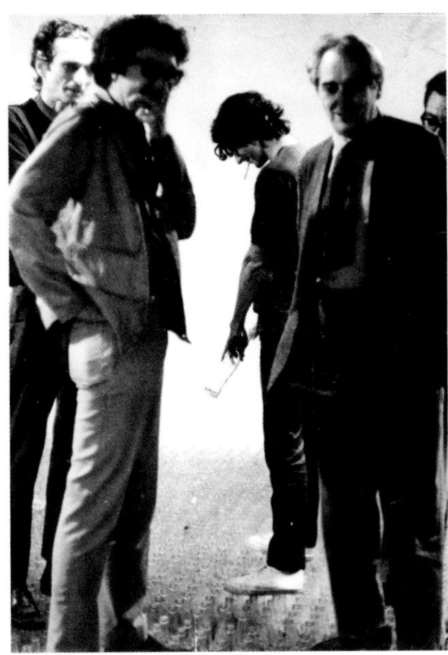

Dionísio del Santo, Frederico Morais, Antonio Manuel, Mário Pedrosa and Jackson Ribeiro at Frederico Morais's *A Nova Crítica* at Petite Galerie, Rio de Janeiro, c. 1969–1970. Image courtesy Antonio Manuel and Vera Pedrosa

BA: Pedrosa's description of *O corpo é a obra* has since become a key concept to describe and understand the artistic experimentation of the period.

AM: *O corpo é a obra* seemed to absorb much of the creative artistic experiments in Brazil at the time like a magnet. A later work of mine, *The Cock,* 1972, shared a strong connection to *O corpo é a obra* because after MAM I felt kind of lost, but continued to work with the body. I felt impotent in face of the reality of the exceptional environment in which we lived. I did two years of intense yoga, and this yoga posture may have inspired *The Cock.* The cock is strong, powerful; it sings at five in the morning, it awakens the city. This the kind of symbolism interested me. A cock sings and is strong even when it needs its nest; so it also has a kind of impotence.

For the work, I made a nest in Barra da Tijuca near a river where there was a hill of shells. The work consisted of a lot of photos of me in the nest.

BA: Beyond the richness of the symbolism, were you thinking about the documentation, how the photographs of you in the nest of shells might look?

AM: I wasn't really worried about registering the work, but making it happen right then and there. I think that there are some things that should be registered, but I never really felt interested in doing so. Photography interested me as a language, as information. I used newspaper photos for some of my work, as a live and immediate situation. Others, such as *O bode* (The Goat) or *The Cock,* are my own photos, ephemeral work; what remains of them is having being registered.

BA: *O bode* was your proposal for a solo exhibition at MAM in 1973, where a black angora goat would appear in a red circle. Why was the work rejected?

AM: *O bode* was banned at the MAM exhibit because of the directory's paternalistic attitude; they didn't feel that *O bode* was representative of my work. The MAM directors thought that one single element couldn't represent my work, and that I needed to show more. I maintained at a number of meetings that this single work was a statement about censorship and political repression. They didn't accept my argument so I couldn't show *O bode.* For me, *O bode* was all about the exceptional environment at that time, much worse than the repressive system itself. But the work also had its playful side and a kind of fusion between this playfulness and malignity was what made me conjure up this particular animal. In my childhood days, goats could be found wandering about the streets, free just like any sacred element. In Umbanda religious practice the goat is used to unload evil from people, while in Quimbanda religion the goat is sacrificed because it absorbs so much evil and tension that only the goat itself can take it. I think it ends up getting sacrificed so that it doesn't just explode. It's a metaphor and a reflection of a very tense and repressive experience of the time.

Having decided to carry out the project, I went to the *Jornal* [*do Brasil*] and proposed the *Exposição Antonio Manuel – De 0 à 24 horas* (Exhibition of Antonio Manuel – From 0 to 24 Hours) to them. It would be an exhibition that you bought at the newsstand.

On Saturday an announcement was released on the first page and on Sunday the show was published using the whole cultural section: "Exposição de Antonio Manuel (de zero às 24 horas nas bancas de jornais" (Exhibition of Antonio Manuel (from zero to 24 hours on the newsstands). Everyone who bought the paper got the exhibition as well.

BA: And how did people react?

AM: Sixty thousand issues went to press nationwide. Publishing was important for me then; the work was out on the street, in the newsstands, in another circuit, distinct from the museums and art galleries.

BA: That's a pretty radical idea. But why didn't the newspapers get into trouble with the military for doing this sort of thing?

AM: Look, I don't know. It was very daring for a newspaper, with all the heavy censorship at that time, to publish a six-page long proposal like this, doing an art exhibition independently from a museum, the dictatorship, etc. It lasted twenty-four hours, just like any newspaper.

BA: How did you decide to work with newspapers for the first time, starting with your drawings and then the flans?

AM: I think it was the appeal newspaper itself. The strong images, the diagramming, all of this interested me. I contoured the newspaper images with crayon; I liked making contours on faces, mouths and bodies.

BA: Were you familiar with Amilcar de Castro's graphic work for the *Jornal do Brasil* in the late 1950s?

AM: I was a passionate *Jornal do Brasil* fan. It was a left-leaning paper. I liked the diagramming and the people who worked there. I took part in the *Jornal do Brasil* graphics shop while, in the evening, I would go find the *flans*, and as such, I made some friends at the paper. Amilcar's graphics renovation was revolutionary.

BA: Amilcar de Castro renovated the graphic aspect of the newspaper, but never engaged in its social potential. Your works investigate and exploit the social, the graphic, as well as the circulatory potential of the newspapers.

PRESO POLICIAL ACUSADO DE MATAR A PROFESSORA

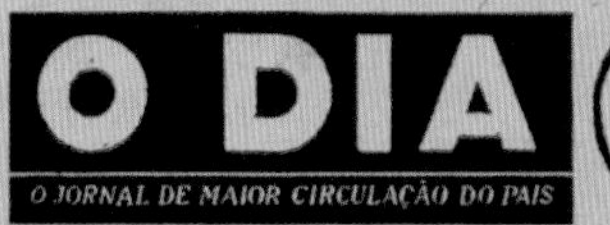
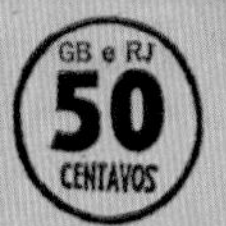

Duas testemunhas o reconheceram no fichário da SPJ — Postas em frente do suspeito, afirmaram, categoricamente, que era ele o matador — É APJ e servia na 10ª Delegacia Policial — Ia saindo para uma ronda, armado de metralhadora, quando chegou a turma da DH para prendê-lo — Ao retornar da missão, apresentou-se e entregou as armas — Tem grande semelhança fisionômica com o Comissário Jairo, que vinha sendo acusado pelo crime ——————————————— (PÁGINA 7)

Redação e Administração: Rua Riachuelo, 359. Tel.: 222-7751 — Telex 386

ANO XXIII   Rio de Janeiro, quinta-feira, 7 de junho de 1973   Nº 7.705

CHUPAVA SANGUE DANDO GARGALHADAS

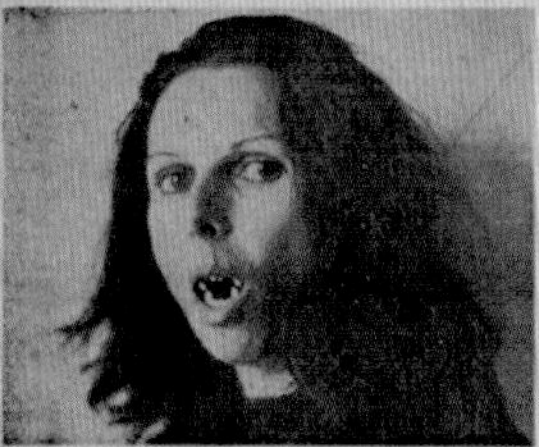

Mlher tranqüila e sem vícios — Foi passar o fim de semana fora — Voltou Vampira — Permaneceu várias horas gargalhando e quebrando sepulturas — Pela manhã acharam o coveiro mordido — Chamaram o pinel — Também foi mordido às gargalhadas — Vampira foi vista hoje, na Cidade de Deus.

Estado constrói parque para proteção da fauna e da flora

Parque Ecológico de Jacarepaguá terá também Centro de Primatologia — Convênio entre o Estado e a UFRJ para pesquisas e estudos sobre conservação da Natureza — Reconstituição do arvoredo atlântico — Secretaria de Ciência e Tecnologia preocupada com as novas indústrias

Execução a qualquer momento

"Comando Justicialista" apoderou-se de figuras de destaque do PC argentino e ameaçou matá-las — Exigem a libertação de todas as pessoas que os terroristas do "ERP" mantêm detidos — Comandante militar é solto, depois de passar 40 dias no cativeiro — Peron de malas prontas para o regresso (P. 7)

Noivos assassinados

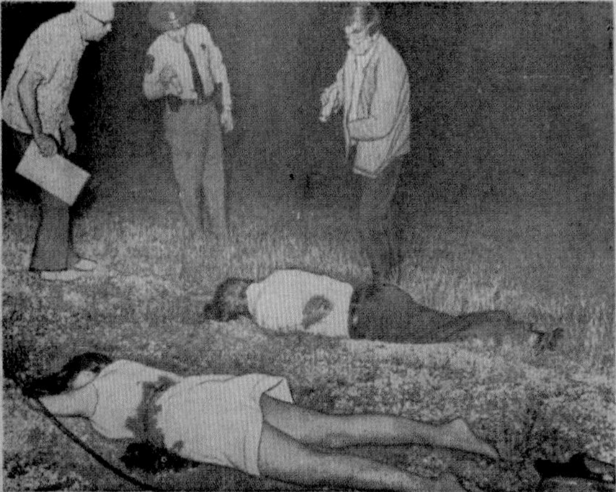

Nas cercanias de Chicago, foram encontrados, lado a lado, de bruços, os corpos de Dorothy Cerny e James Schmidt, ambos de 25 anos de idade e que pretendiam se casar brevemente. Os cadáveres, que apresentavam perfurações a tiros de revólver, não tinham outros sinais de violência (Radiofoto UPI)

Jairzinho vetado na revisão médica

Brasil é favorito mas campo complica outra vez — Televisões começam a mostrar o jogo para todo o Brasil, ao vivo, às 16 horas (hora do Rio) (Leia na pág. dezesseis).

Ancião surrava amante de 15 em 15 dias

Era caixeiro-viajante e só voltava de duas em duas semanas — Jovem aceitava, mas ontem ele exagerou, e ela teve de ser medicada no hospital — (Leia na página treze)

Federais apreendem contrabando de 10 milhões

Desova era feita em Cabo Frio e os agentes seguiram contrabandistas três dias e três noites — Mantidos em sigilo os nomes dos presos — Várias pessoas envolvidas — Uísque, eletrodomésticos e calças Lee, a muamba (Pág. 8).

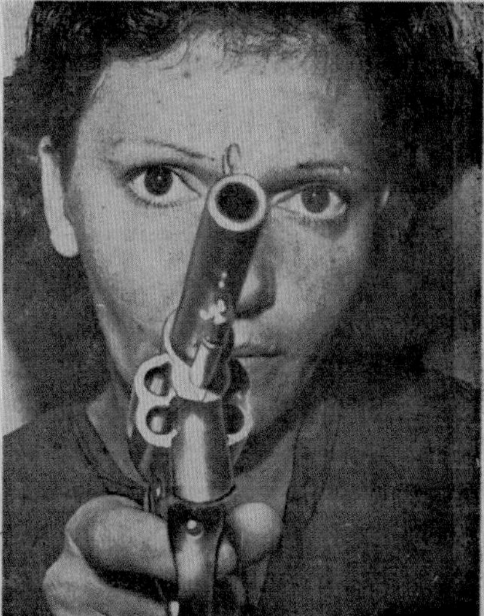

Pistoleira morena

Queixando-se da vida infeliz, que pôs em seu caminho "amantes sem escrúpulos, patrões interesseiros e colegas que a empurravam para o submundo", Nelita Dias (foto) confessou ser a chefe de uma quadrilha de assaltantes a mão armada, na Baixada Fluminense. Negou ter matado, mas a Polícia não acredita e está investigando ——————————— (Página 13)

NAZISTAS SABOTARAM AVIÃO RUSSO

Comitê de Ação para a Libertação de Rudolf Hess assumiu a responsabilidade pelo desastre com o supersônico soviético, que explodiu na França — (Leia na sétima página)

Governo pune frigoríficos que lesavam a população

Chupava sangue danda gargalhadas (Drank Blood Laughing), 1973. From the *Clandestina* series, newspaper, 22 x 15 in. Courtesy the artist

AM: I'm interested in creativity, which in my work, is done using newspapers, *flans*, graphics, but also moves into urban space, onto the streets, as in some of my later installation works, such as *Sucessão de fatos* (Sequence of Facts), 2003, and *Ocupações/descobrimentos* (Occupations/Discoveries), 1998–2000.

In this poetics of the graphic body, which isn't my body, but the body of the font itself, there's a relationship to life as a whole. Choosing the font, larger or smaller, has an impact on one's emotions and on one's body; emotional weights I felt while I was making some of the *flans*. There are a series of *flans* in which my interference is taking the flans, putting talcum powder on them and then paint so that they become visible images. I consider the 1968 *flans* as documents and registries of the political situation in Brazil. In the 1973–1975 *flans*, I actually created the *flan*, inventing the headlines, diagramming the photos and texts as visual poems, within the *O DIA* graphics room.

I did *Flans* parallel to the *Clandestina* (Clandestine) papers with the same logotype as the regular newspaper. There's no difference between my *O DIA* and the regular *O DIA* logotype. Some of the *Clandestinas* (Clandestines) were left at the newsstand and people bought them as if they were the *O DIA* newspaper.

BA: It was art sold as a newspaper. How was this possible?

AM: There were no differences between the paper I created and *O DIA,* because *Clandestina* was made in the paper's own graphic studio, using the same kind of type, the same diagramming. I was able to do this because I knew Ivan Chagas Freitas, the newspaper owner's son, who had studied at MAM.

BA: Can you describe your *fotonovela, A arma fálica* (A Phallic Weapon), from 1970?

AM: Hélio Oiticica was going to London to show work at the Whitechapel Gallery. Lygia Pape, Roberta Oiticica and I took Hélio to the port in Rio de Janeiro. He was going with the poet, Torquato Neto, also his friend, by ship to London.

This was the same port in Praça Mauá, Rio de Janeiro, where I had arrived in Brazil from Portugal when I was five years old. Hélio going to the same place where I had arrived in Brazil created this whole moment. When he returned to the country in 1970, I proposed doing the *fotonovela* to recuperate this port space.

The initial idea was for the *A arma fálica* to be published in *O Pasquim,* a magazine created by comedians and intellectuals. The *fotonovela* ended up not being published in the paper and in the 1990s it was published as a magazine.

BA: Why didn't you publish it then? Was it because of the censorship, the content?

AM: No, I requested Nelsinho Motta, the composer and musical critic, to take the *fotonovela* to the *O Pasquim* office. He took the work there and the *fotonovela* sat there for a year without being published. I don't know why. I went there to get it back because it was the only original I had of the work, the negatives had already been lost. In the 90s, RioArte looked me up to publish a *fotonovela* as a magazine, with Luciano Figueiredo doing the design. It's a beautiful diagramming job and we were able to give it an interesting rhythm.

BA: And you did the *fotonovela* before you worked with film, correct?

AM: Yes, my first film, *By Antonio,* was made in 1972. The *fotonovela* was an interesting resource; photos were taken, dialogues written and everything sort of fell into place, an economical and simple way to produce art. It was a kind of quasi-cinema. I actually find it quite interesting as a language.

BA: When you began experimenting with film in the 1970s, there seems to be a strong connection with your newspaper works.

AM: The films made this kind of graphic noise, as did the newspapers. This has to do with the space and body of the type. The films can be identified with the *Urnas quentes,* the *Jornais* (Newspapers) and the *Flans.* For example, *Semi Ótica* (Semi Otics/Optics) (1975) is a short movie, seven minutes long, which has a relationship to newspapers, since the film was shot using *O DIA* photos. This is where I had made the *Flans* and the *Clandestinas* papers. When I was I boy, I lived right next to the Atlantida Cinematography studio so I saw a lot of filming on the streets and in the studio, in what became known as Brazilian *chanchada* (vaudeville). Later on I met some of the *Cinema Novo* and *Cinema Experimental* directors. I shot a film a day, because I had to borrow everything, the camera, the cameraman had little time and the equipment belonged to friends.

The *Exposição Antonio Manuel – De 0 à 24 horas* shared a relationship with the films in terms of time, and also graphic noise and diagramming.

In the film *Loucura & Cultura* (Madness & Culture) the actors were filmed live with their photos fixed from the front, back and sides, just like police photos. I wanted to use the Brazilian National Anthem in the movie, but I wasn't allowed to, so I used the French *Marsellaise,* because it's a powerful and involving anthem. This is what I wanted for my film *Loucura & Cultura.*

The movie *By Antonio* (1972), has no sound, is in black and white, and was my first experience with 16mm; a hand burns documents in a toilet. In the second frame, the burnt paper is flushed down the toilet. The water took away all that was burned.

BA: Many of the works you have described – the *fotonovela* and films, for example – were collaborative in nature. Collaboration is central to your work from the very beginning of your career.

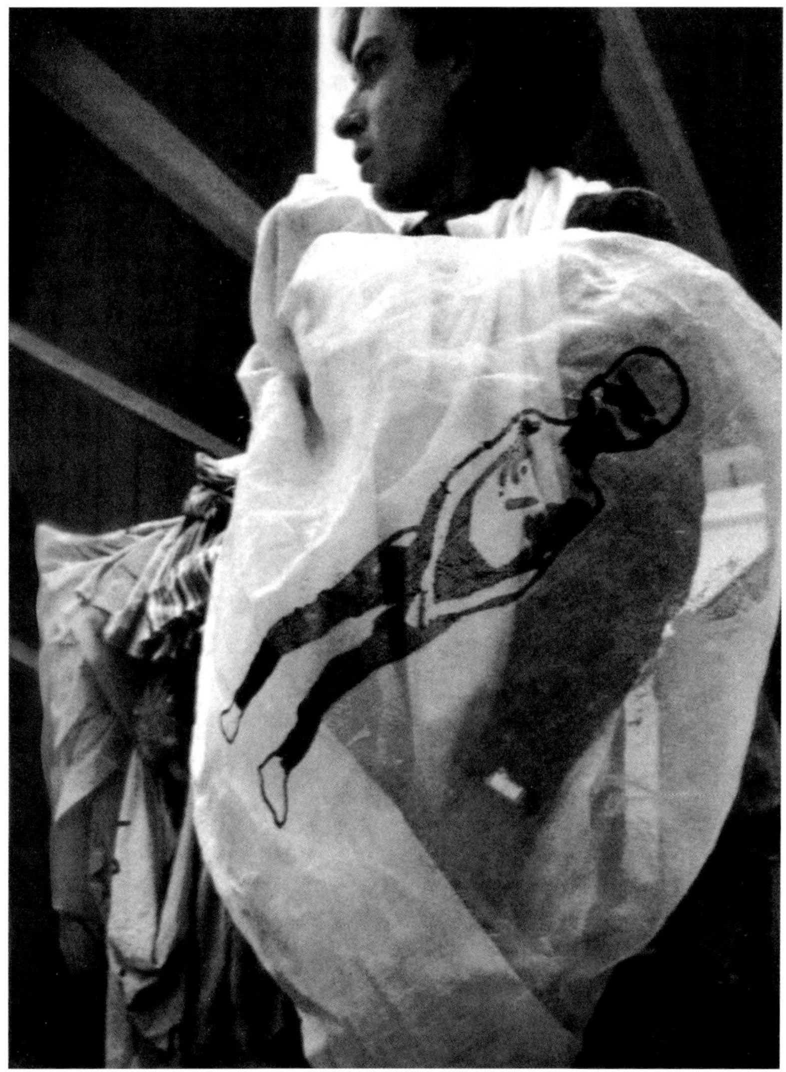

Hélio Oiticica and Antonio Manuel, [Torquato Neto with] *Parangolé P22, Cape 18, Nirvana*, 1968. Courtesy Projeto Hélio Oiticica and Antonio Manuel

AM: People thought of doing collective work at the time. I like to think of that period as a collective time, based on partnerships. My first contact with Hélio Oiticica was in MAM in Rio de Janeiro during the *Nova objetividade brasileira* (New Brazilian Objectivity) (1967) exhibit. On the way to the MAM I saw this newspaper headline: "Matou o cachorro e bebeu o sangue. Mulher vampira age em Ipanema" (Killed the dog and drank its blood. Vampire lady on the loose in Ipanema). I bought the paper and took it out in the MAM cafeteria, and started reworking it with crayon. There were two pictures, a "young miss" side by side with an ugly woman. It was beauty and the beast. I tried doing the opposite, turning beauty into the beast and the beast into beauty. Hélio Oiticica was in the cafeteria and got interested in the work.

At the same time that I was invited to show this and other work of mine in his Tropicália anthology - Roberta Oiticica participated as well with poetry written on bricks. I was 18 or 19 at the time, and this is how I got really close to Hélio and his brothers.

The only thing left is Hélio's letters commenting, saying that he was very happy to have invited me to participate in *Tropicália.* With Hélio we did the *Parangolé P22, Cape 18, Nirvana* (1968), which used an image that was inside one of the *Urnas quentes.* It was a newspaper image of a skinny African child from Biafra. Hélio invited me to do the *Parangolé* with him using that image. Then he projected the *Parangolé,* and I studied how to diagram the image a bit and then we put it together at his house.

Before Hélio, I had gone to Ivan Serpa to show him some of my drawings. I did some work with Serpa, for example I did an image of Guevara, he painted it with colors, and then we co-signed it.

With Lygia Pape, we had a strong friendship, very intense, for over ten years. We did some work together, especially cinema, she had some sort of participation in my work, and I in her work.

BA: You begin working in a collective environment that quickly eroded due to the political circumstances.

AM: There was this collective feeling, but the planetary tendency was individual isolation. I felt this physically because my friends were all abroad and the political situation in Brazil was tense. In 1979 I made a small object-box out of wood with a picture on it, a text and

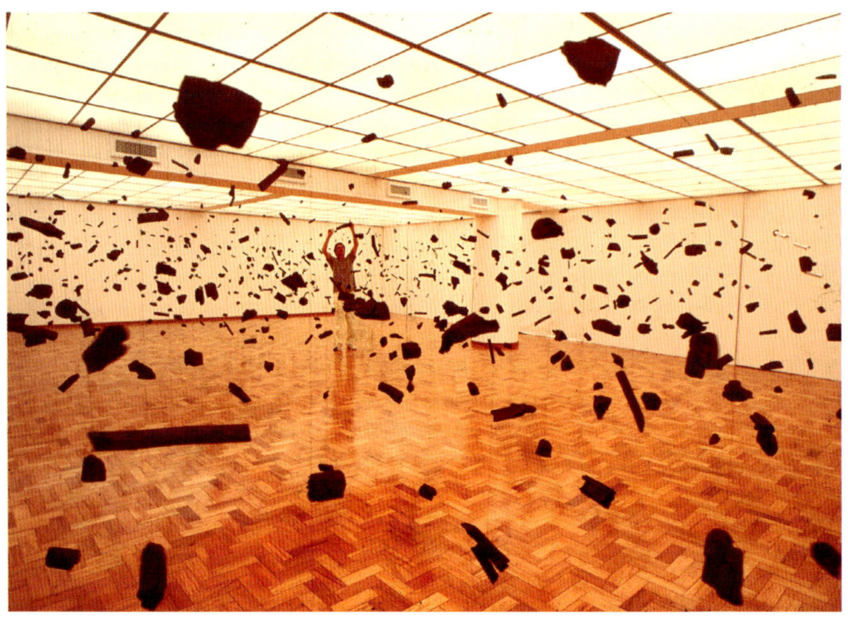
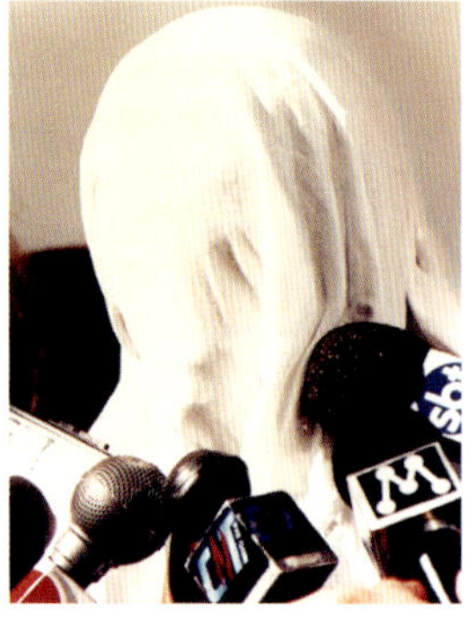

Fantasma (Ghost), 1994. Mixed media installation. Courtesy the artist

also some dried leaves. More than a poem, this object invites the spectator to discover and read among the leaves the text, *ONDE ESTÃO TODOS* (WHERE IS EVERYBODY), which alludes to absence.

BA: And after the dictatorship, how did your work experience change?

AM: I never stopped working and always tried to live from my work, making no concessions; whether during the dictatorship or not. [Giorgio] Morandi, for example, during the war, never stopped painting bottles, and he's a wonderful artist. Art elevates the spirit and gives us knowledge.

I've been working on installations and experiments with time and space, such as the *Sucessão de fatos* installation, which is made of French tiles laid on the ground, and everyone has to walk over them carefully so they don't break. Among these tiles are lakes of fiberglass, making up a poetic space. There's a bucket hanging from the lakes with water drops falling, forming a kind of spring, a water hole. In reality, art is always a creative act, a way to discover and to get to know things.

BA: *Fantasma* (Ghost) from 1995 has this same sort of poetic and political interaction with space and spectator.

AM: *Fantasma* is an installation with thousands of pieces of coal suspended in the air, hanging from threads at different heights. The coal floats in space around a photo of the *Fantasma* fixed on the wall and illuminated.

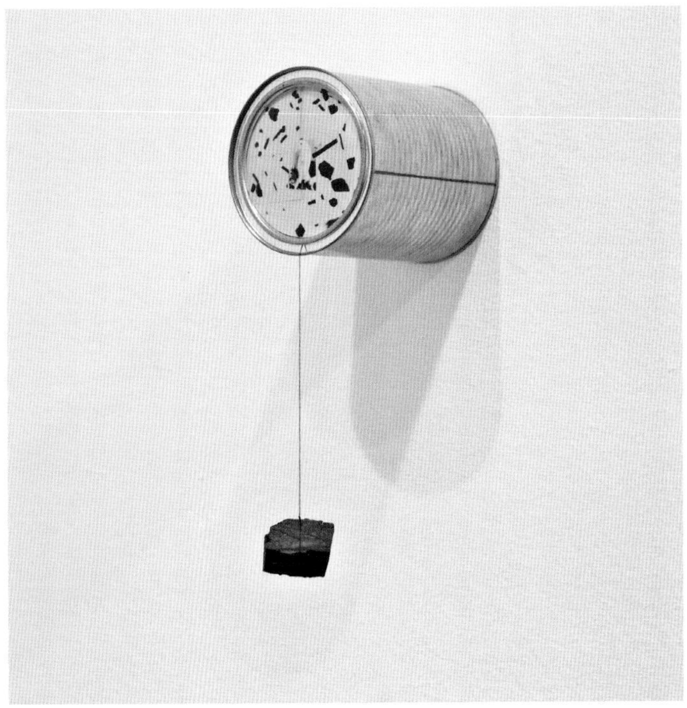

Pêndulo (Pendulum), 1994/2010. Mixed media, 4.7 x 4 in. Courtesy the artist

It is an experience in which the visual strength of the mass formed by the pieces of coal invites the spectator to walk around the installation. By walking across the space and getting closer to the image on the wall, the spectator can touch or be touched by the pieces of coal. The spectator must walk or dance in order not to bump into the work and dirty his clothes – this makes *Fantasma* ambiguous. The specter of violence as revealed by the coal and by the photography is compensated with the lightness of the hanging objects.

Likewise, the work is poetic. If you look at it with your eyes slightly shut you can see the pieces floating about, but when you open your eyes, they look like a dense mass.

BA: There seems to be strong connections between your early works and your later installations, like, for example, the *Urnas quentes* and *O corpo é a obra* with a work done thirty years later, *Ocupações/descobrimentos* (1998–2000).

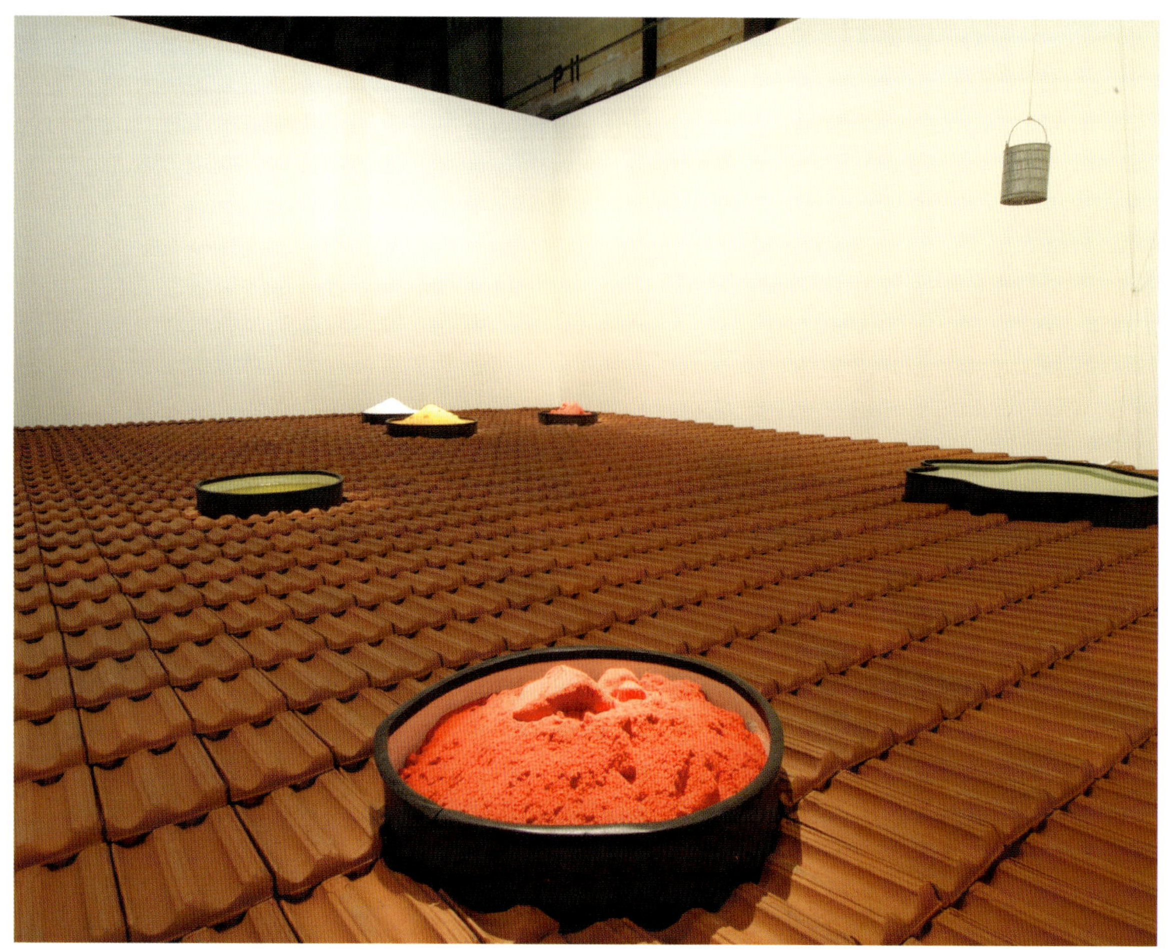

Sucessão de Fatos (Sequence of Facts), 2003. Mixed media installation. Courtesy the artist

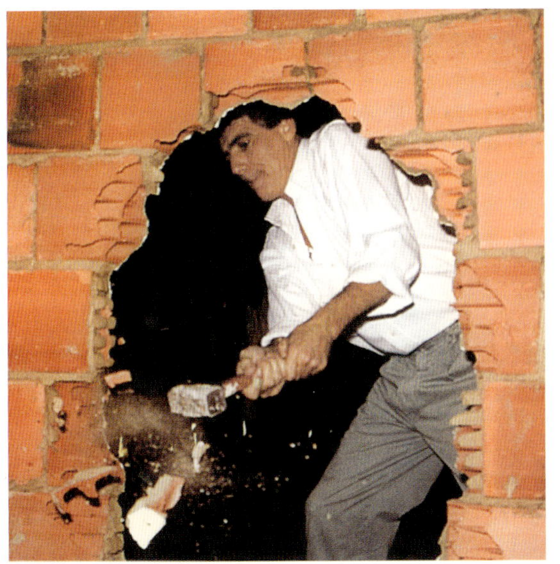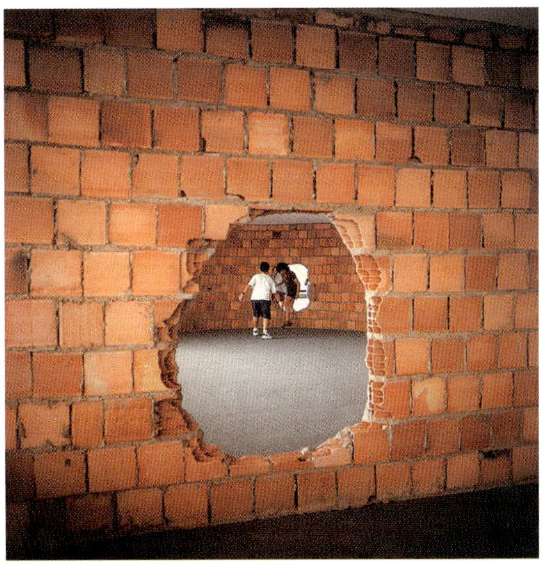

Ocupações-Descobrimentos (Occupations-Discoveries), 1998–2000. Mixed media installation.
Courtesy the artist

AM: *Ocupações/descobrimentos* was done at Museu de Arte Contemporânea in Niterói, which is a magnificent project by Oscar Niemeyer. The museum is like a huge sculpture strategically projected between Pão de Açúcar and Corcovado mountains, a veritable work of art. I was invited to set up an installation there in a spot from which the Atlantic Ocean could be seen, Corcovado mountain and Pão de Açúcar , a difficult space, because it's all glassed in, transparent. In this respect, when I mounted the installation *Ocupações/ descobrimentos,* it was a great challenge to construct the walls inside the museum. There was a total of seven walls that were broken one by one; thus, the visitor was invited to enter the work and come to live that experience. People's gazes no longer turned to the Atlantic Ocean, Corcovado or Pão de Açúcar; body and gaze were enveloped by the space itself, in an interaction between art, architecture and nature. In that sense, it was a marvelous challenge. I wanted people to look into the space and not to the outside, for them to participate in the work, thus the creation of the walls and the holes in them; the gaze turns to the inside and no longer to the outside. The wall is a limit, a boundary. When it's breached, it opens a passage and transcends that limit. In this sense, the work is related to *Urnas quentes,* which you break into in order to discover their contents. I also see a link to *O Corpo é a obra,* which surpasses limits and the concept of art. Even though rejected by the jury, the work was executed, was done. There is a similarity to the earlier works, a bond among them, to break down and question barriers.

PLATES

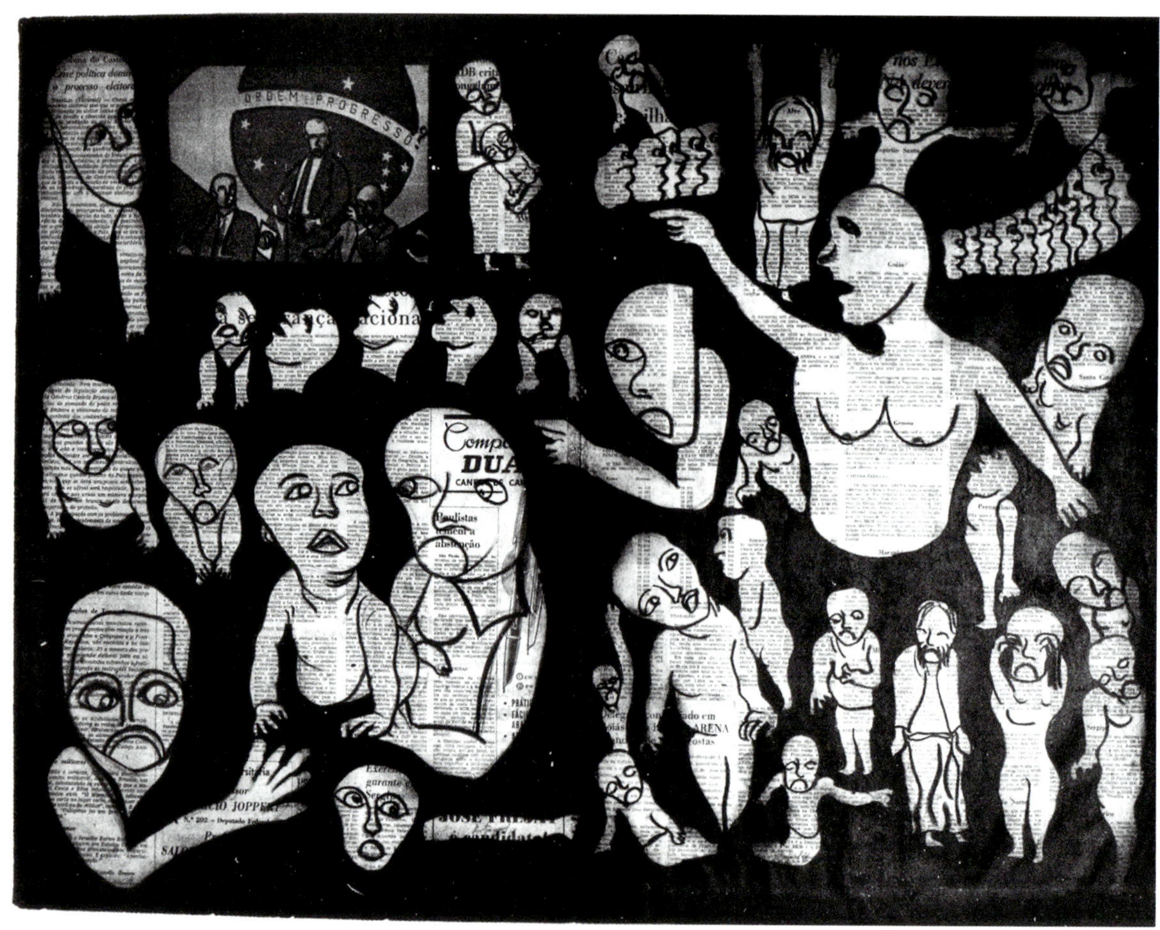

Untitled, 1966. Crayon on newsprint paper, 22 x 31 in. Courtesy the artist

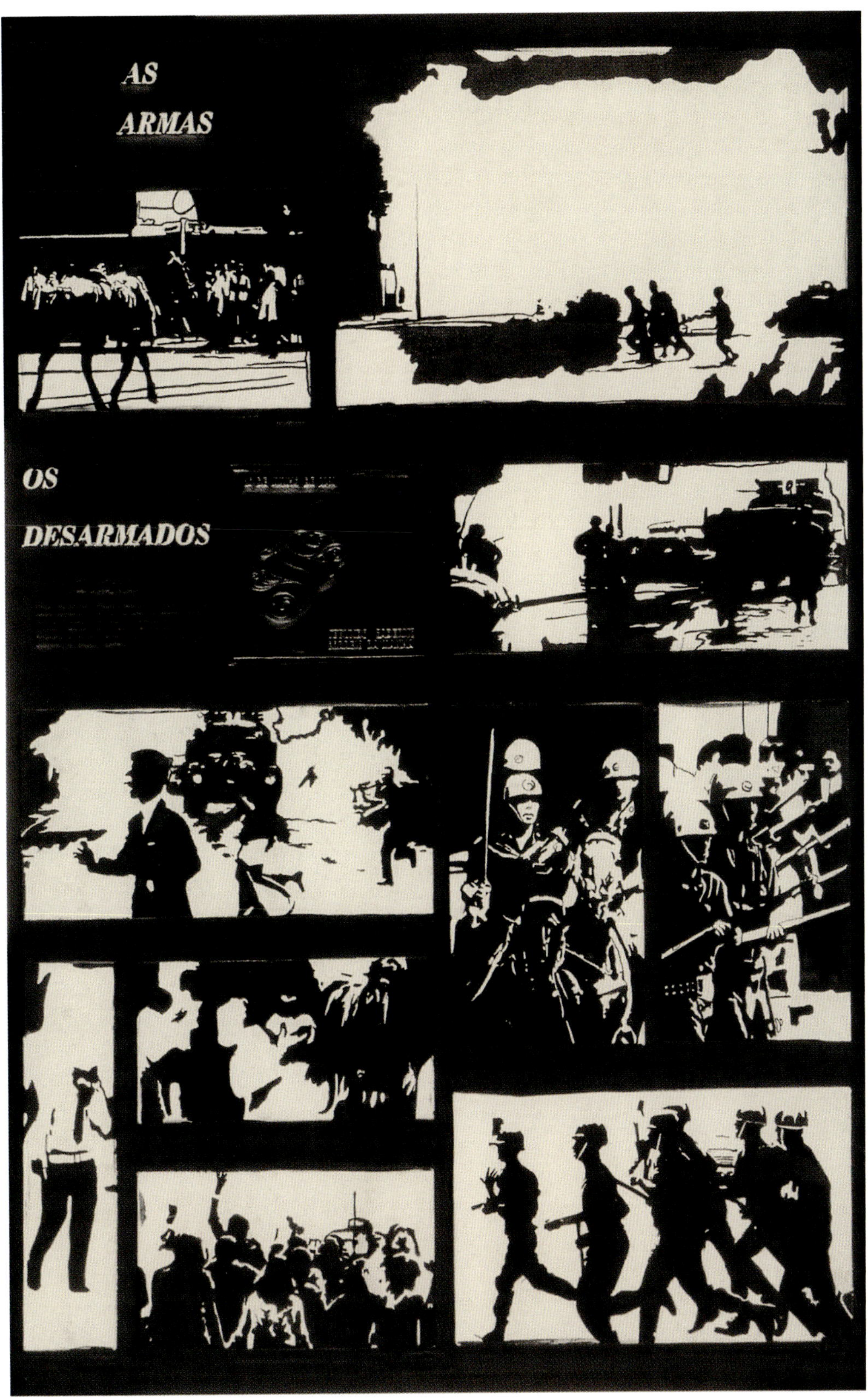

As armas / *Os desarmadaos* (The Armed / The Unarmed), 1968. From the Flan series, ink on papier-mâché stereotype mold, 22 x 15 in. Courtesy the artist

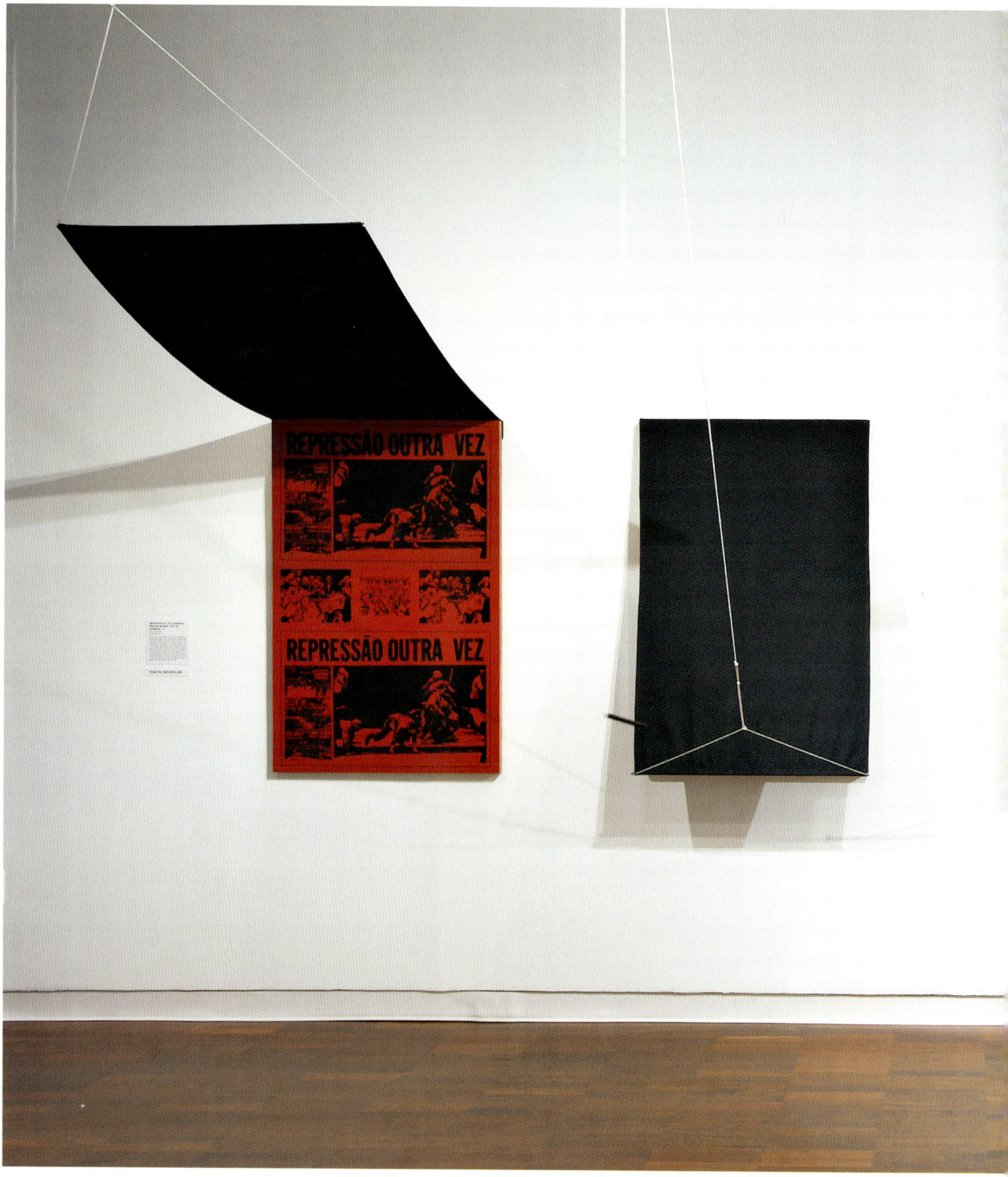

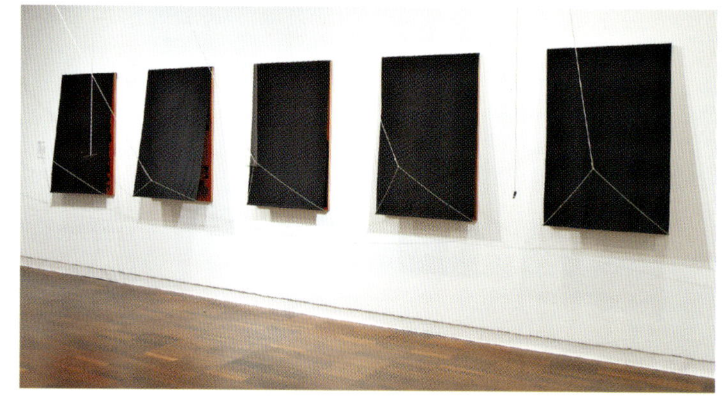

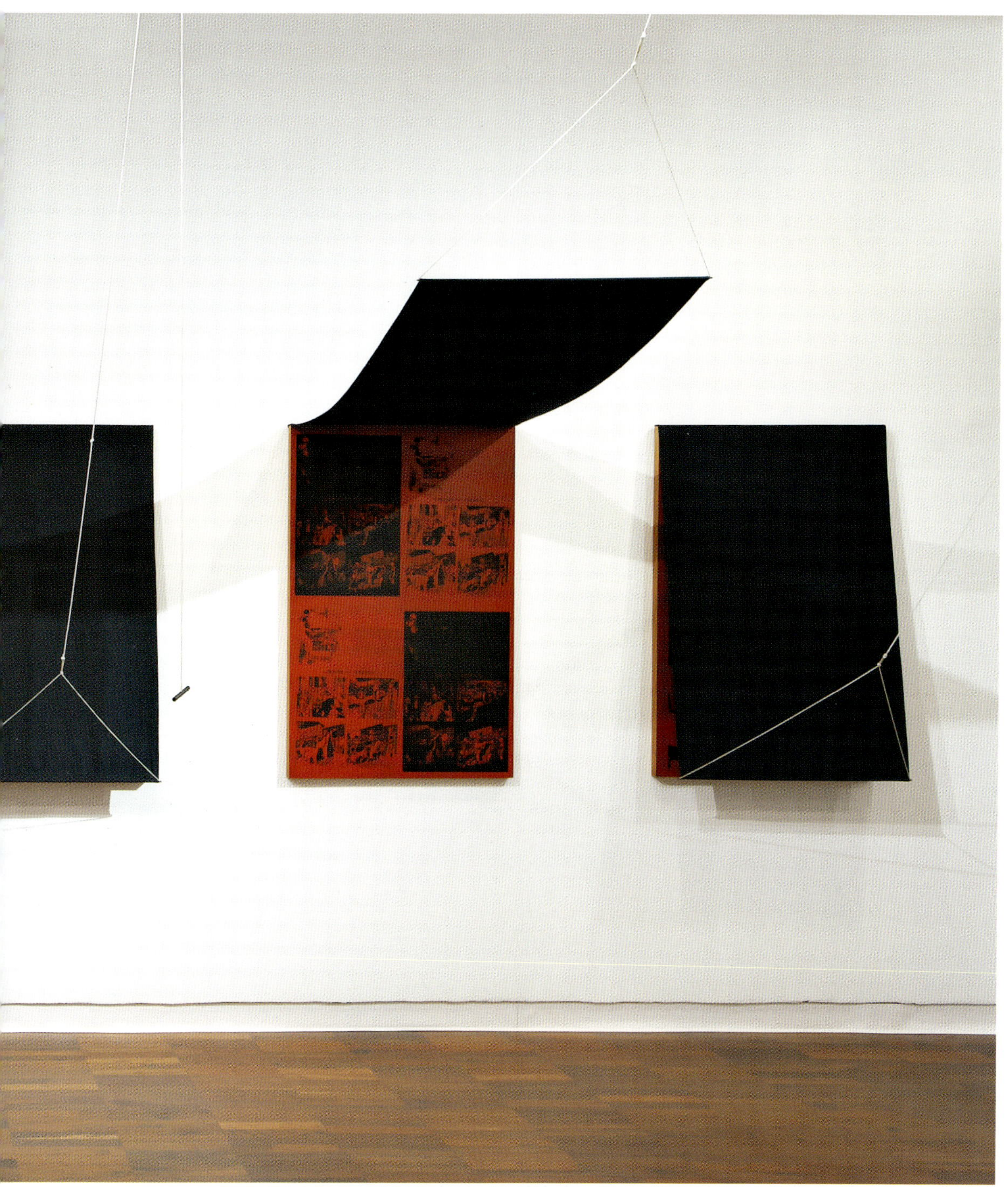

Repressão outra vez – Eis o saldo (Repression Once Again – Here is the Outcome), 1968. Wood, cloth, rope and silkscreen (set of 5), 48 x 31.5 in. each. Courtesy the artist

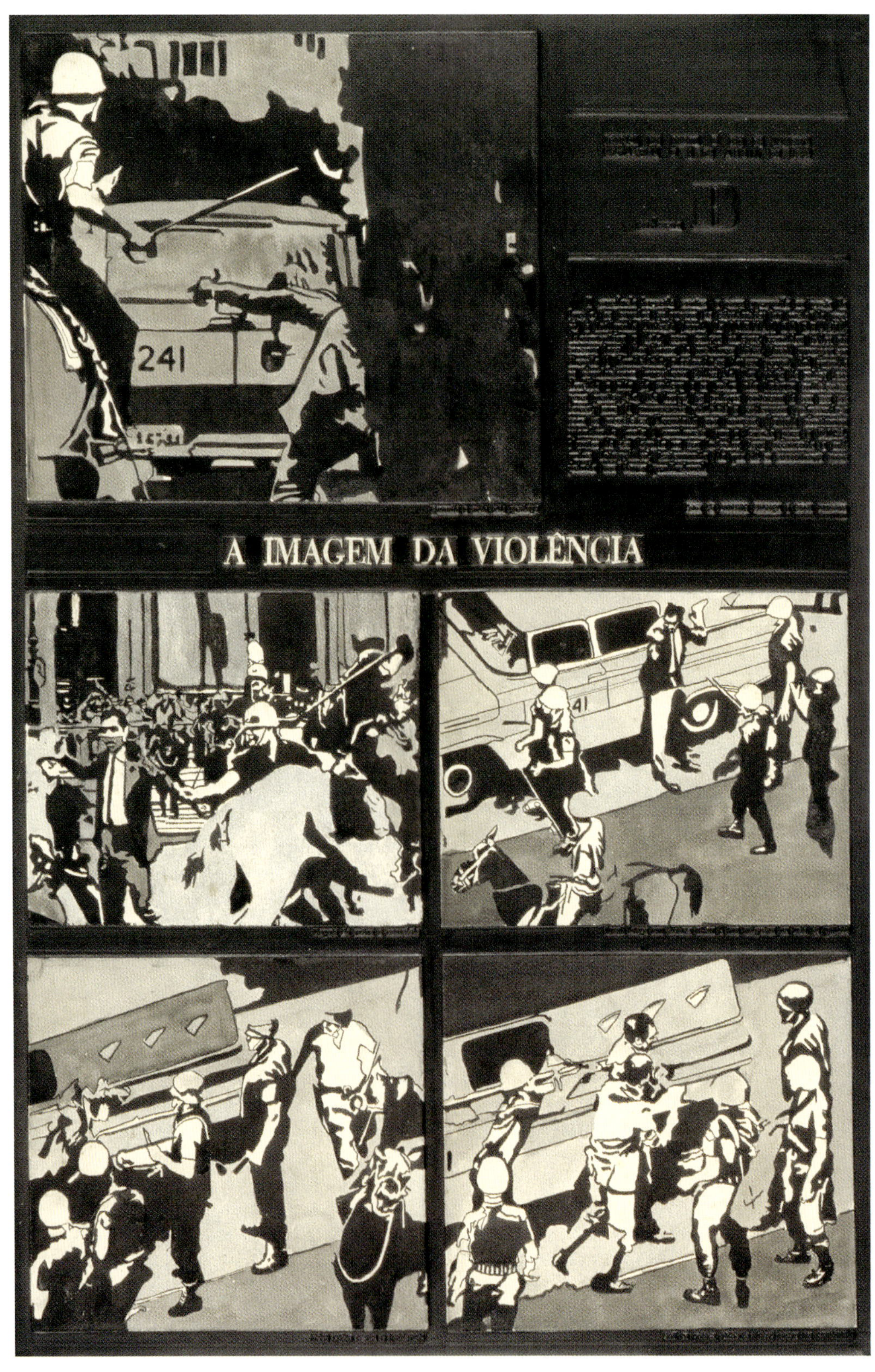

A imagem da violência (The Image of Violence), 1968. From the *Flan* series, ink on papier-mâché stereotype mold, 22 x 15 in. Courtesy the artist

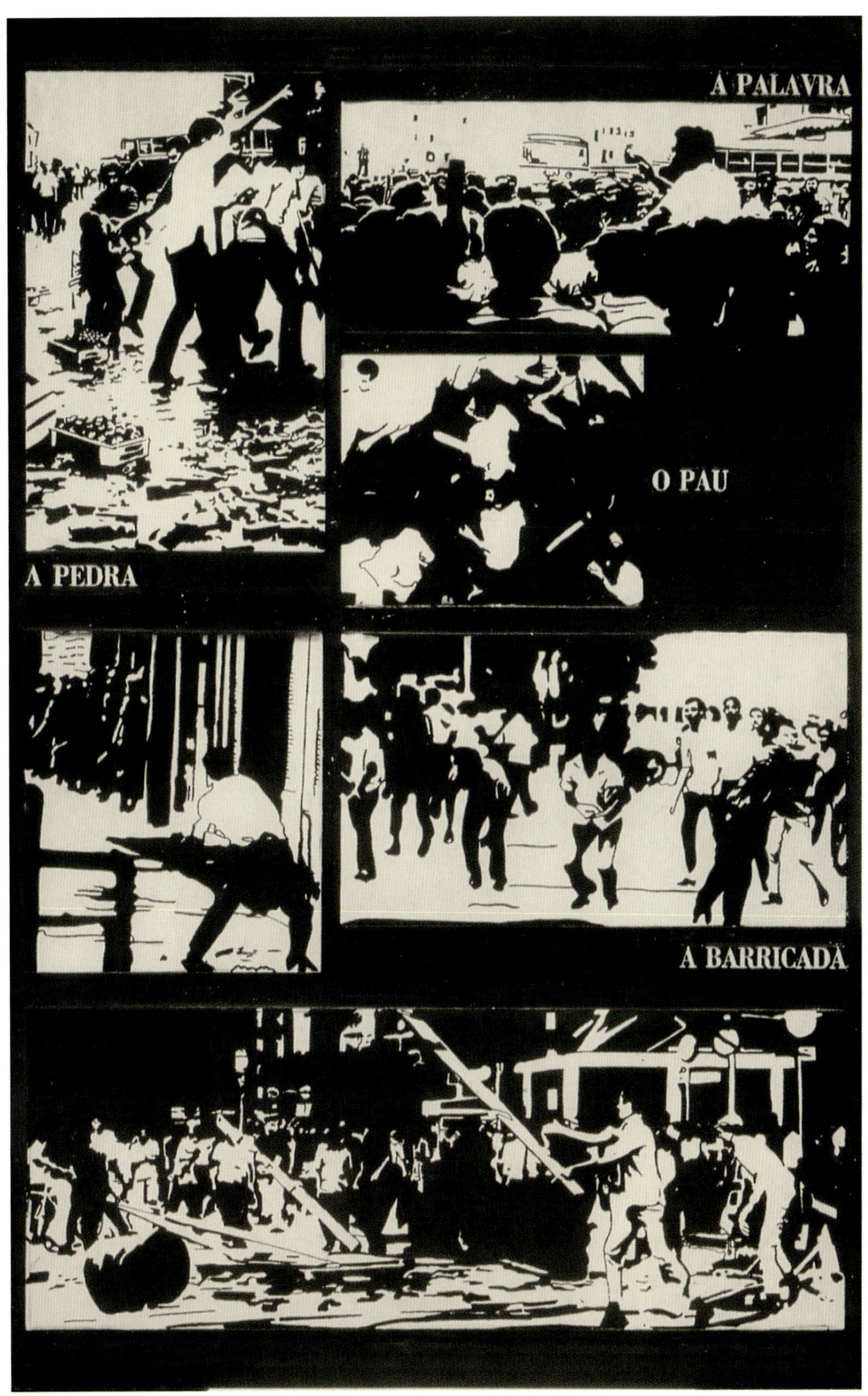

A palavra/o pau/a pedra (The Word/The Stick/The Stone), 1968. From the *Flan* series, ink on papier-mâché stereotype mold, 22 x 15 in. Courtesy the artist

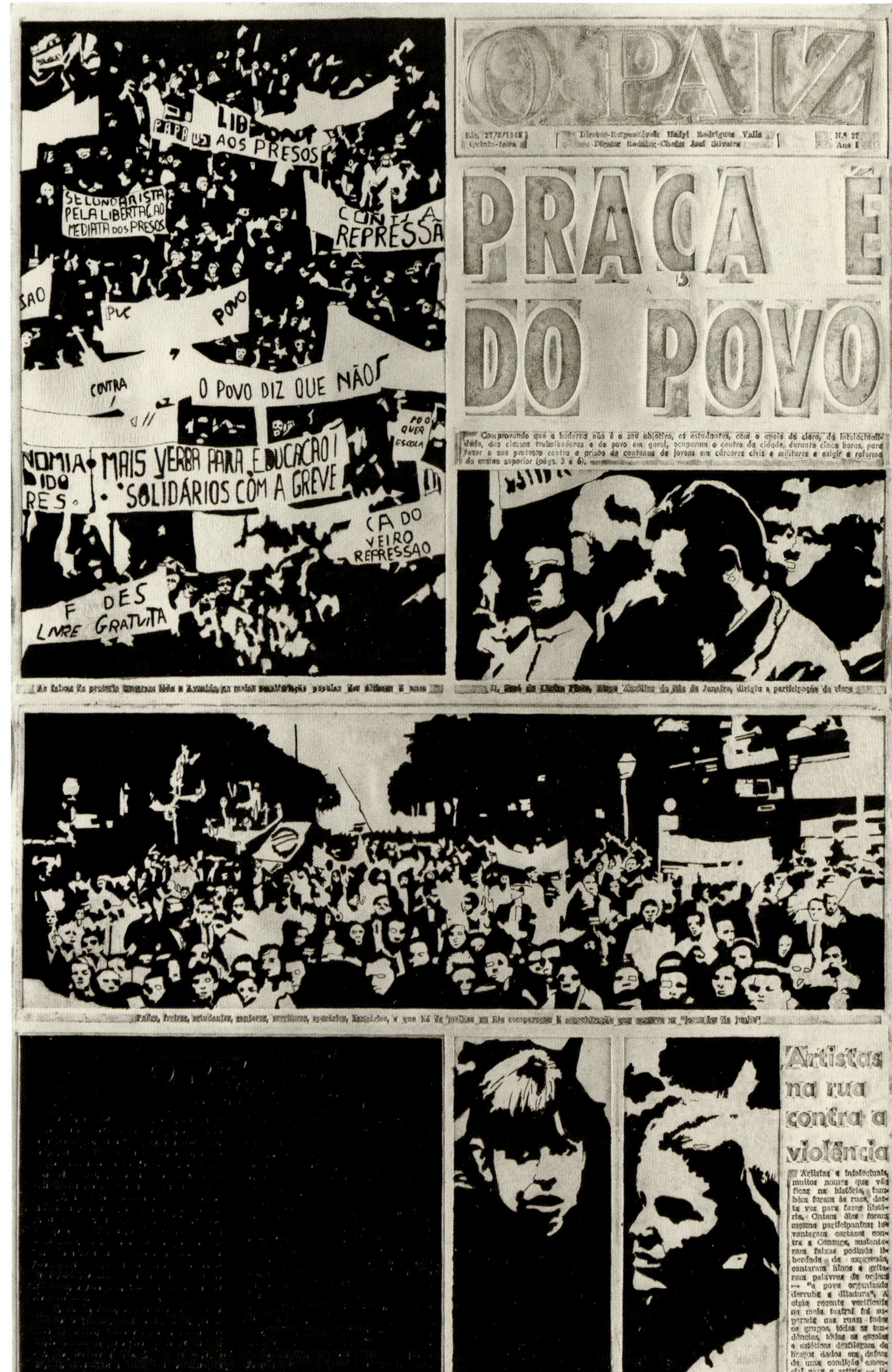

Praça é do povo (Plaza is the People's), 1968. From the *Flan* series, ink on papier-mâché stereotype mold, 22 x 15 in. Courtesy the artist

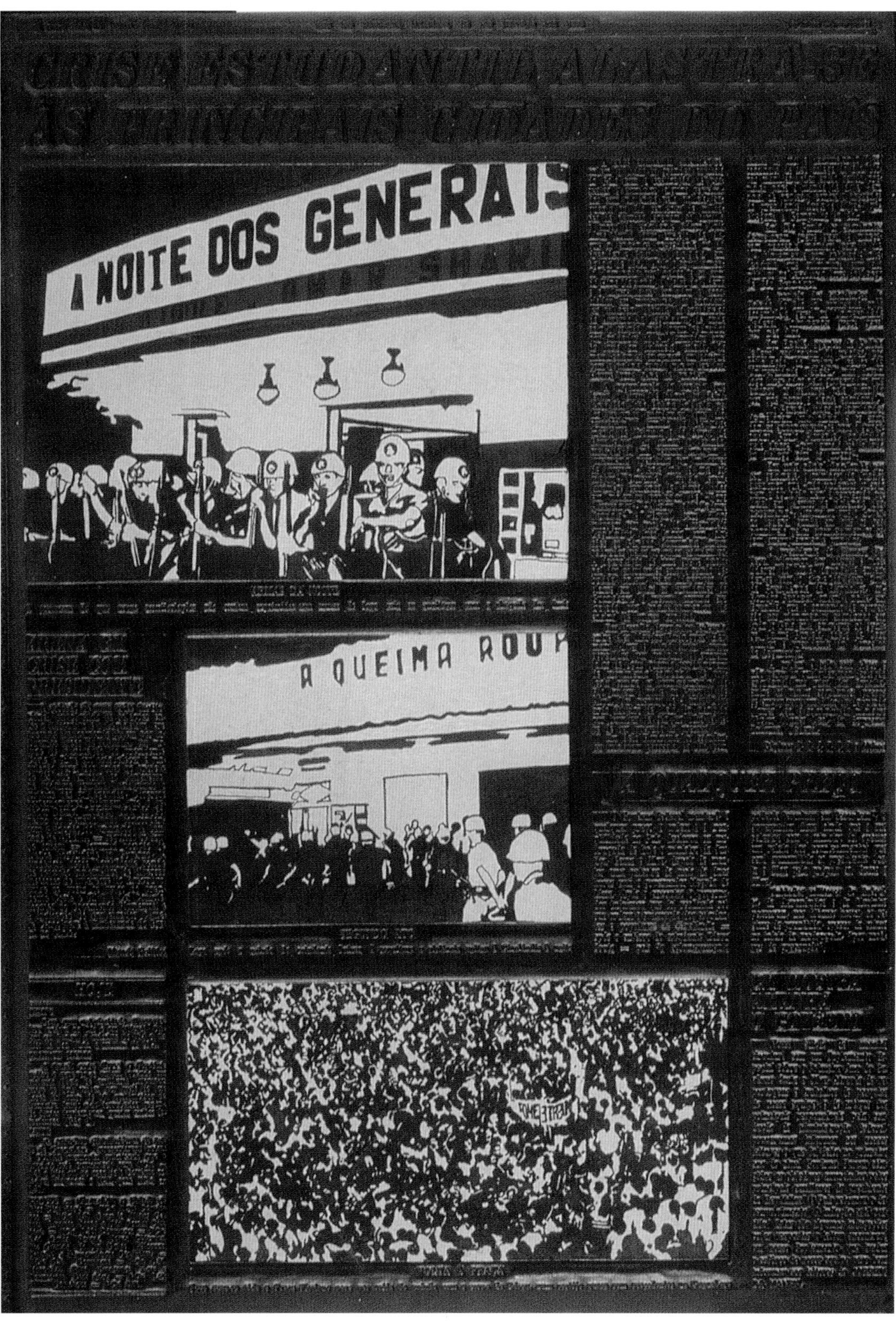

A noite dos generais (The Night of the Generals), 1968. From the *Flan* series, ink on papier-mâché stereotype mold, 21 x 15 in. Courtesy the artist

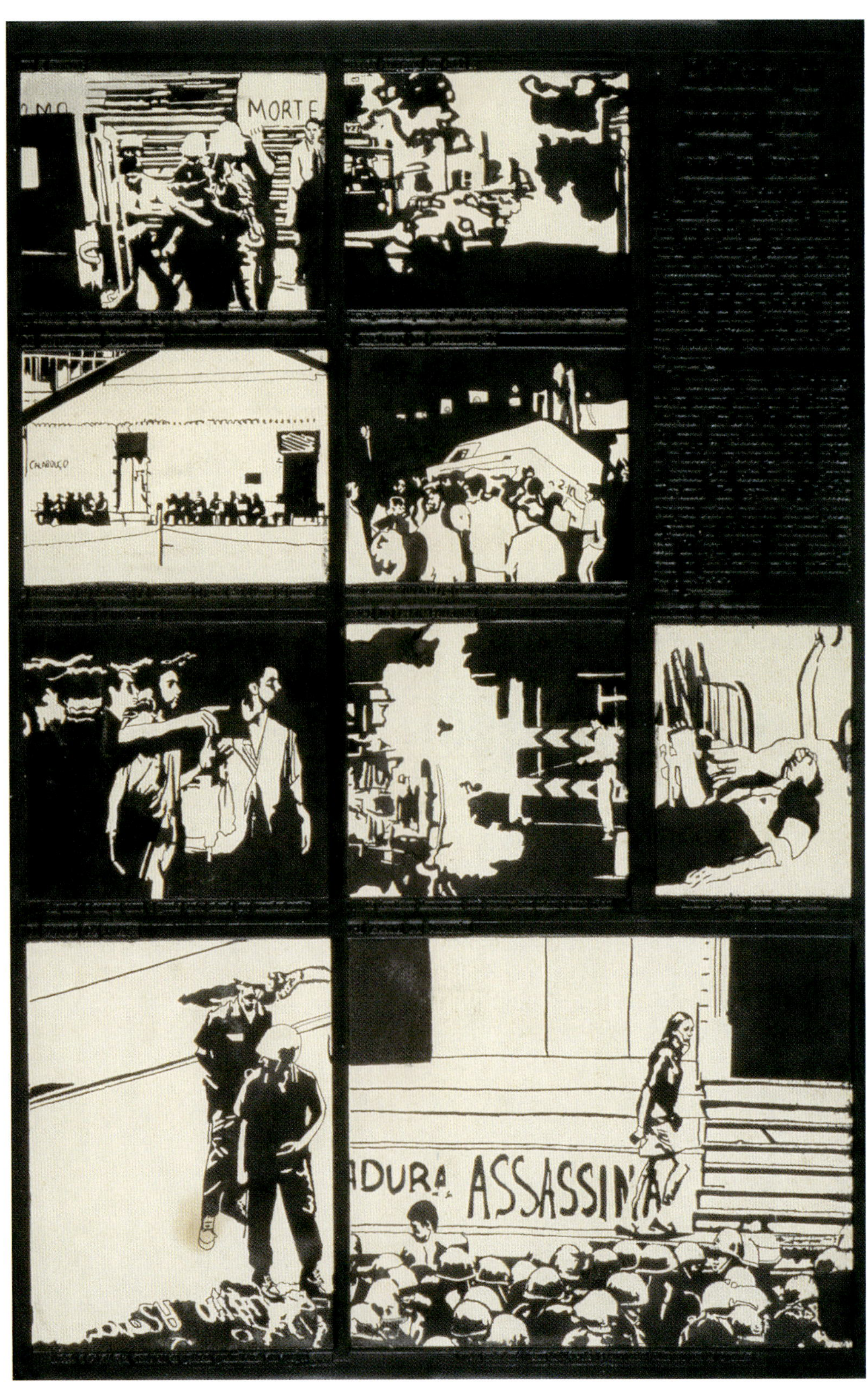

126 *Dura assassina* (Hard Assassin), 1968. From the *Flan* series, ink on papier-mâché stereotype mold, 22 x 15 in. Courtesy the artist

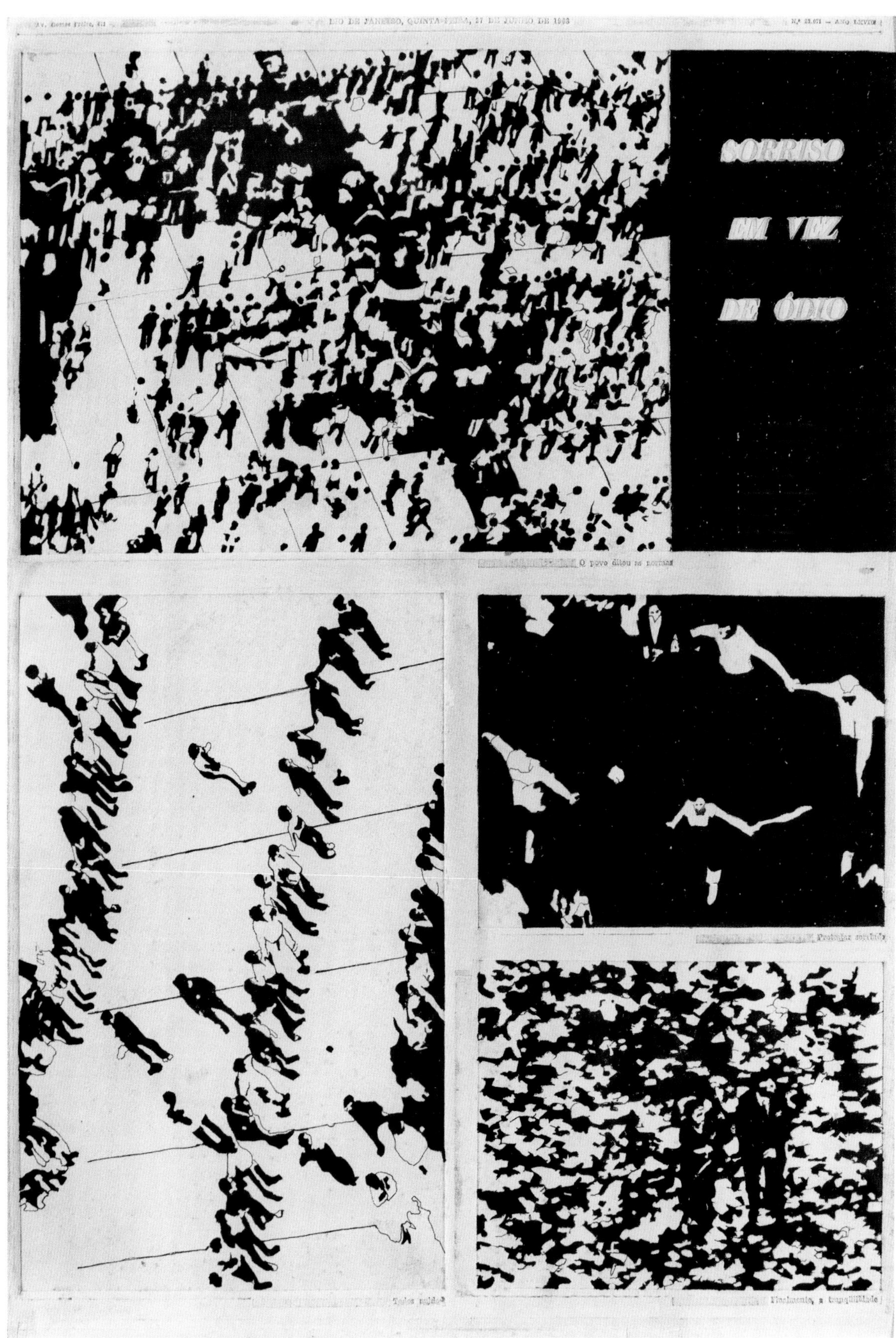

Sorriso em vez de ódio (Smile Instead of Hate), 1968. From the *Flan* series, ink on papier-mâché stereotype mold, 22 x 15 in. Courtesy the artist

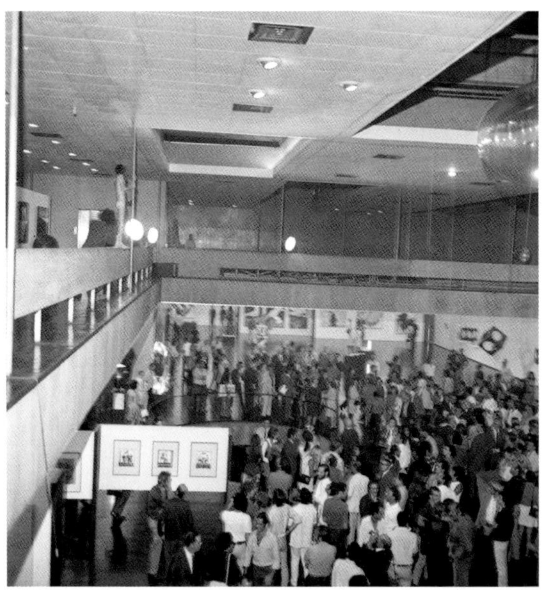
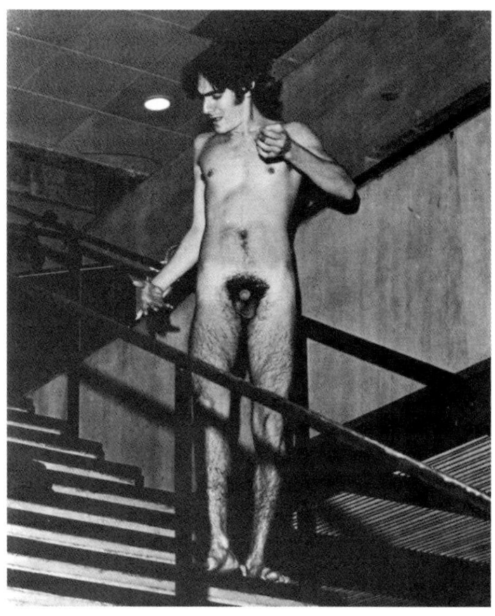
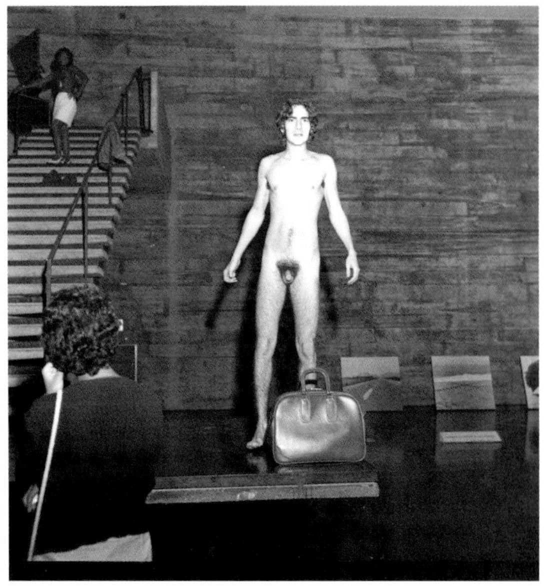
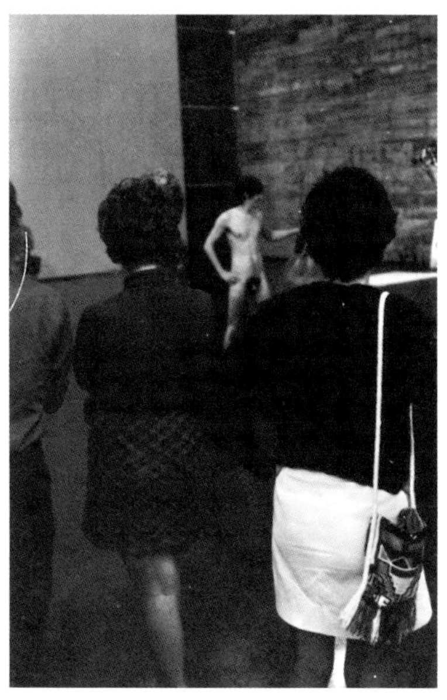

O corpo é a obra (The Body Is the Work), 1970. C-Prints. Courtesy the artist

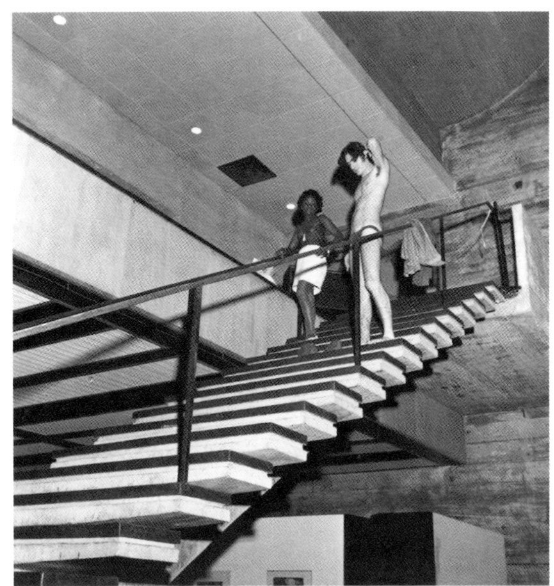 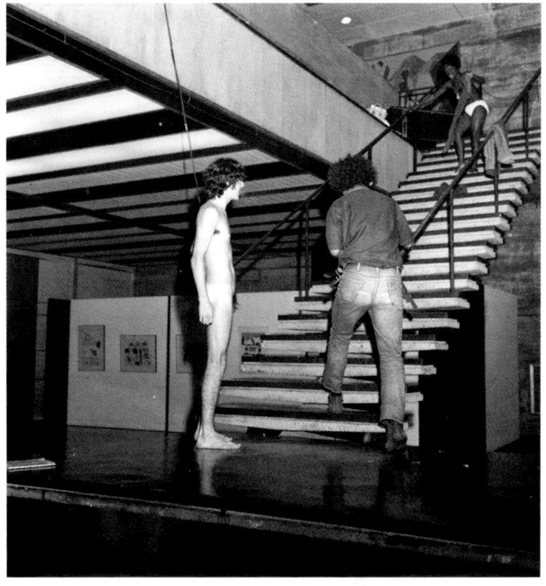

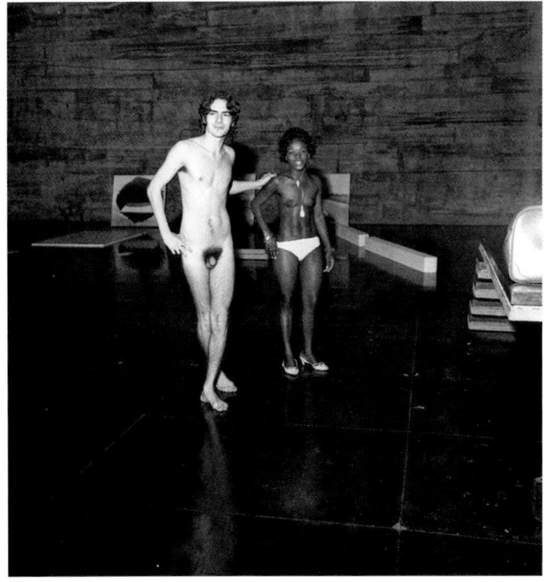 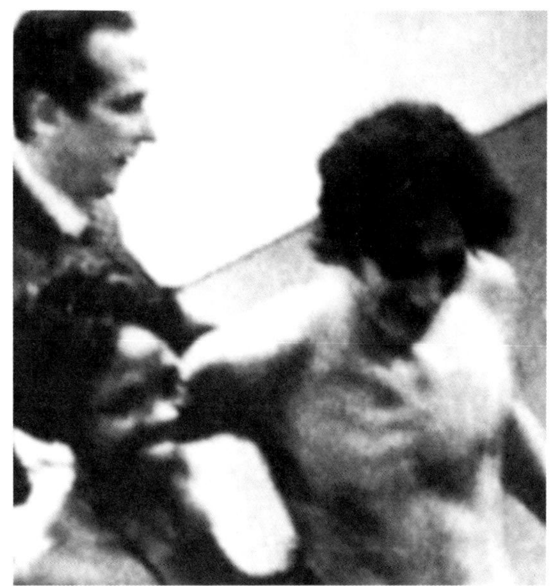

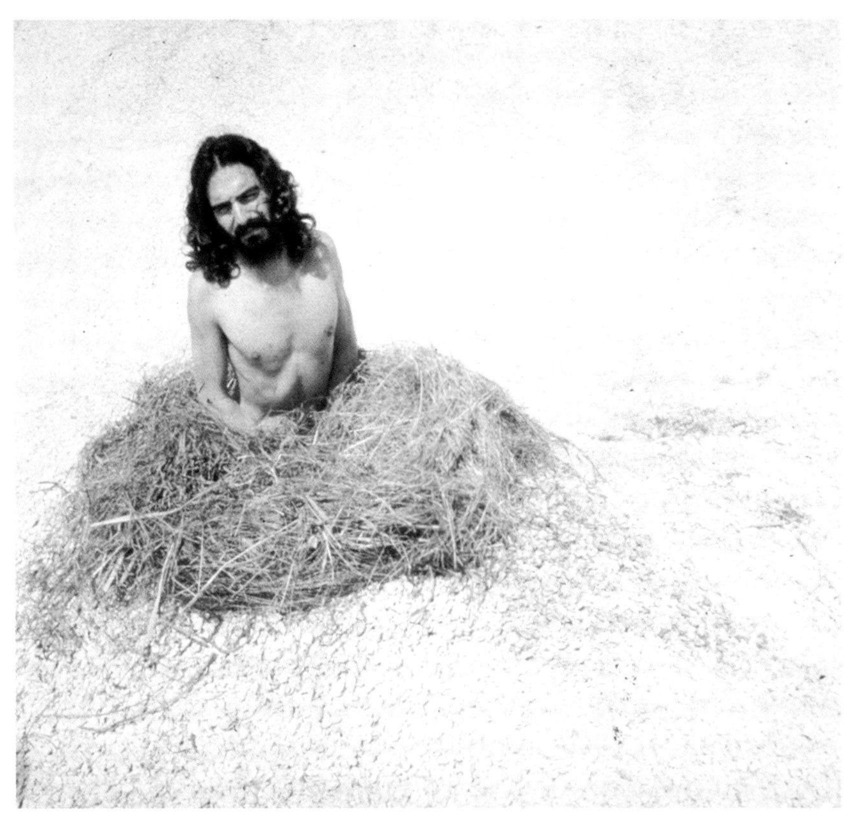

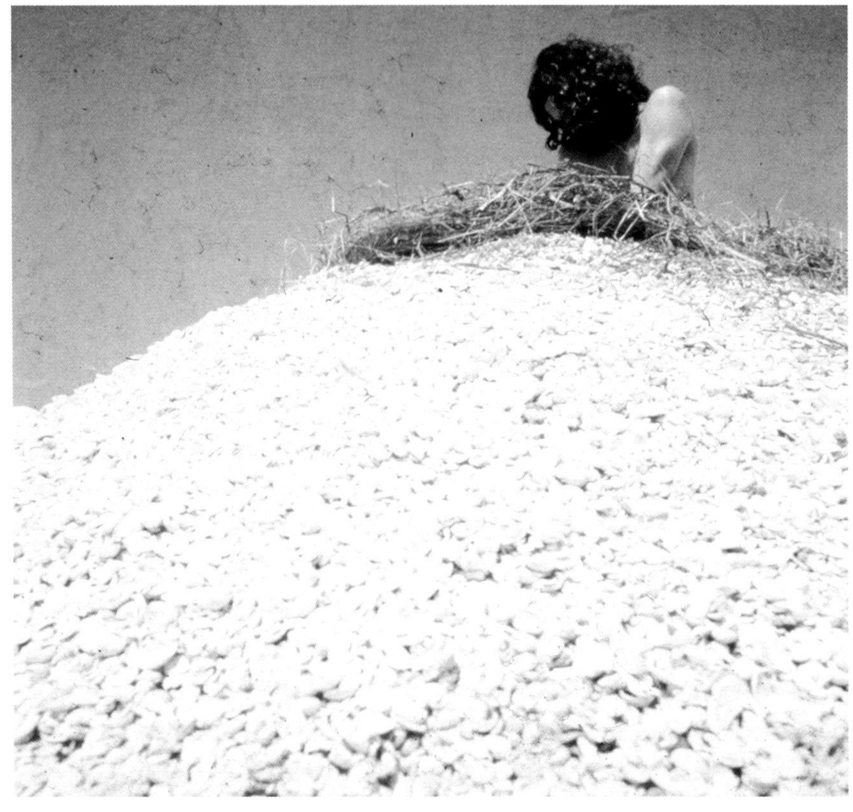

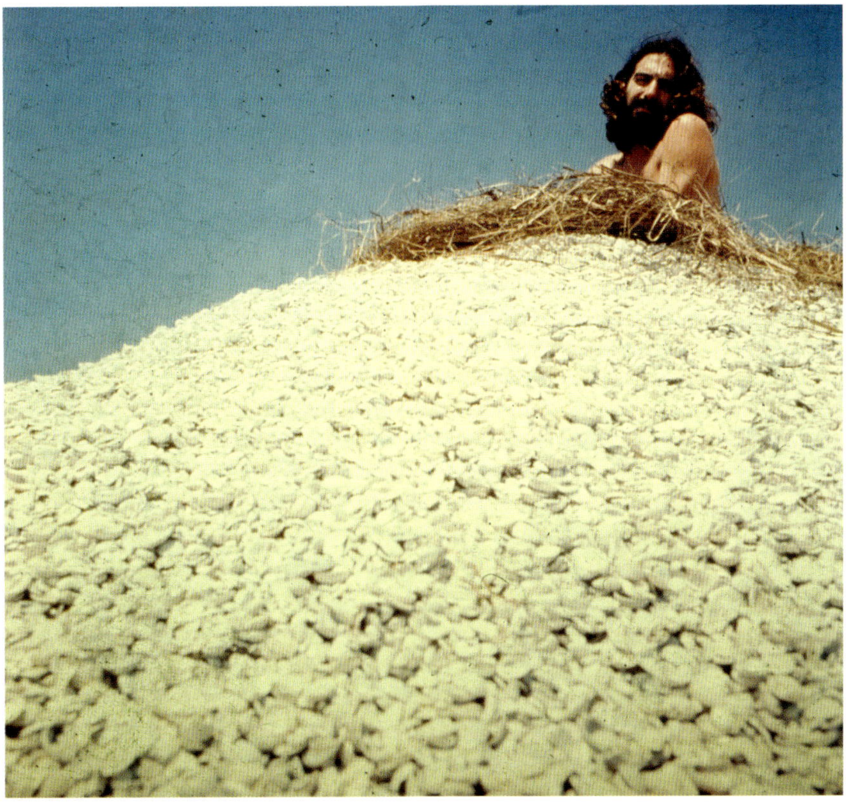

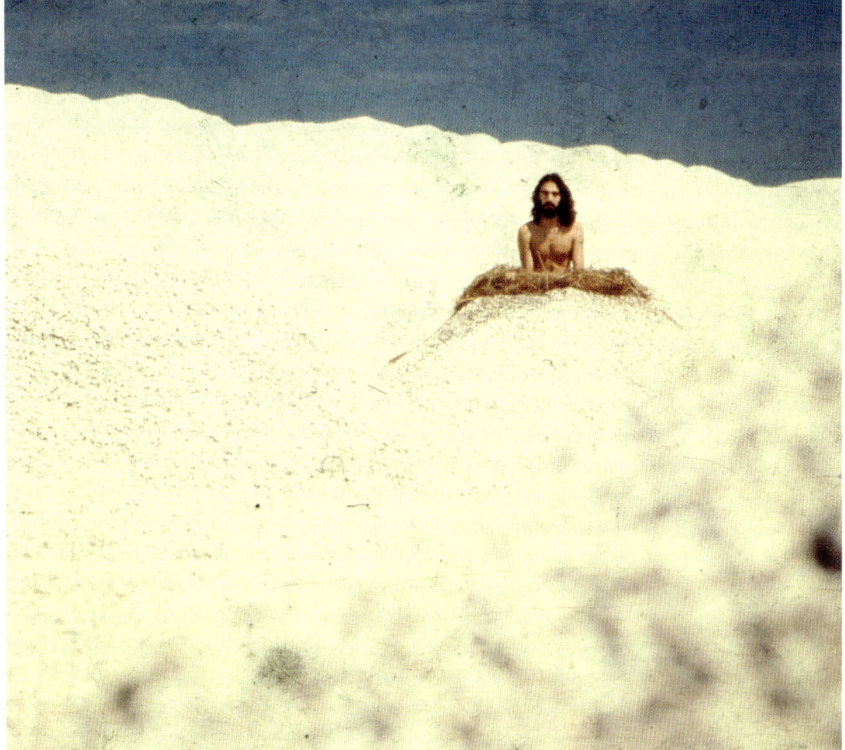

The Cock, 1972. C-Prints (set of 6), 19.5 x 16 in each. Courtesy the artist

Poema classificado (Classified Poem), 1975. From the *Flan* series, ink on papier-mâché stereotype mold, 22 x 15 in. Courtesy the artist

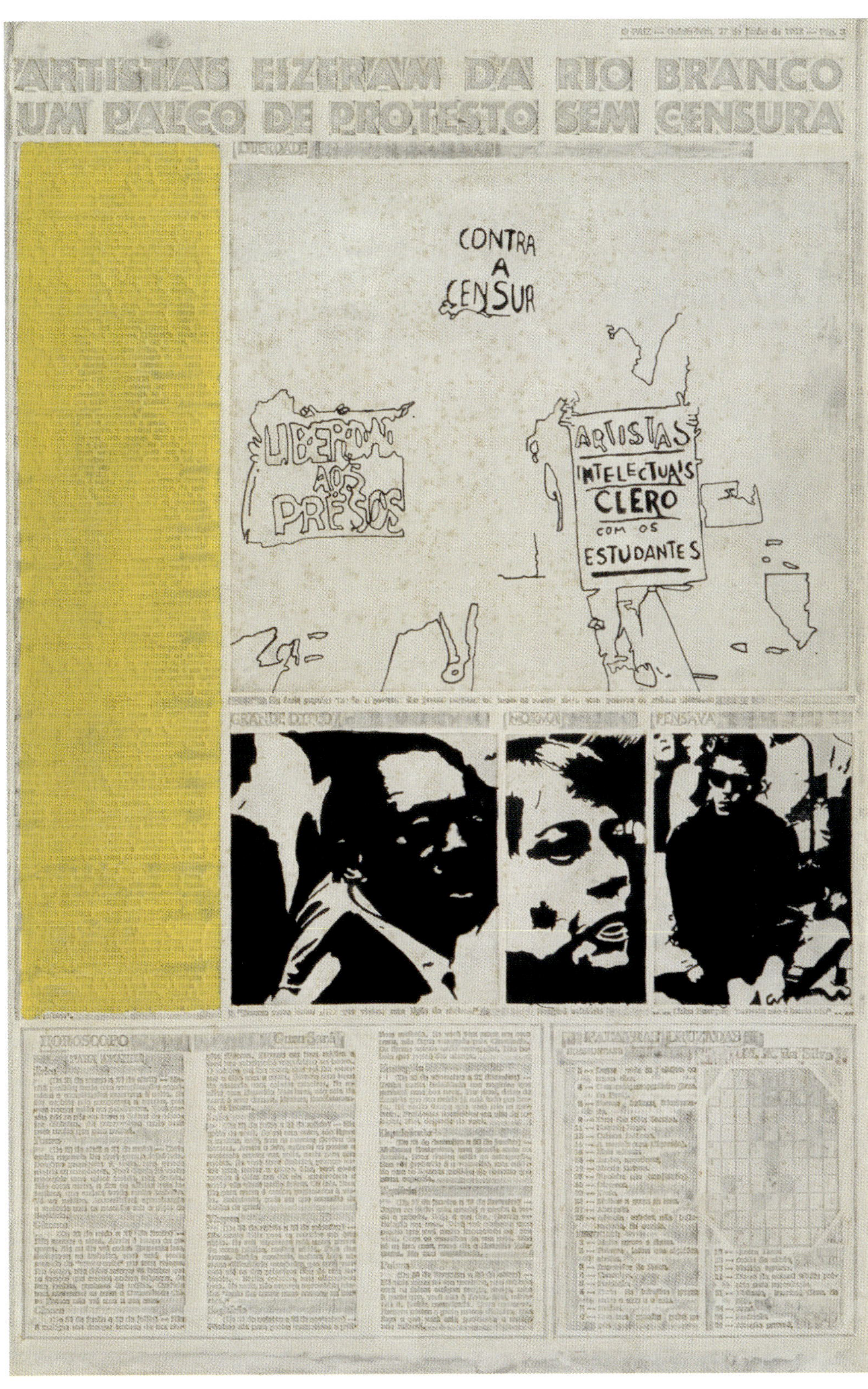

Sem censura (Uncensored), 1975. From the *Flan* series, ink on papier-mâché stereotype mold, 22 x 15 in.
Courtesy the artist

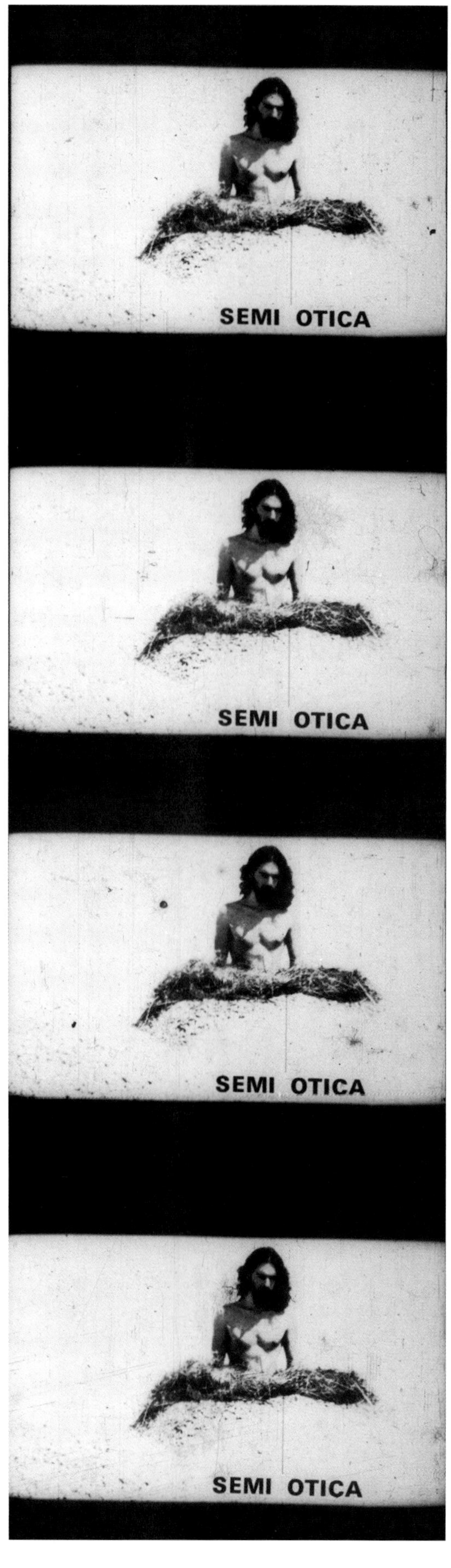

  Stills from *Semi Ótica* (Semi Otic/Optic), 1975. B&W, with sound, 35 mm, 7 minutes. Courtesy the artist

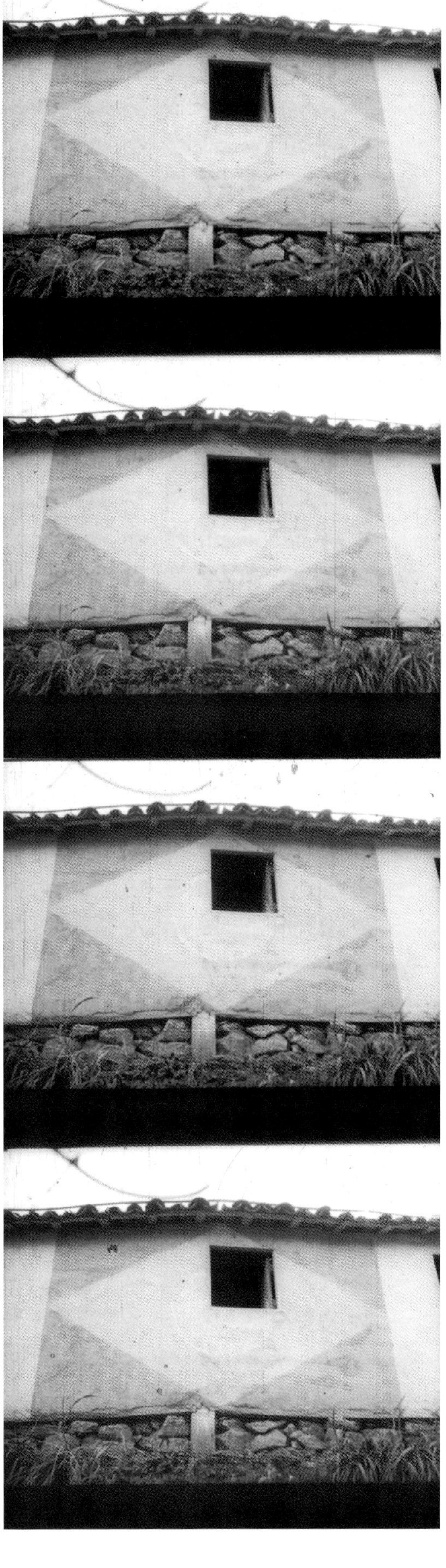

ANTONIO MANUEL: ARTIST'S TIMELINE

COMPILED BY NATALIE BUNNELL AND THEODORA DOULAMIS

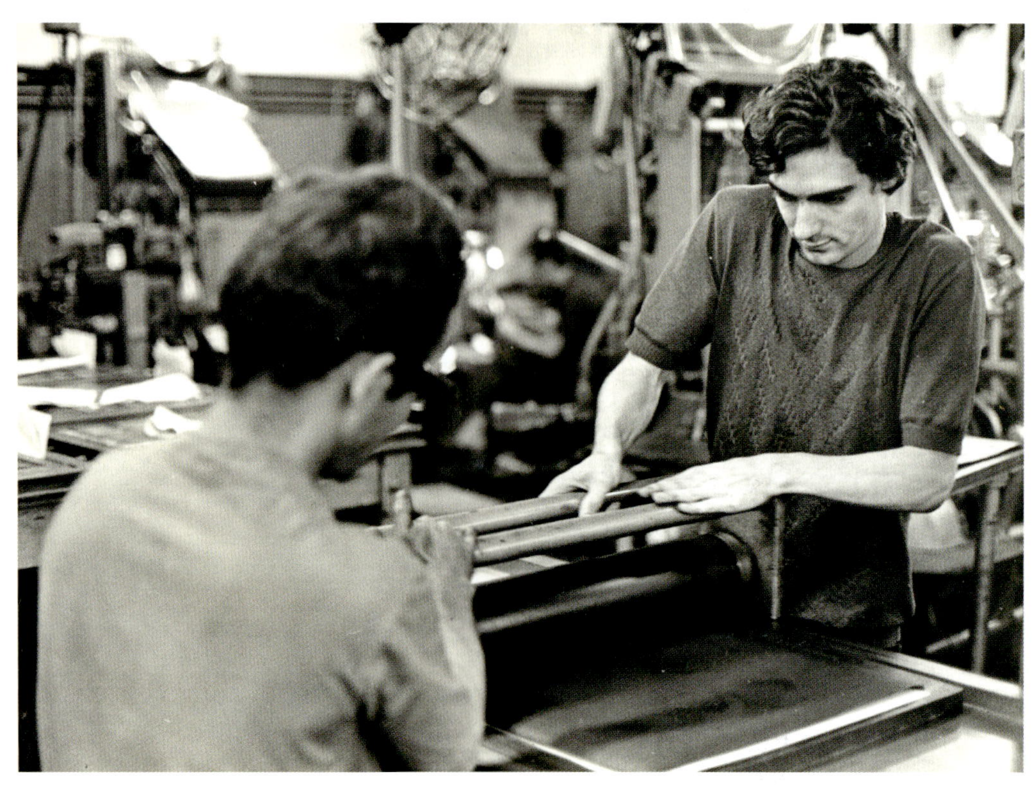

Antonio Manuel making a proof at the offices of *Jornal do Brasil*. Courtesy Antonio Manuel

1947
Born October 22 in Avelãs de Caminho, Portugal.

1953
Moves to Rio de Janeiro, Brazil.

1963
Begins drawing while working at an advertising agency.

1963–1966
Attends Escola Nacional de Belas Artes, Rio de Janeiro.

1965
Begins work at Ivan Serpa's studio. Serpa was a founding member of the *Grupo Frente*, an experimental group of artists who played a key role in Brazilian Constructivism and laid the foundations for Conceptualism and Geometric Abstraction.

1966
Exhibits drawings in crayon on newsprint paper at *I Bienal Nacional de Artes Plásticas*, Bahia, organized by Riolan Coutinho, Harry Laus, Juarez Paraíso, Mário Pedrosa and Clarival do Prado Valladares.

1967
First solo exhibition at Goeldi Gallery, Rio de Janeiro.

Awarded acquisition prize at *IX Bienal de São Paulo*.

Participates in *Tropicália* installation works *Penetrable - PN2* and *Penetrable - PN3* by Hélio Oiticica in the exhibition *Nova objetividade brasileira* (New Brazilian Objectivity), at Museu de Arte Moderna, Rio de Janeiro.

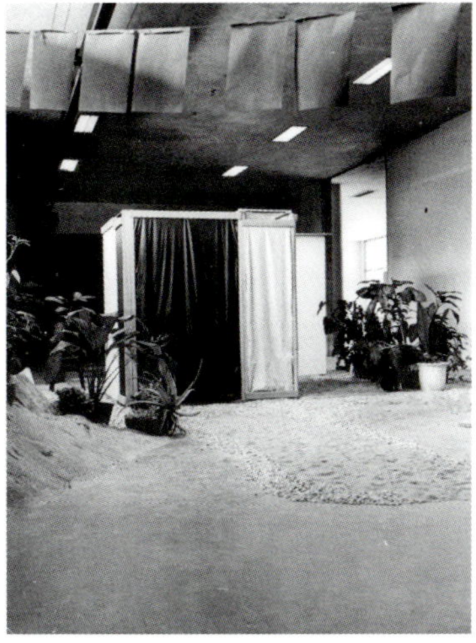

Installation view of Hélio Oiticica's *Tropicália*, 1967. Courtesy Projeto Hélio Oiticica

1968
Produces series of black and white *Flans*, based on stereotype molds; papier-mâché imprints taken from the surface of type formes, used for printing newspaper at the time.

Produces *Urnas quentes* (Hot Ballot Boxes), the first version of the work, and presents it at *Apocalipopótese* (Apocalypothesis), a collaborative art event organized by artist Hélio Oiticica and designer Rogério Duarte held at Frederico Morais's *Arte no Aterro: um mês de arte pública* (Art at Aterro: A Month of Public Art), Aterro do Flamengo, Rio de Janeiro.

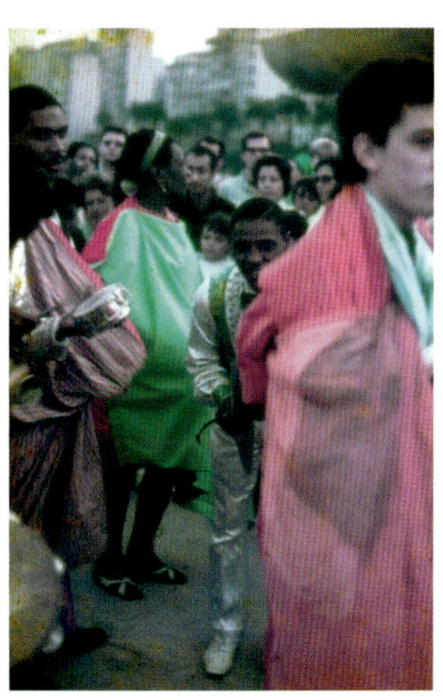

Installation view of *Apocalipopótese* (Apocalypopothesis) with Torquato Neto and Mangueira dancers, 1968. Courtesy Projeto Hélio Oiticica

1968 (CONTINUED)

Exhibits in *II Bienal Nacional de Artes Plásticas*, Bahia. The Biennial is later shut down by the Brazilian military police.

1969

Awarded acquisition prize at *Salão da Bússola* (Compass Salon), Museu de Arte Moderna, Rio de Janeiro, by Salon jury composed of Walmir Ayala, Frederico Morais, and Mário Schenberg. Brazilian artists boycott the X Bienal de São Paulo making the Compass Salon their default artistic forum. The boycott garners international attention and support.

Repressão outra vez – Eis o saldo (Repression Once Again – Here is the Outcome), shown at an exhibition of pre-selected works for the *VI Biennale de Paris* at Museu de Arte Moderna, Rio de Janeiro. Exhibition shut down by the military regime and Brazilian participation in Paris is canceled.

1970

Performs, *O corpo é a obra* (The Body Is the Work), at Museu de Arte Moderna, Rio de Janeiro. The artist removes his clothing in protest of governmental censorship and conservative institutional policies.

Conceives *A arma fálica* (A Phallic Weapon), in collaboration with Lygia Pape including photographs by Kiko (Marcos Lins Andrade, Lygia Clark's nephew). The *fotonovela*, later designed by Luciano Figueiredo, would not be printed until 1995.

1972

Completes *By Antonio*, Antonio Manuel's first 16mm, black and white, 2:56 minute short-film.

1973

Produces *Clandestinas* (Clandestines), a series of newspaper interventions.

Produces *Loucura & Cultura* (Madness & Culture), a 35 mm, black and white, 9:14 minute film, featuring friends and fellow artists Rogério Duarte, Hélio Oiticica, Lygia Pape, Luiz Carlos Saldanha and Caetano Veloso.

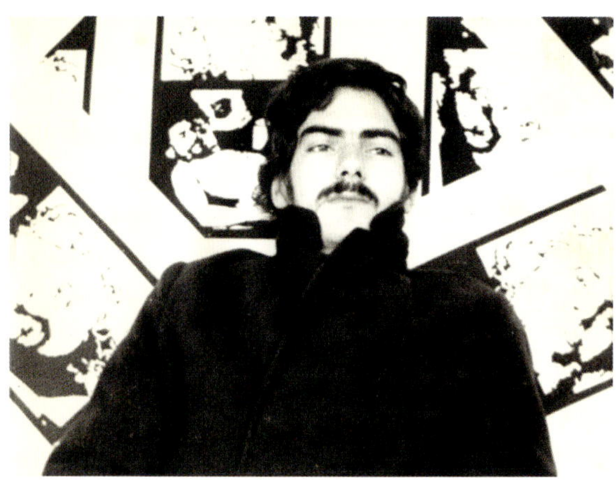

Antonio Manuel standing in front of *Guevara,* 1967–8. Courtesy the artist

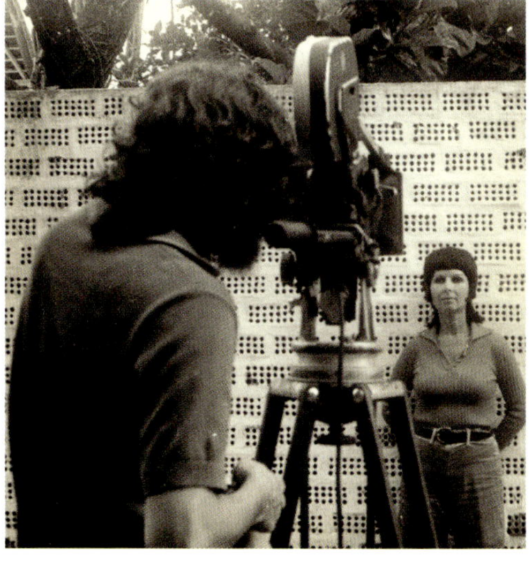

Production image of Antonio Manuel and Lygia Pape from *Loucura & Cultura* (Madness & Culture), 1973. B&W with sound, 10 minutes, 35mm. Courtesy the artist

1973 (CONTINUED)
Proposed solo exhibition cancelled by
Museu de Arte Moderna, Rio de Janeiro.

Produces *Antonio Manuel Exposição – De
0 à 24 horas* (Exhibition of Antonio Manuel
from 0 to 24 Hours). Antonio Manuel
reproduces the artwork from his canceled
solo exhibition as a six-page supplement
to the newspaper *O Jornal*.

1975
Produces color *Flans*, the second in a
series based on stereo-mold imprints.

Solo exhibition, *Isso é que é* (This Is What
it Is), at Petite Galerie, Rio de Janeiro.

1976
Completes *Uma parada* (A Halt / A
Parade), a 16mm, black and white, 5:48
minute film.

Completes *Arte hoje, Histórias verídicas*
(Art Today, True Stories), a 16mm, black
and white, 14:14 minute film.

Semi Ótica (Semi Otics/Optics), a 35 mm,
black and white, 5:00 minute short film,
entered in *XXXVII Biennale di Venezia*
organized by Vittorio Gregotti and Franco
Raggi.

1980
Solo exhibition of sculpture installation,
Frutos do espaço (Fruits of Space), at
Espaço de Arte Brasileira Contemporânea,
Parque da Catacumba, Rio de Janeiro.

Participates in *Quasi cinema: (video tapes
e film d'artisti in Brasile 70/80)* (Quasi
Cinema: Videotapes and Film by Artists in
Brazil 70/80), at Centro Internazionale di
Brera, Milan.

1982
Participates in the group exhibition, *Brazil:
60 Years of Modern Art – Gilberto
Chateaubriand Collection*, organized by
Wilson Coutinho at Fundação Calouste
Gulbenkian, Lisbon, and Barbican Art
Gallery, London.

1984
Wins research grant from Fundação Nacional
de Artes (Funarte), resulting in the publication of the monograph *Antonio Manuel.*
Authors include Ronaldo Brito, Antonio
Manuel, Frederico Morais, Hélio Oiticica
and Mário Pedrosa.

Participates in the group exhibition
Homenagem a Mário Pedrosa (Homage
to Mário Pedrosa), at Museu de Arte
Moderna, Rio de Janeiro.

1991
Participates in the group exhibition *Mário
Pedrosa – arte, revolução, reflexão* (Mário
Pedrosa – Art, Revolution, Reflection),
organized by Franklin Pedroso and Pedro
Vasquez at Centro Cultural Banco do
Brasil, Rio de Janeiro.

1993
Participates in the group exhibition, *Brasil,
segni d'arte. Libri e video 1950–1993*
(Brazil, Signs of Art. Books and Video
1950–1993), organized by Lucilla Saccà
at Biblioteca Braidense, Milan; Biblioteca
Nazionale, Florence; Palazzo Pamphili,
Rome; and Centro Cultural Banco do Brasil,
Rio de Janeiro.

Participates in the group exhibition,
*Emblemas do corpo – o nu na arte
brasileira* (Emblems of the Body – The
Nude in Brazilian Art), organized by
Franklin Pedroso at Centro Cultural
Banco do Brasil, Rio de Janeiro.

1994

Fantasma (Ghost), the installation, shown at Instituto Brasil-Estados Unidos Gallery, Rio de Janeiro.

1995

A arma fálica, designed and printed by Luciano Figueiredo. This *fotonovela* was conceived in 1970 in collaboration with Lygia Pape and includes photographs by Kiko.

1997

Solo exhibition organized by Ronaldo Brito at Centro de Arte Hélio Oiticica, Rio de Janeiro.

Participates in the group exhibition, *Re-aligning Vision: Alternative Currents in South American Drawing*, organized by Mari Carmen Ramírez and Edith Gibson Wolfe at El Museo del Barrio, New York; Arkansas Art Center, Little Rock; Archer M. Huntington Art Gallery, Austin; and El Museo de Bellas Artes de Caracas.

Participates in the group exhibition, *ARTECINEMA: anos 60/70 – filmes experimentais/filmes de artistas plásticos* (ARTCINEMA: Years 60/70 – Experimental Films/Films by Visual Artists), organized by Gloria Ferreira and Ligia Canongia at Centro Cultural Banco do Brasil, Rio de Janeiro.

1998

Solo exhibition, *Ocupações/Descobrimentos* (Occupations/Discoveries), organized by Luiz Camillo Osório at Museu de Arte Contemporânea, Niterói.

Fantasma, the installation, shown at *XXIV Bienal de São Paulo*, organized by Paulo Herkenhoff.

1999

Fantasma, the installation, shown at Galerie Nationale Jeu de Paume, Paris.

Participates in the group exhibition, *Circa 1968*, organized by Vicente Todolí and João Fernandes, at Fundação Serralves, Porto, Portugal.

Participates in the group exhibition, *Global Conceptualism: Points of Origin 1950– 1980*, organized by Luis Camnitzer, Jane Farver and Rachel Weiss at Queens Museum of Art, New York; Walker Art Center, Minneapolis; and Miami Art Museum, Miami.

2000

Solo exhibition, *Antonio Manuel*, organized by João Fernandes at Fundação Serralves, Porto, Portugal.

Participates in the group exhibition, *Heterotopías: medio siglo sin lugar* (Heterotopias: Mid-Century Nowhere), organized by Héctor Ólea and Mari Carmen Ramírez at Museo Centro de Arte Reina Sofía, Madrid.

2001

Participates in the group exhibition, *Experiment/Experiência: Art in Brazil, 1958–2000*, organized by Nelson Aguilar and Astrid Bowron at Museum of Modern Art, Oxford.

Participates in the group exhibition, *Brazil Body & Soul*, organized by Edward J. Sullivan and Nelson Aguilar, at Solomon R. Guggenheim Museum, New York, and Guggenheim Bilbao.

2003

Sucessão de fatos (Sequence of Facts), the installation, shown at the Centro Cultural, São Paulo, by invitation of Roberto Conduru, Célia Euvaldo, Ricardo Resende, Stella Teixeira de Barros.

2004

Participates in the group exhibition, *Beyond Geometry: Experiments in Form, 1940s–70s*, organized by Lynn Zelevansky at Los Angeles County Museum of Art and Miami Art Museum.

Participates in the group exhibition, *Inverted Utopias: Avant-garde Art in Latin America*, organized by Héctor Ólea and Mari Carmen Ramírez at The Museum of Fine Arts, Houston.

2005

Solo exhibition, *Antonio Manuel,* organized by Michael Asbury at Pharos Center for Contemporary Art, Nicosia, Cyprus.

Participates in the group exhibition, *O corpo na arte contemporânea brasileira* (The Body in Contemporary Brazilian Art), organized by Fernando Cocchiarale and Viviane Matesco at Itaú Cultural, São Paulo.

2006

Participates in *Espaço aberto/Espaço fechado – Sites for Sculpture in Modern Brazil*, an exhibition and conference organized by Stephen Feeke at The Henry Moore Institute, Leeds, United Kingdom.

2007

Solo exhibition, *Fatos: Antonio Manuel* (Facts: Antonio Manuel), organized by Paulo Venancio Filho at Centro Cultural Banco do Brasil, São Paulo.

2008

Participates in the group exhibition, *Arte ≠ Vida: Actions by Artists of the Americas, 1960–2000*, organized by Deborah Cullen at El Museo del Barrio, New York.

2010

Participates in the group exhibition, *Río experimental: Más allá del arte, el poema y la acción* (Experimental Rio: Beyond Art, Poem and Action), organized by Mónica Carballas at Fundación Marcelino Botín, Santander, Spain.

Exhibits in *XXIX Bienal de São Paulo*, organized by Agnaldo Farias and Moacir dos Anjos.

2011

Solo exhibition, *Antonio Manuel: I Want to Act, Not Represent!*, organized at Americas Society, New York, co-curated by Claudia Calirman and Gabriela Rangel.

Participates in the group exhibition, *Ordem e progresso: vontade construtiva na arte brasileira* (Order and Progress: Constructive Will in Brazilian Art), organized by Felipe Chaimovich at Museu de Arte Moderna, São Paulo.

Exhibits in *Europalia.Brasil: The Diversity of Brasil in the Heart of Europe*, organized by Ronaldo Brito, Guilherme Bueno, Vanda Klabin and Sonia Salcedo at Palais des Beaux-Arts, Brussels.

BIBLIOGRAPHY

XXIV Bienal de São Paulo – Arte contemporânea brasileira: um e/ entre outro/s. São Paulo: Fundação Bienal de São Paulo, 1998. Exhibition catalogue.

A fronteira dos vazios – Livro objeto. Rio de Janeiro: Centro Cultural Banco do Brasil, 1994. Exhibition catalogue.

Aguilar, Nelson, Astrid Bowron, and Paulo Venancio Filho. *Experiment = Experiência: Art in Brazil, 1958–2000.* Oxford: Museum of Modern Art, Oxford, 2001. Exhibition catalogue.

Alphonsus, Luiz, and Ligia Canongia. *Arte foto.* Rio de Janeiro: Centro Cultural Banco do Brasil, 2002.

Alvarado, Daisy Valle Machado Peccinini de, ed. *Objeto na arte: Brasil anos 60.* São Paulo: FAAP, 1978.

Alves, Cauê, Felipe Soeiro Chaimovich, and Tadeu Chiarelli. *MAM(na)OCA: Arte brasileira do acervo do Museu de Arte Moderna de São Paulo.* São Paulo: Museu de Arte Moderna de São Paulo, 2006.

Americana II- Antonio Manuel. Paris: Éditions du Jeu de Paume, 1998. Exhibition catalogue.

Antonio Manuel. Rio de Janeiro: Fundação Nacional de Arte, MEC / Secretaria de Cultura, 1985.

"Antonio Manuel/ Portfolio." *Concinnitas, Revista do Instituto de Artes da Uerj,* 4, no. 5 (December 2003).

Arnaud, Raquel. *Raquel Arnaud e o olhar contemporâneo.* São Paulo: Cosac Naify, 2005.

Arte brasileira – os anos sessenta e setenta – Coleção Gilberto Chateaubriand. Salvador: Museu de Arte Moderna da Bahia, 1976. Exhibition catalogue.

ArteCinema anos 60/70: filmes experimentais / filmes de artistas plásticos. Rio de Janeiro: Centro Cultural Banco do Brasil, 1997. Exhibition catalogue.

Arte Hoje: XVII salão de arte de Ribeirão Preto. Ribeirão Preto: 1988. Exhibition catalogue.

Artequeune diversidade & confluência Brasil/ Europa. Brasília: Museu de Arte de Brasília / Secretaria do Estado da Cultura, 2003.

Asbury, Michael. "Two Accounts on Art in Brazil from the 50s to the 60s." Paper presented at *International Perspectives on Brazilian Sculpture,* Henry Moore Institute, Leeds, March 10, 2006.

Asbury, Michael, and Garo Keheyan. *Antonio Manuel.* Nicosia: Pharos, 2006.

Ayala, Walmir. "Arte usada ou abusada?" *Jornal do Brasil,* July 3, 1968.

————. "Salão dos Etc." *Jornal do Brasil,* October 28, 1969.

Bento, Antonio. "Dadá no Salão Moderno." *Última Hora,* May 22, 1970.

————. "O Jornal de Antonio Manuel." *Última Hora,* November 9, 1967.

Bienal Nacional de Artes Plásticas. Salvador: 1966. Exhibition catalogue.

La Biennale di Venezia: General Catalogue, vol. 2. Venice: Ed. La Biennale di Venezia, 1976. Exhibition catalogue.

Bittencourt, Francisco. "Entrevista de Antonio Manuel a Francisco Bittencourt." *Vida Das Artes* (Porto Alegre), December 13, 1975.

————. "O revolucionário Antonio Manuel." *Correio do Povo,* November 30, 1975.

Boardman Carneiro, Maria Lúcia, Antonio Manuel, and Ileana Pradilla. *Antonio Manuel: Entrevista a Lúcia Carneiro e Ileana Pradilla.* Rio de Janeiro: Lacerda / Secretaria Municipal de Cultura do Rio de Janeiro, 1999.

Böhm, Heide, and Peter Möller. *Configura 2: Dialog der Kulturen, Texte und Bilder zur Ausstellung.* Erfurt: Configura-Projekt, 1995.

Brett, Guy, Katia Maciel, and Renato Rezende. *Brasil experimental: Arte/vida, proposições e paradoxos.* Rio de Janeiro: Contra Capa, 2005.

Brett, Guy, Ronaldo Brito, João Fernandes, Paulo Herkenhoff, Hélio Oiticica, Roberto Pontual, and Vicente Todolí. *Antonio Manuel.* Porto: Museu de Arte Contemporânea de Serralves, 2000. Exhibition catalogue.

Brett, Guy, and Paulo Venancio Filho. *Antonio Manuel: Fatos.* Translated by Renato Rezende. São Paulo: Centro Cultural Banco do Brasil, 2007. Exhibition catalogue.

Brito, Ronaldo. *Antonio Manuel.* Rio de Janeiro: Centro de Arte Hélio Oiticica, 1997. Exhibition catalogue.

————. *Fluido labirinto.* São Paulo: Gabinete de Arte Raquel Arnaud, 1999. Exhibition catalogue.

————. *Harmonia dos contrários.* Rio de Janeiro: HAP Galeria, 2004. Exhibition catalogue.

————. "Jornais do espaço – esculturas de Antonio Manuel." *Módulo* (January–February 1981): 46–8.

————. *Os gestos de Manuel.* São Paulo: Cosac & Naify, 2005.

————. "Experiência crítica." *Opinão,* November 14, 1975.

Brito, Ronaldo, Antonio Manuel, Frederico Morais, Hélio Oiticica, and Mário Pedrosa. *Antonio Manuel.* Rio de Janeiro: Funarte / Instituto Nacional de Artes Plásticas, 1984.

Bueno, Guilherme, ed. *Antonio Manuel/ Eis o saldo: Textos, depoimentos e entrevistas de Antonio Manuel.* Rio de Janeiro: Funarte, 2010.

Calirman, Claudia. *Brazilian Art under Dictatorship: Antonio Manuel, Artur Barrio, and Cildo Meireles.* Durham, NC, and London: Duke University Press, forthcoming (2012).

————. "Naked Man, Flaming Chickens: A Brief History of Brazilian Performance Art." From *Arte ≠ Vida: Actions by Artists of the Americas 1960–2000,* 102–13. Edited by Deborah Cullen. New York: El Museo del Barrio, 2008. Exhibition catalogue.

Camnitzer, Luis. *Conceptualism in Latin American Art: Didactics of Liberation.* Austin: University of Texas, 2007.

Camnitzer, Luis, Jane Faver and Rachel Weiss. *Global Conceptualism: Points of Origin, 1950s–1980s.* New York: Queens Museum of Art, 1999. Exhibition catalogue.

Campofiorito, Quirino. "A arte 'flanante' de Antonio Manuel." *O Jornal* (Rio de Janeiro), November 22, 1967.

————. "O futuro pertence à mocidade." *O Jornal* (Rio de Janeiro), April 23, 1968.

Canejo, Cynthia Marie. "Antonio Manuel: A Dialectical Response to Brazilian Developments in Modern Art." M.A. Thesis, University of California Santa Barbara, 1998.

————. "Gestos efêmeros e obras tangíveis." *Novos Estudos – CEBRAP* 76 (November 2006).

Canongia, Ligia. *Quase Cinema – Cinema de artista no Brasil 1970/80.* Rio de Janeiro: Funarte, 1981.

Carballas, Monica. *Río Experimental. Más allá del arte, el poema y la acción.* Santander: Fundación Marcelino Botín, 2010. Exhibition catalogue.

Carneiro, Lucía and Ileana Pradilla. *Antonio Manuel – entrevista.* Rio de Janiero: Lacerda / Centro de Arte Hélio Olticica / Secretaria Municipal de Cultura do Rio de Janeiro, 1999.

Cavalcanti, Lauro, Luciano Figueiredo, and Mônica Almeida Kornis. *Caminhos do contemporâneo: Paço Imperial.* Rio de Janeiro: Eventual, 2002.

Coehlo, Teixeira, ed. *Coleção Itaú Contemporâneo – arte no Brasil, 1981–2006.* São Paulo: Itaú Cultural, 2006.

Coleção Gilberto Chateaubriand: O desenho moderno no Brasil. Rio de Janeiro: Museu de Arte Moderna do Rio de Janeiro / Serviço Social da Indústria (SESI), 1993.

O Corpo na arte contemporânea brasileira. São Paulo: Itaú Cultural, 2005. Exhibition catalogue.

Costa, Eduardo, and Luiz Camillo Osório. "Antonio Manuel at the Centro Hélio Oiticica." *Art in America* 87, no. 3 (March 1999): 126.

Coutinho, Wilson. "Antonio Manuel, ações radicais." *Jornal do Brasil* (Rio de Janeiro), March 12, 1985.

————. "Antonio Manuel: 'é possível fazer uma revolução com as cores.'" *Jornal do Brasil* (Rio de Janeiro), March 29, 1983.

Doctors, Marcio, and José Mindlin. *Livro-objeto: A fronteira dos vazios.* Rio de Janeiro: Centro Cultural Banco do Brasil, 1994.

Duarte, Paulo Sérgio. *Arte brasileira contemporânea: Um prelúdio.* São Paulo: Silvia Roesler, 2008. Exhibition catalogue.

————. *Da escultura à instalação.* Porto Alegre: V Bienal do Mercosul, 2005. Exhibition catalogue.

————. *Formas transitivas: Arte brasileira; construção e invenção 1970/1998.* São Paulo: Gabiente de Arte Raquel Arnaud, 1998. Exhibition catalogue.

————. *Anos 60: transformações da arte no Brasil = The '60s: Transformations of Art in Brazil.* Rio de Janeiro: Campos Gerais, 1998.

É hoje na arte brasileira contemporânea: Coleção Gilberto Chateaubriand. Porto Alegre: Santander Banespa, 2006. Exhibition catalogue.

Ecoart. Rio de Janeiro: Spala, 1992.

Emblemas do corpo: O nu na arte moderna brasileira. Rio de Janeiro: Banco do Brasil / O Centro Cultural, 1993. Exhibition catalogue.

Fantasma. Rio de Janeiro: Galleria do Instituto Brasil-Estados Unidos, 1994. Exhibition catalogue.

Feeke, Stephen. "Espaço aberto / espaço fechado – Sites for Sculpture in Modern Brazil." Paper presented at *International Perspectives on Brazilian Sculpture,* Henry Moore Institute, Leeds, March 10, 2006.

Ferreira, Gloria, ed. *Wilton Montenegro: Notas do observatório – Arte contemporânea brasileira.* Rio de Janeiro: Centro Cultura Telemar, 2006.

Freitas, Artur. "Arte e Movimento Estudantil: Análise de uma Obra de Antonio Manuel." *Revista Braileira de História* 25, no. 49 (January–June 2005), 77–97.

————. "A pop art brasileira contra a ditadura: a arte de vanguarda e a resistência poética de Antonio Manuel." *Revista de História* 15 (2006).

Frutos do Espaço. Rio de Janeiro: Espaço Arte Brasileira Contemporânea, 1980. Exhibition catalogue.

Gullar, Ferreira. "É ferro na boneca." *O Pasquim,* May 28, 1970.

Herkenhoff, Paulo. *Fotografia brasileira contemporânea – espessura da luz.* São Paulo: Câmara Brasileira do Livro, 1994.

Hillings, Valerie L., and Lynn Zelevansky. *Beyond Geometry: Experiments in Form, 1940s–70s.* Cambridge: Massachusetts Institute of Technology Press, 2004.

IBEU, 60 anos. Copacabana: Galeria IBEU Copacabana / Instituto Brasil-Estados Unidos, 1997. Exhibition catalogue.

Lagnado, Lisette. "Telas de Manuel evocam o tema da violência." *Folha de São Paulo,* October 25, 1990.

Lins de Magalhaes, Marcelo. "Antonio Manuel: Arte em jornal." PhD diss., Pontifícia Universidade Católica do Rio de Janeiro, 2005.

Machado, Milton. "Power to the Imagination: Art in the 1970s and Other Brazilian Miracles." Paper presented at *International Perspectives on Brazilian Sculpture,* Henry Moore Institute, Leeds, March 10, 2006.

Manuel, Antonio. "O corpo é a obra." *Item 4* (November 1996): 30–33.

Marra, Heloísa. "A multiarte de Antonio Manuel." *O Globo,* June 10, 2000.

Martel, Richard, ed. *Art Action 1958–1998.* Quebec: Intervention, 2001. Exhibition catalogue.

Martins, Luiz Renato. "A situação da arte e o 'pensamento único.'" *Margem Esquerda Ensaios Marxistas* 5 (2005).

Morais, Frederico. "Antonio Manuel: 'meus desenhos são a expressão de uma revolta.'" *Diário de Notícias,* March 23, 1968.

————. "Antonio Manuel, tudo existe na sua pintura." *O Globo,* May 5, 1986.

————. "Antonio Manuel: velar, des-velar, re-velar." *O Globo,* January 14, 1976.

————. "Arte Brasil hoje – Guanabara." *Revista de Cultura Vozes* 64, no. 9 (November 1970): 701–9.

————. "O vazio ocupado pelos frutos do espaço." *O Globo,* March 28, 1983.

————. "Três exposições." *Diário de Notícias,* March 16, 1967.

Museu de Arte Contemporânea de Niterói: General Catalogue. Rio de Janeiro: Museu de Arte Contemporânea de Niterói, 1996.

Ólea, Héctor, and Mari Carmen Ramírez. *Heterotopías: Medio siglo sin-lugar, 1918–1968.* Madrid: Museo Nacional Centro de Arte Reina Sofía, 2000.

Osório, Luiz Camillo. *Antonio Manuel, Artur Barrio: Ocupaçoes: descobrimentos.* Niterói: Museu de Arte Contemporânea, 1998. Exhibition catalogue.

Pedroso, Franklin, and Pedro Vasquez. *Mário Pedrosa: Arte, revolução, reflexão.* Rio de Janeiro: Centro Cultural Banco do Brasil, 1992.

Pereira Rego, Norma. "Arte de vanguarda foi golpeada?" *Última Hora* (Rio de Janeiro), December 5, 1969.

Pignatari, Décio. "Antonio Manuel: The Cock of the Golden Eggs." From *Semiótica e Literatura – Debates Semiótica,* 165–166. São Paulo: Perspectiva, 1974.

Pontual, Roberto. *Arte brasileira contemporânea. Coleção Gilberto Chateaubriand.* Translated by John Knox and Florence Eleanor Irvin. Rio de Janeiro: Jornal do Brasil, 1976.

————. *Arte Brasileira no Século XX.* Rio de Janeiro: JB, 1987.

————. "De uma arte/ corpo por um corpo/ arte." *Revista de Cultura* Vozes 65, no. 1 (January–February 1971): 73–74.

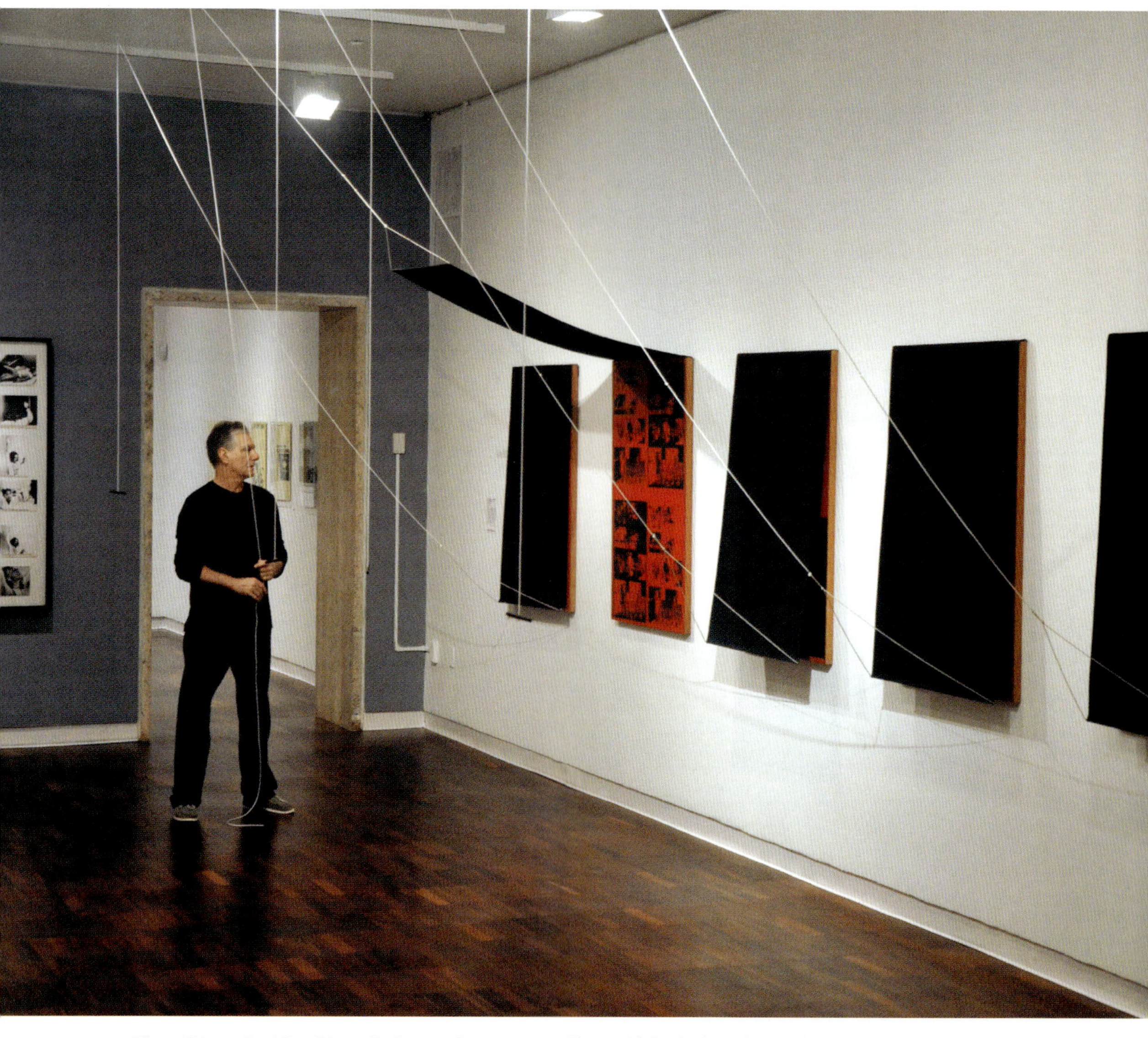

The artist manipulating his work, *Repressão outra vez – Eis o saldo* in the installation of *Antonio Manuel: I Want to Act, Not Represent!*

________. Entre dois séculos: *Arte brasileira do século XX na coleção Gilberto Chateaubriand.* Rio de Janeiro: JB, 1987.

________. "Materiais transfigurados." *Revista de Cultura Vozes* 64, no. 9 (November 1970): 694–5.

________. "Na selva da comunicação." *Revista de Cultura Vozes* 64, no. 4 (May 1970): 321–2.

________. "O belo e a bala." *Jornal do Brazil,* November 13, 1975.

Ramírez, Mari Carmen, ed. *Re-aligning Vision: Alternative Currents in South American Drawing.* New York: El Museo del Barrio, 1997. Exhibition catalogue.

Ramírez, Mari Carmen, and Héctor Ólea. *Inverted Utopias: Avant-Garde Art in Latin America.* New Haven, CT: Yale University Press / The Museum of Fine Arts Houston, 2004. Exhibition catalogue.

Reis, Paulo. "Instalado na trincheira dos 70." *Jornal do Brasil,* September 2, 1994.

________. "Os fantasmas do dia-a-dia." *Jornal do Brasil,* April 26, 1994.

Restany, Pierre. "La crise de la conscience sud-américaine." *Domus* 486 (May 1970): 49–54.

________. "L'art brésilien dans les sables mouvants." *Domus* 544 (March 1970).

Roels, Jr., Reynaldo. "Círculo rompido." *Rio Artes* (May 1993).

________. "Em telas lúdicas um artista oprimido." *Jornal do Brasil,* Revista de Domingo, March 4, 1986.

Salamão, Wally. "Apocalipopótese." From *Hélio Oiticica,* 69–74. Rio de Janeiro: Relume Dumará / Rio Arte, 1996.

Salgado, Renata. *Imagem escrita.* Rio de Janiero: Graal, 1999.

Salzstein, Sônia. *Observador em órbita.* São Paulo: Gabinete de Arte Raquel Arnaud, 2002. Exhibition catalogue.

Santiago, Silviano. "Frutos do Espaço." From *Vale Quanto Pesa,* 161–2. Rio de Janeiro: Paz e Terra,1982.

Sullivan, Edward J., ed. *Brazil Body & Soul.* New York: Guggenheim Museum, 2001. Exhibition catalogue.

Tassinari, Alberto. *O Desequilibrista.* São Paulo: Centro Cultural São Paulo, 2003. Exhibition catalogue.

Terranova, Marco, and Paola Terranova. *Petite Galerie, 1954–1988: Uma visão da arte brasileira.* Rio de Janeiro: Paço Imperial, 1996.

Tokyo kokusai hanga biennare ten; dai 7-kai = The 7th International Biennial Exhibition of Prints in Tokyo. Tokyo: Tokyo Kokuritsu Kindai Bijutsukan, 1971.

Traba, Marta, ed. *Art of Latin America, 1900–1980.* Baltimore: Johns Hopkins / Inter-American Development Bank, 1994.

Trinta anos de 1968. Rio de Janeiro: Centro Cultural Banco do Brasil, 1998. Exhibition catalogue.

Venancio Filho, Paulo. *Espaço Ativo.* Belo Horizonte: Manoel Macedo Galeria de Arte, 2004.

________. *Sombras e cintilações.* São Paulo: Gabinete de Arte Raquel Arnaud, 1990. Exhibition catalogue.

________. *Sucessão de fatos.* São Paulo: Gabinete de Arte Raquel Arnaud, 2006. Exhibition catalogue.

ABOUT THE AUTHORS

BEVERLY ADAMS is the curator of the Diane and Bruce Halle Collection of twentieth- and twenty-first-century Latin American art in Scottsdale, Arizona. She received her Ph.D in Art History from the University of Texas at Austin. She served as assistant curator of Latin American art at the Archer M. Huntington Art Gallery (now the Jack Clanton Museum of Art), University of Texas at Austin, and as the curator of Latin American art at the Phoenix Art Museum. Her recent publications include "The School of the North: The New York Graphic Workshop in New York" in *The New York Graphic Workshop: 1964–1970* (UT Austin, 2009); *Constructing a Poetic Universe: The Diane and Bruce Halle Collection of Latin American Art* (MFA Houston, 2007) and "Latin American Art at the Americas Society: A Principality of its Own" in the eponymous publication (Americas Society, 2006).

MICHAEL ASBURY is a British/Brazilian art historian, critic and curator. He is a Reader at Chelsea College of Art and Design, University of the Arts London, where he works in conjunction with the CCW Graduate School and the Research Centre for Transnational Art, Identity and Nation (TrAIN). He received a M.A. from Liverpool University and a Ph.D. from University of the Arts, London. His writing on modern and contemporary art has been published by: *Arte e Ensaios, Art History Journal, Art Nexus, Dardo,* Documenta 12, and *Untitled,* among others. As a curator he has worked with institutions such as Tate Modern, Camden Arts Centre, and The Henry Moore Institute in the United Kingdom; Museo de Arte Contemporânea do Dragão do Mar, Galeria Nara Roesler and Galeria Milan in Brazil and Pharos Centre for Contemporary Art in Cyprus. Currently, he is involved with the project "Meeting Margins: Transnational Art in Latin America and Europe 1950–1978" funded by the Arts and Humanities Research Council.

CLAUDIA CALIRMAN is Assistant Professor at John Jay College of Criminal Justice of the City University of New York, where she teaches Art History and Curatorial Studies. She received her Ph.D. in Art History from the Graduate Center of the City University of New York. Calirman is a lecturer at the Museum of Modern Art, New York, and has taught at Parsons the New School of Design, New York, and the Fashion Institute of Technology, New York. In 2008–09, she was selected as a Visiting Scholar at the David Rockefeller Center for Latin American Studies at Harvard University.

She also serves as Chief Curator at Location One, a non-for-profit residency program for international artists in New York City. Calirman has curated several exhibitions including *"But enough about me-now let's talk about my work": Artoons by Pablo Helguera* (John Jay College, 2011), *Adel Abidin: I am Sorry* (Location One, 2010), and *Elizabeth Jobim: Endless Lines* (Lehman College Art Gallery, 2008). Her book *Brazilian Art under Dictatorship: Antonio Manuel, Artur Barrio, and Cildo Meireles* is forthcoming by Duke University Press (2012).

GABRIELA RANGEL is the Director of Visual Arts and Chief Curator at Americas Society, New York. She holds a B.A. in film studies from the International Film School at San Antonio de los Baños, Cuba; an M.A. in media and communications studies from the Universidad Católica Andrés Bello; Caracas, and an M.A. in curatorial studies from the Center for Curatorial Studies, Bard College. She has curated and co-curated a number of exhibitions on contemporary art, including *Arturo Herrera: Les Noces (The Wedding)* (Americas Society, 2011); and *Gordon Matta-Clark: Undoing Spaces* (Paço Imperial de Rio de Janeiro, 2009–10); and *Dias & Riedweg …and it becomes something else* (Americas Society, 2009). Some of her catalogue contributions include *Arturo Herrera* (Trasnocho Arte Contacto, 2009), *Claudio Perna* (Galería de Arte Nacional de Caracas, 2004), *Liliana Porter: Fotografía y ficción* (Centro Cultural Recoleta, 2003), and *Da Adversidade Vivemos: Contemporary Latin American Conceptual Artists* (Musée de Art Moderne de la Ville de Paris, 2001). Her articles have appeared in *Parkett, Trans>, Atlántica.* More recently, she has edited *SITAC 8. Blind Spots: Film, Performance and Feminism* (Patronato de Arte Contemporáneo de Mexico, 2011).

JUDITH RODENBECK is a professor of Modern and Contemporary Art at Sarah Lawrence College. She received a B.A. in Art History and English from Yale University, a B.F.A. from Massachusetts College of Art and a Ph.D. in Art History from Columbia University. Rodenbeck was Editor-in-Chief of *Art Journal* from 2007 to 2009, and regularly contributes art criticism to magazines such as *Artforum, Grey Room, Modern Painters,* and *October.* Her recent publications include *Radical Prototypes: Allan Kaprow and the Invention of Happenings* (MIT Press, 2011) and, with Benjamin Buchloh, *Experiments in the Everyday: Allan Kaprow and Robert Watts, Events, Objects, Documents* (University of Washington Press, 2000).

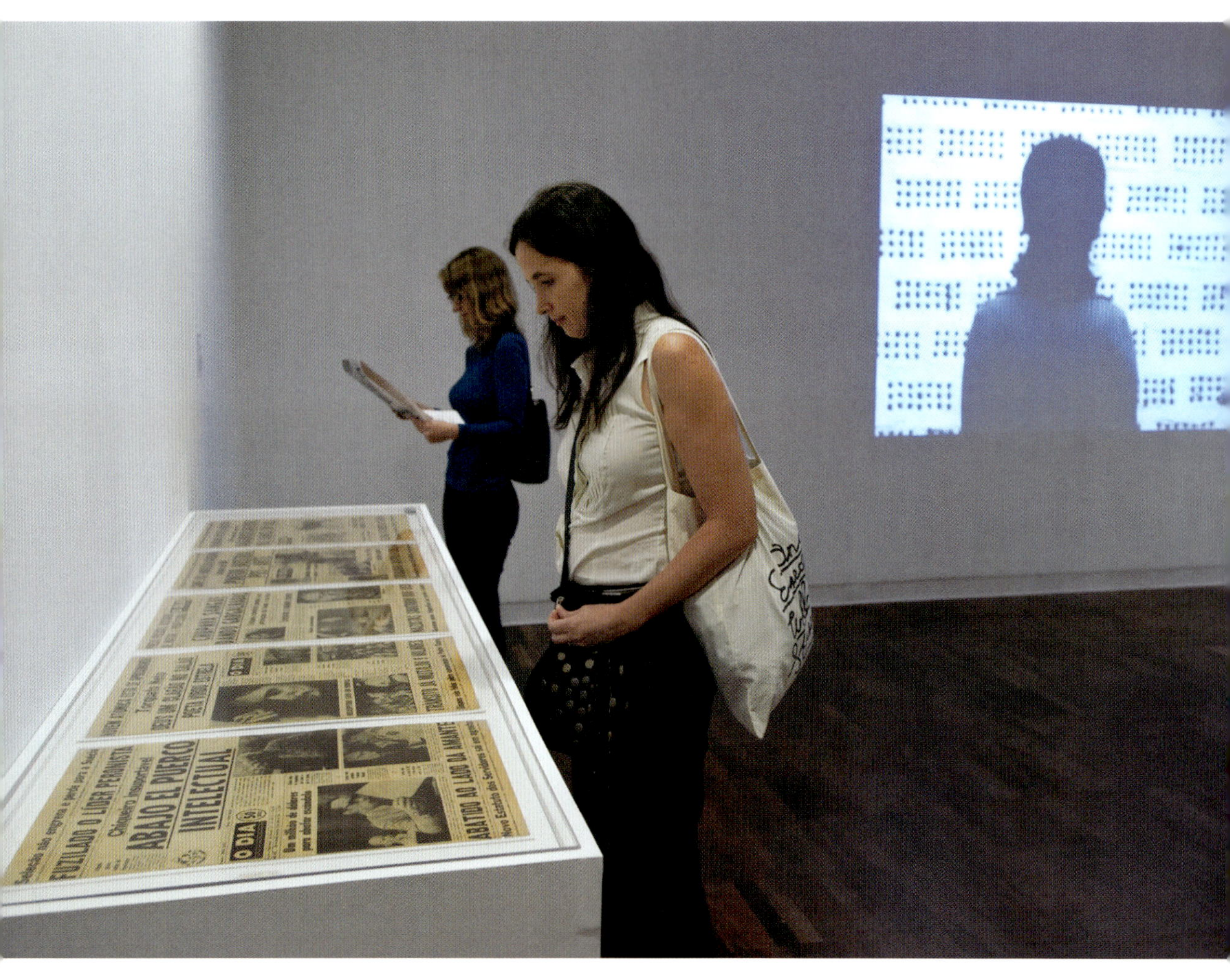

Installation view of *Antonio Manuel: I Want to Act, Not Represent!*

ACKNOWLEDGMENTS

A special acknowledgment is extended to Guy Brett and Ronaldo Brito, who inspired the title of this exhibition and publication, *Antonio Manuel: I Want to Act, Not Represent!*

PHOTOGRAPHY CREDITS:
Sebastião Barbosa: 130, 131
Guy Brett: 36
Bazilio Calazans: 136
Pedro Oswaldo Cruz: 117 (r)
Beto Felicio: 114 (l)
Rômulo Fialdini: 116
Michel Filho: 114 (r)
John Goldblatt: 113
Carlos Foto: 11, 128–29
Magno Mesquita: 117 (l)
Mario Caillaux Oliveriras: 31, 124, 127, 146
Cristina Pape: 14
Lygia Pape: 38
Fabio del Re: 116
Lula Rodrigues: 6, 13, 22, 26, 30, 39–40,
96, 101, 110, 118–19, 122–23, 125–26,
132–33
Arturo Sánchez: 4, 16, 17, 19, 84, 93, 94,
115, 120–21, 150

IMAGE COPYRIGHT CREDITS:
Vito Acconci, Terezinha Colares, Luiz
Chrysostomo, Luciano Figueiredo, Galerie
LeLong, New York, Gilberto Chateaubriand
Collection (Museu de Arte Moderna, Rio de
Janeiro), Anna Maria Maiolino, Cildo
Meireles, Projeto Hélio Oiticica, Projeto Lygia
Pape, the Estate of Mário Pedrosa, and
VALIE EXPORT.

**ANTONIO MANUEL AND THE EDITORS
WOULD LIKE TO THANK:**
Marisa Abate
Vito Acconci
Hannah Adkins
Seth Becker
Sabine Breitwieser
Beatriz Caillaux
The Honorable Osmar Chohfi
Terezinha Colares
Valeria Souza Cruz
Chris Dierks
The Drawing Center
Rafaela Ferreira
Ariane Figueiredo
Luciano Figueiredo
Mari Hayman
Paulo Herkenhoff
Anna Maria Maiolino
Victor Manuel
Marli Matsumoto
César Oiticica
Claudio Oiticica
Mario Caillaux Oliveira
Paula Pape
Vera Pedrosa
Quito Pedrosa
Priscila Piantanida
Iara Pimenta
Paulo Uchôa Ribeiro Filho
Daniel Roesler
Nara Roesler
Arturo Sánchez
Paulo Roberto Santi
VALIE EXPORT
Monica Vieira
Erica Watanabe Patrón

Americas Society is the premier organization dedicated to education, debate, and dialogue in the Americas. Its mission is to foster an understanding of the contemporary political, social, and economic issues confronting Latin America, the Caribbean, and Canada, and to increase public awareness and appreciation of the diverse cultural heritage of the Americas and the importance of the inter-American relationship.

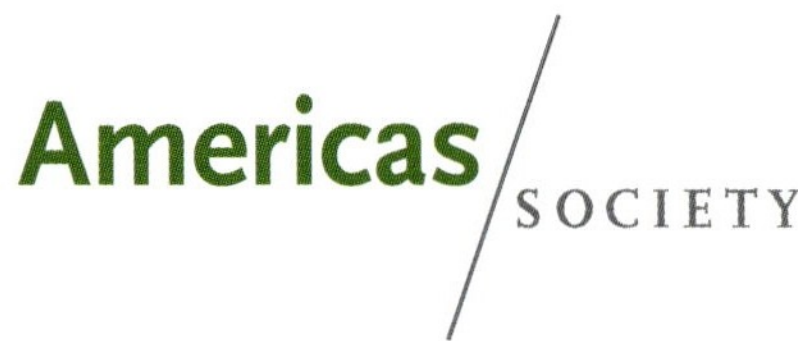

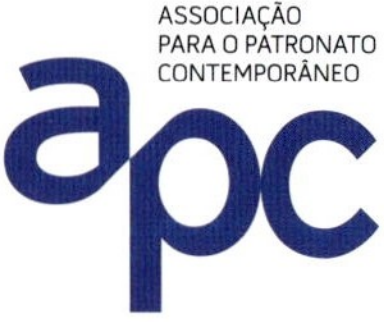

680 Park Avenue, New York, NY 10065
Phone: (212) 249-8950 Fax: (212) 249-5868
e-mail: artgallery@as-coa.org
Web site: www.as-coa.org/visualarts

Rua Doutor Oliveira Pinto, 145
São Paulo, SP 01444-010
e-mail: info@apcbrasil.org
Web site: www.apcbrasil.org